PHANTOMS OF REMEMBRANCE

PHANTOMS OF REMEMBRANCE

MEMORY AND OBLIVION AT THE END
OF THE FIRST MILLENNIUM

Patrick J. Geary

PRINCETON UNIVERSITY PRESS

PRINCETON, NEW JERSEY

LIBRARY OF CONGRESS CATALOGING-IN-PUBLICATION DATA

GEARY, PATRICK J., 1948–

PHANTOMS OF REMBRANCE : MEMORY AND OBLIVION AT THE END

OF THE FIRST MILLENNIUM / PATRICK J. GEARY.

PHANTOMS OF REMEMBRANCE : MEMORY AND OBLIVION AT THE END

OF THE FIRST MILLENNIUM / PATRICK J. GEARY.

P. CM.

INCLUDES BIBLIOGRAPHICAL REFERENCES (P.) AND INDEX.

ISBN 0-691-03422-2 (ACID-FREE PAPER)

1. HISTORY—PHILOSOPHY. 2. HISTORY—METHODOLOGY.

3. MEMORY. I. TITLE

D16.9.G35 1994 901—DC20 94-15608 CIP

PUBLICATION OF THIS BOOK HAS BEEN AIDED BY THE MELLON FUND.

THIS BOOK HAS BEEN COMPOSED IN GALLIARD

1 3 5 7 9 10 8 6 4 2

For Anne Irène

CONTENTS

LIST OF ILLUSTRATIONS

ACKNOWLEDGMENTS

THE INTELLECTUAL ODYSSEY that has led to the present book has been circuitous, and if it has produced anything of value, it is largely because of the generosity of a great number of individuals and institutions that have assisted me over the past years. They deserve more than the usual terse listing of names that recalls some tenth-century *liber memorialis*: people and institutions organized according to some arbitrary system of social or cultural division with little explanation of why each deserves to find its *memoria* preserved for the readers of the book. My debts are too great to leave such a phantom remembrance. I would like rather to thank those who contributed to this volume by evoking not only the shadow of their names but also something of those memories that have remained for me the proof of their continued presence.

During the first phase of my gropings toward how to understand social memory, the L. J. Skaggs and Mary C. Skaggs Foundation provided me funds which I could pass on to the remarkable team of medievalists and computer scientists at the University of Münster in the *Sonderforschungsbereich* 7 under the direction of Joachim Wollasch. This grant made possible the completion of the *Gruppensuchprogramme* (GSP), an extraordinary series of computer programs allowing for the recognition of repeating name groups across vast bodies of charters. These funds came just as the funding for the *Sonderforschungsbereich* 7 had ended and it appeared that Friedrich-Wilhelm Westerhoff, who had developed the program, might never be able to perfect it and prepare the documentation necessary for its use by others. Little did we know how crucial the timing was—just after he had completed perfecting the program and started to draft the documentation, Wilfried Westerhoff disappeared on a solitary climb in the Italian Dolomites. His friend and colleague Maria Hillebrandt completed and published the documentation.[1] Without the timely assistance of the Skaggs Foundation, Wilfried's brilliant contribution to medieval social history would have disappeared with him. In my use of the GSP, I have benefited far more than the present volume shows from the patience and collegiality of Joachim Wollasch, Wilfried Westerhoff, Maria Hillebrandt, Franz Neiske, Dietrich Poeck, and their colleagues, and from the Skaggs Foundation, which made our collaboration possible.

Before I quite knew where my investigations were headed, the American Council of Learned Societies provided me a year to explore the literature of memory as well as the valleys and mountains of the Piedmont and the Maritime Alps, which form part of the geography of this book. During that year of 1987–88, I also learned that the book I thought I was writing—a monographic study on memory in the Rhône watershed—was not the book that wanted to be written. An invitation from the Shelby Cullom Davis Center at Princeton University in the spring of 1988 to present a paper on transmitting the past forced me to take on the broader implications of what I was studying. Only then did I realize that I was writing something broader and less comprehensive than a regional study, although its form was not yet clear.

The École des Hautes Études en Sciences Sociales, by inviting me in the spring of 1990 to discuss the history of memory in the seminars of Lucette Valensi and Jocelyne Dakhila and of Jean-Claude Schmitt, forced me to face the theoretical and epistemological problems of studying not only memories but memory systems in the past. At the same time, an invitation from Georges Duby to discuss the memory of women in his seminar at the Collège de France gave me the opportunity to think about memory and gender.

During two extraordinary months as a guest of the Max-Planck-Institut für Geschichte during the summer of 1990, I began to realize the parameters of a different and more ambitious comparative study of memory. During long discussions with Otto Gerhard Oexle while we explored together the new-old world that would soon cease to be the German Democratic Republic and walked the fields on the edge of Göttingen, I learned from that scholar more about how the past lives in the present than I can ever say. In the meantime his colleagues Gadi Algazi and Jan Gerchow educated me about German history and forced me to face the inconsistencies and inadequacies of early drafts while J. Clifford Hubby assisted me with Bavarian materials.

An invitation from the Institute for Advanced Study to spend the academic year 1990–91 in that exquisite institution set among tranquil fields and silent woods gave me the opportunity to begin writing the fragments that would become this book. There Giles Constable and John Freed read and criticized drafts and taught me much about the worlds of medieval France and Germany. Joan Scott led me to realize the importance of political systems in the development of gender-based memory. The members of the Princeton University history department, especially Peter Brown, Judith Herrin, Natalie Davis, Anthony Grafton, and William Jordan, also helped me come to terms with memories of my own of that very special community in the 1970s.

I returned to Gainesville with ninety-nine separate computer files relating to memory and oblivion. The John Simon Guggenheim Foundation provided time to rethink and rework these fragments into something resembling a whole. John Freed, Peter Brown, and Barbara Rosenwein took time they could little spare from their own lives to read a first draft of the book and provide pages of criticisms and suggestions, all of which were appropriate and some of which I have followed.

In Gainesville and away, every aspect of this study has been generously supported by the Department of History of the University of Florida. Within the constraints of available resources, the university has been very liberal in supplementing grants and fellowships, in allowing me to adjust teaching schedules around travel, and in every possible way investing in me and my work.

Faculty and students at Notre Dame, the University of Chicago, Yale University, Barnard College, Cornell University, the University of Pennsylvania, and the University of California at Los Angeles have patiently listened to bits of preliminary musings on memory and have assisted me in rethinking them. Thomas Waldman has generously shared his notes and photographs of St. Denis Charters, and Richard Landes provided me with transcriptions of his forthcoming edition of Ademar of Chabannes' *Chronicle*. The late Joachim Jahn, in one of his last acts of professional generosity, read and corrected my Bavarian sections. Barbara Rosenwein has read and critiqued numerous drafts of chapters and the completed manuscript. Chris Wickham, who was writing his own book on memory at the same time, not only scrutinized early portions of my study but risked sharing his own original and insightful chapters with me in draft.

Thomas Head and a second, anonymous reader for Princeton University Press went far beyond what could have been expected of them in their detailed and insightful criticisms and suggestions for how to make a rough manuscript into a book. Their reports, each well over fifteen single-spaced pages of comments, not only pointed out what was wrong with the manuscript in content and form but suggested how to make it right.

Maribel Dietz worked valiantly with the revised manuscript to eliminate as many errors and traces of my dyslexia as possible. Those that remain are my fault, not hers. Finally, it would be unfair to acknowledge only the positive support and advice that I have received in the course of studying memory and oblivion. I am particularly grateful to an anonymous reviewer who convinced the National Humanities Center not to support me in my project. He or she wrote in part:

> Historians from their earliest training are warned against arguments from silence, but Patrick Geary is proposing to study the sounds of medieval silences. But whatever the song affirms, silences remain silent. How can one study what people in the Middle Ages forgot? Because something is not mentioned in the scanty written records of the early Middle Ages does

not prove that it has fallen into oblivion. He wants to write on "structures of forgetting." My counsel to him would be: forget it.

This is generally well-founded and well-intentioned advice. Listening to the silences of the past is fraught with the very real danger of filling past silences with present concerns. But perhaps it is not so much the silences that I have tried to hear in the texts I have studied as the whispers, those faint rustlings of the past which can at times announce that which is more important than the tumult to which we are first attracted. One thinks of Elijah on Mount Horeb who ignored the great wind, the earthquake, and the fire, but when he heard the whispering of a light breeze, "he wrapped his face in his mantle and went out and stood at the entrance of the cave."

I am grateful to the Publications de l'Université de Provence for permission to incorporate into chapter two material that has appeared as "Mémoire monastique et oubli onomastique en Provence," in *Histoire et société: Mélanges offerts à Georges Duby*, Vol. 3, *Le moine, le clerc et le prince* (Aix-en-Provence: Publications de l'Université de Provence, 1992), 61–65. The illuminations from the Warmund Sacramentary are reproduced by permission of Priuli and Verlucca (copyright 1990). The folio reproduced from the Fulda Kopialbuch is by permission of the Staatsarchiv Marburg. The folio from the Freising Kopialbuch is by permission of the Bayerisches Hauptstaatsarchiv. The photograph from the Bamberg Apocalypse is reproduced with the permission of the Staatsbibliothek Bamberg.

ABBREVIATIONS

MGH	Monumenta Germaniae Historica
SS	Scriptores
SSRM	Scriptores rerum merovingicarum
SSRG	Scriptores rerum Germanicarum in usum scholarum
Epist.	Epistolae
Capit.	Capitularia regum Francorum
Poet.Lat.	Poetae Latini medii aevi
Nec.	Necrologia Germaniae
MIÖG	Mitteilungen des Instituts für österreichische Geschichts-forschung
PL	J.-P. Migne, ed. *Patrologiae cursus completus, Series Latina.* (221 vols., Paris, 1844–64)

PHANTOMS OF REMEMBRANCE

INTRODUCTION

ARLY in the eleventh century Rodulfus Glaber, apparently expressing the sentiment of his former abbot William of Volpiano, assailed the new styles that had entered Burgundy and the Capetian kingdom with the marriage in 1002–1003 of Robert the Pious and Constance:[1]

> About the year 1000 of the Incarnation of the Word, when King Robert took as his wife Queen Constance, a woman of Aquitaine, for her sake a great flood of strange men from the Auvergne and Aquitaine began to flow into France and Burgundy; they were flippant and vain fellows with strange manners and clothes; their weapons and the equipment of their horses were curious, and they were close-shaven from half-way down their heads; they were beardless like actors, wore indecent hose and shoes, and were totally devoid of good faith and respect for agreed peace.[2]

This attack is an echo of one launched in October 1016 by William of Volpiano himself against those who wore short clothes and shaved their necks and beards (also reported by Rodulfus).[3] A tirade against tonsorial styles may seem a strange place to begin a study of memory. And yet, this attack on the Capetian king and his wife, at first glance strangely misdirected toward something as trivial as hair style and shoes, presents many of the problems and strategies of memory and identity common to the early eleventh century. The diatribe is not simply about style but about authority and, ultimately, the legitimate exercise of power. It uses style in order to identify and stigmatize regional opposition. But the presentation of the two opposing parties as distinct regional groups is possible only when those so identified are denied a past, or when their relationship to the past is seen as unproblematic. William (or perhaps Rodulfus' version of William), in attacking dress and custom, is involved in a double reproduction of the past: one for Robert, Constance, and her southern followers; another for himself and the supporters of the old imperial order.

The attack was as imprecise as it was vehement. As usual for him, Rodulfus' report is at a certain level inaccurate and confused.[4] Constance was not, as he suggests, from Aquitaine but rather from Arles, the daughter of Count William of Provence;[5] nor, apparently, had William of Volpiano meant to attack southern novelties as such, if indeed he had actually preached the sermon Rodulfus attributes to him.[6] The context of William's harsh words was the sermon he preached at the dedication of the basilica of St. Benigne of Dijon and was intended as a funeral oration for the fortunes of Carolingian and Ottonian legitimatists in Burgundy.[7] On 30 January 1016 Bishop Bruno of Langres, a relative of the Ottonians, the last anti-Capetian magnate in Burgundy, and the particular patron of William's reconstruction of the basilica of St. Benigne had died. His death left his enemy Robert the Pious free to orchestrate an episcopal election that would guarantee his control over Dijon and hence over Burgundy. This he promptly did, and Robert's choice, Bishop Lambert, presided nine months later over the dedication ceremony that was to have been his predecessor's moment of glory. William's attack on the dress of the southerners must be seen in relation to his background and in the context of the rest of the sermon pronounced at this critical occasion. He challenges those present to declare if anyone among them had contributed so much as five solidi to the construction. None could meet the challenge. The implication was clear—it had been the men of the old order, with their traditional customs and their imperial connections (Bruno was related to the Carolingians through Lothar III as well as to the Ottonians) to whom credit was due for the reconstruction, but none could be present to receive their deserved praise. The sermon thus contrasted the actions of the old and new orders—the one adorning the Church of God, preparing it, in William's metaphor, as a bride for her wedding; while the other frivolously adorned itself with shameful and disgusting styles of tonsure and dress.[8]

But even if Rodulfus was factually inexact and deficient in his historical presentation, his testimony remains extraordinarily useful for penetrating the perceptions and categories of his generation. Far from being a naive monastic chronicler, his writings are carefully constructed and ideologically sophisticated texts closely in tune with the ideology of William of Volpiano and the reform monastic movement most strongly represented by Cluny.[9] His Constance is particularly interesting as an image of a dangerous influence on Francia, both because she was southern and because she was a woman. Constance was perhaps born in Provence, but for Rodulfus and other contemporaries she was Aquitanian, in part by virtue of her mother—Adelaide/Blanche—who was the daughter of Fulk the Good of Anjou and the repudiated wife of the Carolingian Louis V, and in part because to northerners since at least the seventh century "Aquitaini" had been a general term for the "Romani" of the South when they wanted to emphasize their separateness.[10]

This "Romanness" that Rodulfus/William and their contemporaries found so significant was, however, of very recent vintage. This "Aquitanian" was not a member of some ancient Gallo-Roman family either through her maternal or paternal ancestors but belonged rather to the Frankish aristocracy which had been installed, in the case of her father in particular, only one generation previously in the South. In the 940s Count William's father Boso had probably descended the Rhône from

Burgundy along with the uncle of his wife, Hugo of Arles, Marquis of Provence and then king of Italy from 927–947. After the collapse of the fragile and complex network of lands controlled by the latter, he had extricated himself from the "Burgundians" by divorcing his wife.[11] Within less than two generations this family had become, in the eyes of their contemporaries and, no doubt too, in their own eyes, part of a world that stood in strong contrast with the northern, Carolingian world of Burgundy and Francia. Memory of family traditions could be extremely short when such memories could be politically embarrassing.

Not only was Constance a southerner, but she was a woman. By marrying into the Capetian family, she brought her husband novelty and frivolity rather than sage counsel and a respect for the old ways such as he would have received from reform-minded monks such as William himself. This too was a deliberate construction of woman as danger: her contemporaries, the Ottonian empresses, were seen as powerful forces for the preservation of stability and continuity within the royal family. For a reforming monk such as William, such politically active women as Constance offered only instability and discontinuity.

The choice of dress and hair style as indications of regional identity and as the focus of hostility toward the Capetians and their meridional allies was in keeping both with an ancient tradition of ethnic self-identification and with the fluidity of these identities.[12] By their dress and customs (*mores*) these southerners presented themselves as different, foreign. These external cultural symbols were particularly shocking perhaps because they represented a choice (in William's view, the choice of the devil's temptations) of identity that was more dangerous and damning than an accident of birth.

William was himself, after all, from the South, from Lombardy. His father's family had been among those northerners who had established themselves in Lombardy in the previous century and who had put up a valiant if futile resistance to the Ottonian absorption of the region. After his capitulation, however, he had reaffirmed his ties to the north by submitting to Otto II and making him the godfather of his son William.[13] William himself had chosen to return north to the roots of his family's tradition beyond the Alps. His return to the world of Ottonian politics and monastic reform emphasized his ties, through his parents and his godfather Otto II, to the traditions of northern, Frankish Europe. By contrast these other southerners had returned not to rediscover the good old ways of their grandfathers but to introduce the dangerous novelties of the new world into the old. They had assimilated into meridional culture; he had not.

Or better, William thought that he had not. But if he had not adopted the frivolities of the South, he had become affected with another of its values—a reforming monasticism primarily created, it is true, at Cluny but also nurtured on Northern Italian aesthetic and monastic traditions and led by such southerners as Maiolus of Cluny.[14] These traditions were in their own ways as alien and as threatening to the old Frankish order as were the shaven necks and frivolous clothing of the Provençals.[15] Both the southern nobles and the reforming abbot embody aspects of an alien, Mediterranean world, which, in the first years of the new millennium, began to spread its influence to the North, eliciting both the fears and the hopes of the peoples who had dominated for over three centuries the world between the Loire and the Alps.

However, only a superficial understanding of this Mediterranean world would suggest that it had heretofore preserved intact Gallo-Roman traditions in contrast to a northern Germanic world beyond the Loire. In fact, this meridional culture now spreading north was itself a product of centuries of the creative fusion of Frankish, Gothic, and Gallo-Roman societies, and its principal agents of dissimilation such as Constance and, in his own way, William of Volpiano, were descendants of northern Frankish families that had been introduced into Provence, Lombardy, and Aquitaine in the eighth through tenth centuries.[16] These groups had for a time preserved their social, political, and institutional ties with their homelands and could still, when useful, recall something of these former relationships. Increasingly, however, in the later tenth and eleventh centuries new forms of southern social, political, and cultural structures were emerging. With them, new identities were being forged, identities compounded not only of perceptions of contemporary circumstances but also, necessarily, of recollections of the past that could give meaning to the transformed present. The memory of the past then was fundamental to the understanding of the contemporary world. The right to speak this tradition, whether in matters of dress and hair style, or in law and lordship, was a claim to a fundamental power. Those who could control the past could direct the future.

The differing cultural, geographical, and political identities William constructs for himself and for Constance thus represent two different relationships to the past: one of radical discontinuity, the other of artificial continuity. William (or perhaps Rodulfus) is suppressing some elements of the past, selecting others, and organizing them to present a programmatic understanding of how the present ought to be. He is also pressing claims about who should be allowed to speak for the past.

The novelty of the new age is to be rejected. One must instead return to the old lost world just as William himself returned first physically to the North of his ancestors and then to the spiritual reformation of monastic life. This return must be mediated by reformed monks, who, unlike women, are the only guarantors of the proper continuity. He is creating himself and his opponents through his manipulation of memory, both personal, familial, and regional.

The manner in which William of Volpiano rethought these questions of the relationship between past and present is no isolated incident. Across the former Carolingian world, people of the eleventh century seemed as interested in questions of continuity and discontinuity as subsequent historians, with some emphasizing the novelty of their age and others its continuity with the past.

Creating the Past

Listening to how people such as William of Volpiano created their pasts first aroused my interest in understanding how he and his contemporaries reformed their pasts for their present. Not only did their recollections seem to contradict the image that modern historians have reconstructed of their relationship to the past, but they seemed to suppress or transform evidence that they themselves had available. This inability or disinclination to make the same sense of the past that one would today seemed far from random. Rather, it seemed part of a way of creating a present within a broadly political process in which the nature of that present, and thus of the past which created it, was in contention.

The right to speak the past also implied control over that which gave access to the past—the "relics" by which the past continued to live into the present. How these tangible or written relics of the past were preserved, who preserved them, and who could therefore make them to disappear were thus fundamental aspects of power and authority. The creation of the past, then, whether individual or collective, seemed far from a natural and spontaneous development from "collective memory" or the inevitable result of the transition from "oral" to "literate" modes of recalling. These were issues that I wished somehow to explore.

This competition for power over the past needs to be explored for two reasons. First and most obviously, by examining the creation of a past, we can understand better the modes of perception and structures of understanding of the people of the eleventh century and how people used these mental categories to construct their world and to order their lives.[17] But as important, this creation determined not only contemporaries' understanding of the past but ours as well. Much of what we think we know about the early Middle Ages was determined by the changing problems and concerns of eleventh-century men and women, not by those of the more distant past. Unless we understand the mental and social structures that acted as filters, suppressing or transforming the received past in the eleventh century in terms of presentist needs, we are doomed to misunderstand those earlier centuries.

This selectivity of memory is hardly a novel discovery. Some people in the eleventh century were quite aware of what they were doing. Arnold of Regensburg, a Bavarian monk writing around 1030, expressed it clearly:

> Not only is it proper for the new things to change the old ones, but even, if the old ones are disordered, they should be entirely thrown away, or if, however, they conform to the proper order of things but are of little use, they should be buried with reverence.[18]

This sentiment encapsulates the dilemma that he and his contemporaries faced as they went about the Herculean task of reproducing their world from the scattered fragments of the past. A society that explicitly found its identity, its norms, and its values in the inheritance from the past, that venerated tradition and drew its religious and political ideologies from precedent, was nevertheless actively engaged in producing that tradition through a complex process of transmission, suppression, and re-creation. Individuals and communities copied, abridged, and revised archival records, liturgical texts, literary documents, doing so with reference to physical reminders from previous generations and a fluid oral tradition in order to prescribe how the present should be because of how the past had been. This transformative process necessarily meant that something new would come into being. To a greater or lesser extent, many were aware of this process, some deeply troubled by it, others accepting it with resignation or even relish. This book is concerned less with the past itself or even the end product of this process than it is with the way that men and women around the turn of the millennium determined what was, in Arnold's terms, "ordinaria" and "inordinata," what was useful and less useful—that is, with how individuals and groups remembered and forgot. It is also concerned with how that discarded past continued to live in the discordances, inconsistencies, and lacunae of the created past as well as in the dreams, visions, and anxieties of those who suppressed it. For if the past was "buried with reverence," then like the human dead for whom Arnold and his brothers prayed, it was not to be forgotten altogether but rather transformed, both memorialized and commemorated so that the past might be honored, but in a such a way that it might no longer control the lives of the living.

This concern with rethinking the past is hardly unique to the eleventh century. John Pocock has observed that when traditional relationships between present and past break down, those most affected by this rupture respond by reshaping an understanding of that which unites past and present in terms of some new continuity in order to defend themselves from the effects of this rupture.[19] Such a response may be common to many periods, but in the context of the eleventh century it is particularly worth investigating because the end product of the forgetting, remembering, and reorganizing of the past would be the model for

the origins of high medieval society on which subsequent generations of
historians, even into our century, would build.

This model emphasized creativity and freedom from the past represented by the "golden age" of the Carolingian world and the "dark age"
of the tenth century, the latter characterized by radical discontinuity
largely blamed on external forces such as Saracen, Magyar, and Norse
raids and invasions. Those living on the other side of this caesura felt
themselves separated by a great gulf from this earlier age. Already in the
eleventh century those people who undertook to preserve the past in
written form, for their contemporaries or their posterity, seemed to
know little and understand less of their familial, institutional, cultural,
and regional past. To them, theirs was a brave new world for which the
past was but a series of disjointed and isolated persons and events. And
yet they were deeply concerned with this past, possessed by it almost,
and their invented past became the goal and justification of their programs in the present.[20]

Toward a History of Memory

A simple comparison of "ideal" and "reality," a juxtaposition of this created past and the past that modern scholars create, would not do justice
to the creative process of reforming the relationship between past and
present. Instead, we must consider the process by which this created
memory was formed—in other words, the history of memory itself.

The history of memory can mean different things to different people.
The most obvious and frequent meaning is historiography, or the study
of explicitly elaborated and cohesive accounts of the past. Annalists,
chroniclers, and historians alike consciously select from a spectrum of
possible *memorabilia* those which are *memoranda*—that is, those worth
remembering.[21] The study of historiography thus implies the study of
the content of memory. This may mean a source-critical approach to the
content in an attempt to assess its accuracy and to determine the range
of written and oral *memorabilia* on which the author drew. It also means
a study of the value system according to which certain portions of this
memorabilia were deemed *memoranda* and the transformations these
sources underwent in the process of placing them within a new written
context. In this sense the study of historical memory is a study of propaganda, of the decisions about what should be remembered and how it
should be remembered.[22]

The second kind of history of memory is the study of the intellectual
traditions within which memory was understood and cultivated. This
includes both what people in the past thought about memory and the

techniques of memory training by which people sought to enhance human memory faculties.[23] As we shall see, memory, both as a reflection of the divine nature and as a faculty of human reason, loomed large in medieval psychology. Likewise, the ability to remember, to store, and to reproduce imaginatively the past—especially persons from the past—was particularly important to certain specialist groups, particularly reformed monks. Thus techniques of memorization and commemoration were developed to facilitate these abilities.

This book discusses both kinds of history of memory, but its concentration is on something slightly different: it seeks to understand how people actually remember, the structures in which the past is preserved, reorganized, and recalled. It assumes that how one stores the past affects what is remembered, and thus that a change in the storage causes change in the content.[24] The two are inseparable. Moreover, it focuses on the personal, familial, and communal pasts of society rather than on the storage and *verbatim* recollection of discrete data such as liturgy or texts. My interest is less on the "arts of memory" than the ordinary practice of recollecting, transforming, and using the past.

I am not the first to look at the process of memory in the past, but three characteristics separate what I am attempting to do from what has usually been done: First, historians of memory have focused too much, I think, on the putative dichotomy between individual and collective memory and collective memory and history. Second, historians and anthropologists have overstressed the distinction between oral and written remembering. Finally, previous studies have focused primarily on the formation of conscious narrative memory rather than on the structures by which memories of all sorts are transmitted and created.

The French sociologist Maurice Halbwachs set the parameters for much of what has been written on the history of memory in his 1925 study of collective memory.[25] Halbwachs wrote in opposition to a pseudogenetic tradition that grounded collective memory in an inherited racial memory.[26] Against such a racial determinist approach, he emphasized the influence of family, religion, and class through the very structures of language, the rituals of ordinary life, the delimitation of space, to constitute the system of social conventions through which and in which we create our memories.

Although Halbwachs' analysis of memory remains the touchstone of all understandings of social memory, one aspect of his analysis has led to a false dichotomy—that is, the difference not only between individual and collective memory but between collective memory and history. Perhaps because he failed to see the political parameters of collective memory formation, he assumed that collective memory was a natural, nonpurposeful creation of a group while history was an intentional, political, and manipulative process. He thus postulated a fundamental opposition between the two. The former creates a bond between present and past, the latter disrupts this continuity; the former is highly selective, retaining those aspects of collective identity, while the latter recovers and reorganizes this lost difference. Collective memory is made up of a multiplicity of group memories, while history unifies the past into one. Collective memory is oral, history written. History begins where collective memory ends.[27]

In recent years, as memory has become a much discussed historical subject, historians have taken up Halbwachs' formulations and applied them to their analyses of the creations of group and national pasts. This interest is most pronounced in the United States. In a recent issue of the *Journal of American History* dedicated to the subject of memory, David Thelen wrote an extremely valuable presentation of the issues of exploring how national perception uses the past.[28] Thelen is particularly interested in how people construct and narrate memories, in the "social dimensions of memory," which he approaches within the Halbwachs paradigm of collective memory and its formation.[29] One of the few European historians to address directly the history of collective memory is Pierre Nora, who has reformulated the investigations of Maurice Halbwachs into collective memory in order to elaborate a theory of collective memory even more strongly opposed to historical memory.[30] Nora argues that one can distinguish, at least in the modern world, between collective and historical memory. The former is the fluid, transformative and enveloping lived tradition of a social group. The latter is analytic, critical, and rational, the product of the application of specialized scientific methodology.

Such distinctions are deceptive, particularly for understanding history and memory in the Middle Ages, but even for understanding the role of history in the present. Postulating a dichotomy between collective memory and history ignores the social and cultural context of the historian. Writing around the year one thousand, the hagiographer Letaldus of Micy, when preparing his *Miracula S. Maximini*, first circulated a draft of his text among the older monks of his community, who reminded him that he had omitted much from his account "and they recalled to our memory among many things this miracle which we should recount."[31] He then revised his text in accordance with the collective advice of his elders. Here individual and communal memory are not opposed but rather work as one. Likewise, written and oral memory blend together, as oral traditions are incorporated into a written text, which is then circulated among those responsible for collective oral memory. These elders then corrected and revised, but probably also incorporated into their oral memory the essential content of Letaldus' text, which itself underwent subsequent revision based on criticisms advanced by these memory experts.

This dichotomization of memory and history also ignores the political or intentional dimensions of both collective memory and history. Historians write for a purpose, essentially to shape the collective memory of the historical profession and ultimately of the society in which they live. As Keith Baker has pointed out, documentary records often have prescriptive force in society, thus materially affecting the development of collective memory.[32] Successful history is assimilated into collective memory. Likewise, oral tradition plays an essential role in the manner in which historians elaborate their texts. This is true not only of the traditions collected by oral historians but also of the oral culture of the historical profession which determines how and what we write more than we would perhaps like to admit. If the writing of modern historians appears analytic, critical, and rational, the reason is that these are the rhetorical tools that promise the best chance of influencing the collective memory of our age. Similarly, if historical memory is essentially political, so too is collective memory. If collective memory is enveloping and identity forming, it is so for a reason. Rather than an unreflected sharing of lived or transmitted experience, it too has been orchestrated no less than the historical memory as a strategy for group solidarity and mobilization through the constant processes of suppression and selection. For this reason ethnologists and oral historians must often cover the same ground repeatedly before dissident elements of individual memories can be recovered—if they can be recovered at all.[33] All memory, whether "individual," "collective," or "historical," is memory *for* something, and this political (in a broad sense) purpose cannot be ignored. If the distinction between collective and historical memory appears clear in the present and obscured in the distant past as Nora argues, this is so only because of the difficulty of recovering the context within which the memory of the distant past was formed.[34]

For similar reasons, James Fentress and Chris Wickham chose to speak, not of "collective memory" but rather of "social memory."[35] As they point out, social memory "does more than provide a set of categories through which, in an unselfconscious way, a group experiences its surroundings; it also provides the group with material for conscious reflection."[36]

A second dichotomy often proposed is the distinction between written and oral. We are told that literate society, merely by having no system of elimination, no "structural amnesia," prevents the individual from participating fully in the total cultural tradition to anything like the extent possible in nonliterate society.[37] This hypothesis has been taken up by historians, among them Michael Clanchy, whose study of the increasing use of written instruments in England postulates just such a transition.[38] Clanchy shows with enormous perception the process by which the growth of written instruments of government transformed the legal, social, and mental processes of English people from kings to peasants between the eleventh and fourteenth centuries. He is particularly perceptive in discussing the elaboration and uses of archives and the discontinuous changes in storage and retrieval systems whereby these archives could serve the purposes of royal government.

However, Clanchy recognizes that one cannot postulate linear development from a largely oral culture in the early Middle Ages to a literate culture by the late thirteenth century. He points out that reading and writing were widely common in early medieval Italy as well as in Merovingian Gaul and Visigothic Spain,[39] and that writing was already sufficiently established in England at the time of Augustine's mission in 597 that the laws of Aethelbert were written in Old English rather than in Latin.[40] Moreover, he acknowledges that nonliterate habits and methods of proof long persisted in various areas of life. However, his central argument remains that in the twelfth and thirteenth centuries, "the accumulation of documents, and their bureaucratic use, made more people literate."[41]

While Clanchy focused primarily on literacy and government, Brian Stock, in an equally ambitious and insightful study, extended the examination of the effects of the growth of literacy and, more importantly, of a text-oriented culture, to wider cultural and social issues.[42] He argues that prior to the eleventh century, Europeans functioned in a world that was essentially governed and made intelligible by oral discourse. This oral culture was suited to and supportive of "small, isolated communities with a strong network of kinship and group solidarity."[43] Writing in this oral culture certainly existed, but it did so as reminders intended to jog the memory of the reader or listener of that which had been communicated orally.

Gradually, Stock argues, over the later eleventh and twelfth centuries, certain specific groups reorganized around the written word. These "textual" communities redirected the source of authority from the oral tradition which might be noted by texts to the texts themselves. These communities were not necessarily composed exclusively of "literati" nor indeed did the text necessarily exist. What mattered was that texts, real or imagined, became the essential "intermediary between group interests and their ideological expression."[44]

Both of these authors are much more successful in describing the developments of the later eleventh and twelfth centuries than the point of departure for these developments. That the nature and quantity of writing changed during these centuries is certain. That it was a development from an oral culture is less clear, as Clanchy acknowledges in the revised edition of his study. This sort of argument may apply to traditional African societies or, possibly, to fifth-century Greece.[45] However, one cannot describe the civilization of western Europe in the tenth and eleventh centuries as an oral culture. Anglo-Saxon England is increasingly seen as the most governed realm of the later tenth and eleventh centuries, and this governance relied on written instruments and literate agents to a far greater degree than Clanchy assumed. Counting extant documents from the earlier period is an unsatisfactory way of dealing with the problem since, as we shall see in the following chapters, preservation of documentation was seldom random. We thus do not have random samples of either the quantity or quality of documentation from different periods of the Middle Ages but rather documents from previous ages selected for particular reasons by subsequent generations.

Much more important than quantitative comparison is the consideration of the types of documents that survive and the assumptions about later use-value of these survivals. One might well argue that the very commonplace nature of writing mitigated against saving most sorts of written communications, particularly after the Norman Conquest. To take but one example, while Clanchy rightly points out that very few Anglo-Saxon writs survive, the number matters less than the pattern of survival: the bulk come from one monastery—Westminster Abbey. Surely Westminster was not the only or the principal recipient of royal writs but was unique only in its systematic conservation of some of them. Moreover, since most writs, by their very nature, were ephemeral directives to sheriffs, there would have been no reason to preserve such documents once they had served their purpose. Those that Westminster decided to preserve were kept because they might be useful as title deeds or privileges. The very preservation of this small group of writs of a particular nature by a single institution could be seen as evidence of a much wider practice, if one could extrapolate to other types of writs and other recipients across the kingdom.[46]

Writing on the Continent was even more widespread in the early Middle Ages, and it reached far down into the social order.[47] Since much of this writing was done on papyrus in the sixth and seventh centuries and, in some areas of southern Europe into the tenth century, almost all of it has disappeared. However, formularies, fragments, chance survivals, and codicological studies all permit a reassessment of the early Middle Ages as a period during which writing penetrated deeply into medieval society.[48] As we shall see in the following chapters, the same sorts of selective processes one can observe in the Westminster writs explain the survival and the disappearance of Continental documentation from the early Middle Ages.

Moreover, as Chris Wickham has argued, the distinction between oral and literate genres in any society in which writing has appeared is not particularly helpful.[49] As he points out, writing may transform memory by fixing it, but even heavily text-oriented societies communicate values (and, one should add, the interpretative structures within which to understand these written memories) orally.

What Clanchy, Stock, and others are observing in the eleventh century is less the result of a evolution from oral to literate society than the result of two rather different factors. First, the sparse evidence of documentation quite likely comes from a different understanding of the purposes and uses of writing and the relationship between text, action, and object rather than from a lack of writing. Second, and for our purposes far more interesting, is that the paucity of evidence at our disposal today is the result of losses of written evidence, much of which is attributable to decisions made in the eleventh century about the utility of the masses of written material inherited from previous centuries. In other words, the paucity of written evidence from the early Middle Ages tells us less about written records of that period than it does about the preoccupations of its heirs.

Thus Europe in the tenth and eleventh centuries was one of restricted literacy, but literacy organized around the book, interpretative communities even accustomed to using written archives in fairly modest landholding families. Written memory played an important role in the eleventh century, but as Stock and Clanchy rightly observe, it does not necessarily have a privileged position over oral memory.[50] The context established by the oral culture was essential for the training in selecting and interpreting that which was written. As Mary Carruthers suggests, the cultivation of oral memory was essential to all literate societies of antiquity and the Middle Ages.[51] As we shall see, the two work closely together, both subject to the same processes of transformation.

How then should we approach the history of memory? First, we must examine the understanding of memory in late antiquity and the Middle Ages. The central place of memory in the understanding of human cognition as well as in the understanding of the relationship between the human and divine natures placed an enormous memorial burden on medieval society. As Jacques Le Goff has shown, the Judeo-Christian tradition of the Middle Ages placed enormous importance on memory and commemoration.[52] *Memoria* in its many forms was at the heart of Christianity with its eucharistic injunction: "Do this in memory of me" and with the monastic obligation of the liturgical remembrance of the living and the dead. But *memoria* was also central to secular spheres such as legal and institutional legitimization with their dependence on *consuetudo* and precedent. All of these obligations demanded faculties and systems of memory that could provide adequate and accurate, even if admittedly partial, recovery of the past.

Second, we must investigate modern understanding of memory and its functioning. Memory is recognized as a dynamic, creative process, quick to transform that which is remembered and capable of elimination, simplification, and distortion of the past. Although they expressed their anxieties about memory in terms different from those of modern experimental psychologists, medieval rememberers were well aware of the dangers and weaknesses of memory even while acknowledging its centrality: "Because the human memory is very weak . . ." begins the *arenga* or harangue of many medieval charters.[53] The conclusion of this preliminary examination is the recognition of a dilemma in medieval consciousness: memory is at once essential and impossible. The subsequent chapters of this book will examine how people attempted to resolve this dilemma.

The Burden of Augustinian Memory

The Middle Ages inherited two classical memory traditions. First, memory played the essential role in Platonic and neo-Platonic epistemology. Remembering (ἀνάμνησις, μνῆμα) is the means by which one acquires true knowledge. While one is not actually born with innate ideas, sense experience suggests truths and thus starts a process of thinking which leads the mind to recover knowledge that had been lost.[54] The second, more prosaic but no less important classical tradition is that of artificial memory, the techniques of memory training that were essential tools of the well-trained rhetorician.[55]

For both of these traditions, Augustine was the essential conduit through which classical understanding of memory took definitive form and was transmitted to subsequent generations. His understanding and, more importantly, his misunderstanding of memory are seminal in the Western tradition.

Augustine, in book 10 of his *Confessions*, presented the basic understanding of memory in antiquity and the early Middle Ages: "Great is the force of memory, enormously great, my God, a chamber vast and infinite. Who has ever sounded its depths?"[56] His analysis of memory was not an empirical examination of the human memory in the context of psychology or rhetoric but rather an examination of *memoria* as a transcendent phenomenon.[57] Both in the *Confessions* and as developed further in books 9–15 of *De Trinitate*, memory plays much the same role in Augustine's neo-Platonic psychology that *intellectus* does later for Aquinas. With memory one moves through a three-step process of knowledge: first, what is external and known by the senses; second, what is internal and known by introspection; and, finally, what is beyond man and can be known through participation. The process of thought involves gathering together (*colligere*) the data stored in the vast chambers of the memory.[58] But beyond the knowledge of the world, memory is the fundamental means by which one knows oneself. Augustine is fascinated by the process of remembering, of finding continuity between his infancy, of which he retained no memory, his past life, and his present adulthood.[59] It is this memory of past memories, combined with an even more mysterious memory of forgetfulness, which constituted and defined the self.

Even while interpreting transcendent *memoria*, Augustine was deeply influenced by his rhetorical training. For him, as for other classical rhetors, memory was conceived of spatially, as fields and meadows or "vast courts" and "boundless chambers," in which are found innumerable things that can be brought forth when needed.[60] Although the process, and particularly the process of moving from forgotten to remembered, is mysterious for Augustine and others, how and what is remembered is not. Physical things are remembered through images and according to their distinct properties.[61] Ideal things are actually present in the memory without images.[62] Intellectual acts are both actually present and perceived as past acts.[63] Finally, his only uncertainty is about how emotions are present in memory, whether actually or through images.[64] Thus all of one's past is present, "either through images, as all bodies; or by actual presence, as the arts; or by certain notions or impressions unknown to me, as the affections of the mind."[65]

The centrality of Augustine's understanding of memory can be seen in his *De Trinitate*. Here, psychological memory is a fundamental element of the manner in which the human soul reflects the image of God. Just as the Father is the first person of the Trinity, the *memoria* is the first part of the psychological trinity with *intelligentia* and *amor* or *voluntas* comprising the other two.[66] *Memoria* is consciousness, at once of the external world, of the remembering subject, and of God. Thus it corresponds to the first Person of the Trinity. *Intelligentia* results from *memoria* and thus corresponds to the second Person, the Son, who is engendered by the Father. *Amor* or *voluntas*, impossible without consciousness and thought, bonds these two together and corresponds to the Holy Spirit, the third Person of the Trinity.[67] Thus for Augustine memory is the highest intellectual faculty and the key to the relationship between God and man. In the words of Gerhart Ladner, "Memory of sin and of God, memory as distraction and as consciousness, is the bridge between the timeless perfection of the Triune Creator and the temporal and multiple nature of the imperfect creature man."[68]

This trinitarian analogy continued to have great influence throughout the Middle Ages, appearing in the ninth century in Alcuin's *De animae ratione liber ad Eulaliam virginem*:

> The soul thus has in its very nature, as we have said, the image of the holy trinity, in that it has intelligence, will, and memory. . . . I understand that I understand, I will and I remember; I will to understand and remember and will; and I remember that I understand and will and remember.[69]

At a more prosaic level, even a hagiographer such as Arnold, as he wrote a book recording the miracles of his community's patron, Saint Emmeram, was aware that in publishing as a young man those useful things that he had learned as a child, he was participating in the great mystery of the Trinity, "that is of intellect, memory, and will."[70] Thus human memory mirrors the very nature of the godhead.

The centrality of memory in Augustinian epistemology and theology only reinforced the importance of the past in the traditional society of the Middle Ages. Even for those unaware of the philosophical implications of memory, precedent, the tradition of the Fathers, and ancient custom were the fundamental criteria by which the present was judged and the future planned.[71] Thus *memoria* was a key organizing principle, not only in medieval theology but in every aspect of medieval life.[72] It meant memory, but also those objects and actions by which memory was preserved. These included first of all tombs and funerary monuments but could also mean trophies, objects especially associated with important persons or events, relics sacred or profane. By extension, *memoriae* were the churches or altars that held these objects. Finally, *memoria* was the ritual commemoration of the dead: funerary processions; the anniversary of deaths; the liturgical celebration of the dead, both the ordinary dead and the "very special dead" who were the saints.[73] *Memoria* not only commemorated the departed but made them present through the manipulation of words (especially names) and objects.[74] The importance assigned to the past by medieval society was such that this past had to be considered essentially knowable, and thus static and accessible. The names of the dead commemorated in *libri memoriales* and necrologies had to be scrupulously recorded so that they could be made present once more at the Mass or when the necrology was read in chapter.[75] The memories retrieved by Augustine in the "vast courts" and "boundless chambers" had to be, if not the things themselves, then adequate images of them. The faculty of memory had to be able to recover the real past, not a distorted or transformed version of it. Thus memory in the Augustinian tradition carried a great burden, one that both medieval people and modern psychologists recognized as beyond its ability.

The Inadequacy of Human Memory

Modern studies of how memory actually operates present a radical contradiction to the Augustinian belief that memory could recover the real past. What is remembered is a creation of the rememberer. In general, psychological studies of memory develop from one of two experimental traditions.[76] The first, that of the nineteenth-century German psychologist Hermann Ebbinghaus, has concentrated on studying the ability to remember nonsense data, normally series of syllables. Such studies have been able to quantify the rate at which people forget and the various external factors (fatigue, time, and so on) that influence retention and forgetting.[77]

These carefully controlled experiments are, however, quite inadequate to examine the process by which people remember and forget complex, real-life data.[78] Between the first and second world wars the British psychologist F. C. Bartlett began a series of studies of the means by which people store, transform, and retrieve meaningful data, including complex stories and images.[79] While these studies in what is called reconstructive memory lack the quantification and precision possible in studying the ability to remember random syllables, they are much more useful to historians who want to understand how people have actually remembered and forgotten. In very general terms, the work of Bartlett and successors has shown that memory is an active process of creation.[80] It is intimately connected with the present: we perceive a world already meaningful because of the background of memory within which it is perceived. Conversely, there is a direct relationship between what is remembered and the present: to the extent that memories can be made meaningful and connected to the present, memory is retained. Even recent events or knowledge that is disjointed or dissident are quickly lost or transformed beyond recognition.

Psychologists disagree about the structure and types of memory. Endel Tulving has argued that one should distinguish between semantic memory (those things that one remembers but cannot date the acquisition of) and episodic memory (those things that are remembered within a chronological framework).[81] Others, such as J. L. McClelland, argue that it is more helpful to think of three sorts of memory: a generic memory, which is the structure in which memories are entered, organized, and retrieved; the atemporal memory, sometimes called semantic memory, of the sort necessary for the use of language in which is organized knowledge about symbols, rules, concepts, and the relationships among them; and episodic memory, that part of memory which concerns the storage and retrieval of temporally dated episodes and events and the temporal-spatial relationship among them.[82]

Without attempting to resolve the disagreements among experimental psychologists, for our purposes it is necessary to recognize the usefulness of the reconstructive tradition of Bartlett and Bransford, and the fundamental insight into the distinction between the structure within which memories are entered, organized, and retrieved and the content of this structure, whether temporal or not. Since, unlike a computer that stores data and then retrieves it intact, memory transforms its data, the various processes of assimilation and selection are extremely important in understanding creative remembering. This assimilation takes place through four primary processes. The first is visual association: unfamiliar objects are recognized (or made to appear) similar to known objects. The second is analogy—if something can be understood as being like something else, then it can be retained. Third, by logic—if a pattern can be perceived, then the complex data of memory can be recalled by using the formula of the logical pattern. Finally and perhaps most important, memory can be activated by labels, names. Experiments indicate that the ability to name the data of memory is extremely important in the process of remembering.

Toward a History of Medieval Memory

To apply all this to remembering around the millennium, we must examine the semantics of medieval memory. To paraphrase Lévi-Strauss, who asks, "What things are good to think with?" we need to know "What things are good to remember with?" What are the systems in which memory is retained, retrieved, and transformed? How do changes in these systems change the memories themselves? We return to visual association, analogy, logic, and labels. People's names were good things to remember with as were land and physical objects that by analogy or physical association might connect the present and the past. Logic, the logic of repeating patterns or typologies, preserved the past in the present. Texts were good for remembering with as well, but they, like all the rest of memory's contents, were subject to the same transformations caused by the structures of memory.

The following chapters will examine how people used these things "good to remember with" to overcome the dilemma of memory in the tenth and eleventh centuries. The first presents the general problem of the continuity between the eleventh century and its past, a continuity seen already in the late eleventh century as irreparably broken. Across much of the former Carolingian empire, laypersons and clerics were engaged in a similar process of rethinking and rerembering their familial, institutional, and regional pasts. The process, and the resulting pasts they constructed, were not uniform across Europe. And yet striking commonalities did appear in regions as diverse as the north of France long known as Neustria, Bavaria in the south of Germany, and the Mediterranean coast where the Alps meet the sea. Because of their very diversity, I have chosen to examine how these three regions came to terms with their distinct kinds of deep pasts in order to investigate both the spectrum of possible interactions and their commonalities. As necessary background to examining eleventh-century memory in these three regions, this first chapter therefore concludes with an overview of the transformations in these three regions of the former Carolingian empire that provide the particular contexts within which these topics are explored in later chapters.

The second examines family memory, looking at the memory specialists within eleventh-century society and considering the effects of institutional and social changes on the social dimensions of memory. As we shall see, memory was gender specific, with women traditionally assigned a primary responsibility for the preservation of memory (although reformed monks increasingly disputed this social role). We shall also see how changes in family strategy, onomastic patterns, and relationships with religious foundations might affect how and what lay society could remember about itself.

The third chapter concerns archival memory and the complex process by which decisions were made concerning what records of property, rights, and patrons would be preserved and what would be discarded. In particular it examines the appearance of cartularies and their gradual transformation from the ninth through eleventh centuries from administrative to memorial texts and considers how these texts were then used for other types of remembering. An essential part of this process was the destruction of the archives on which these memorial texts were based, thus closing routes to creating alternative pasts.

The fourth chapter examines two similar attempts, in different regions, to exploit monasteries' archival and memorial records to create a useful past. It explores the ways that charters, necrological texts, and oral traditions were selected and transformed to create a structure of the past mirroring claims for the future.

The fifth chapter examines memory in relation to power and lordship. Claims to memory are political claims to speak the past in a way that clarifies and justifies the present. This chapter examines the interrelated processes of forgetting, preserving, and appropriating visions of the past mobilized to justify or condemn power relationships seen through the memories of three unsuccessful claimants to regional power: Charles III (the Simple), Hugh of Arles, and Arnulf of Bavaria.

In the sixth chapter, the recollections of one Bavarian monk are examined in order to see how an individual brings to bear his personal experiences, familial traditions, and monastic archives to construct a past that is at once personal and universal.

The final chapter attempts to survey all of these interrelated topics to understand the creation of formalized pasts that would become constituent elements of European collective memory.

I

REMEMBERING AND FORGETTING IN THE

ELEVENTH CENTURY

THE NEW PAST forged in the eleventh century by Rodulfus Glaber, Arnold of Regensburg, and their contemporaries, with its emphasis on radical discontinuity, is an enduring creation: its central outlines, accepted and elaborated upon by subsequent medieval generations, have been largely accepted by modern historians. The image of destruction, disintegration, and confusion in the tenth century, followed by painful rebirth of a new society, is at the heart of what historians call the "Renaissance of the Twelfth Century" and is remarkably similar to that in the opening chapters of Marc Bloch's *Feudal Society*. This great monument of twentieth-century interpretative scholarship begins with volume one, *The Last Invasions*, whose first chapter, "Moslems and Hungarians," starts with "Europe Invaded and Besieged." In the concluding chapter of this first section, Bloch describes some consequences and lessons of the invasions:

> From the turmoil of the last invasions, the West emerged covered with countless scars. The towns themselves had not been spared . . . the trading centres had lost all security. . . . The cultivated land suffered disastrously, often being reduced to desert. . . . Peasants were driven to despair, . . . the lords were impoverished. But the material damage was not all. The mental damage must also be reckoned. . . . A society cannot with impunity exist in a state of perpetual terror. The incursions, whether of Arabs, Hungarians, or Scandinavians, were certainly not wholly responsible for the shadow that lay so heavy on men's minds, but they were without doubt largely responsible.[1]

From this "ground zero," Bloch and his successors rebuilt a Europe that historians have come to accept as the most creative period of the Middle Ages. Echoes of this view are heard in the two most influential studies of post–World War II medieval scholarship, both of which appeared in 1953—Georges Duby's monumental study of the society of the Mâconnais and Richard Southern's brilliant synthesis of European society between 972 and 1204.[2] Since then, the discontinuities and transformations of the eleventh and twelfth centuries have been echoed in countless studies of both synthesis (such as Jean-Pierre Poly and Eric

Bournazel's *La mutation féodale*)[3] and in the most focused of micro-histories (such as Guy Bois's *La mutation de l'an mil*).[4] The emergence of a new feudal society dominated by parvenu castellans and characterized by new patterns of labor exploitation, the discovery of the individual, the creation of courtly society, the emergence of literate, "textual communities," all stand in sharp contrast to a radically different ninth- and tenth-century past. At least this was until recently the scholarly consensus.

And yet, contemporary scholarship is making it increasingly clear that such a view, particularly when described in terms of rapid rupture and striking originality, is overstated. The parvenus of the eleventh century often have their origins in the Carolingian aristocracy. The continuity between Carolingian and eleventh-century intellectual traditions in such ancient cities as Laon, Reims, Regensburg, and Auxerre as well as in such monasteries as Fulda, Fleury, Reichenau, and St. Gall was stronger than many have supposed. The monarchs east and west of the Rhine in the eleventh century pursued agendas and operated within parameters largely established by their predecessors in the first half of the tenth century. In society, culture, and politics, the later eleventh and twelfth centuries are closely connected with their immediate past.

As a result, the "mutationist" tradition has come under sharp attack in recent years. These attacks have been directed not only against the quality of the scholarship of some who want to see a radical transformation in European society around the year one thousand[5] but, more significantly, against the very conceptualization of European history in terms of a radical break and "takeoff" in the eleventh century.[6] In France, criticism of the mutationist tradition focuses on the social and institutional continuities. While Marxist historians have argued for the prolongation of "classical" slavery to the eleventh century, others question the significance of the linguistic evidence and the possible interpretations of the scarce documentary material for proving the significance of chattel slavery in the tenth century.[7] Likewise, the image of a crisis in public order around the year one thousand, long a mainstay of political and institutional historians, is being questioned by historians more attuned to the fluid nature of the exercise of power between the ninth and twelfth centuries. Much of what appears to be a break in the means by which peace and justice are secured may be the nature of our documentation.[8]

In German scholarship, where both the Investiture controversy and, more generally, a desire to place German history within the established French "takeoff model" of European history have long led scholars to postulate the eleventh century as a moment of decisive novelty, more cautious scholars are questioning the basis for such generalizations.[9]

Even in English language scholarship, a much needed understanding of the deep importance of early medieval literacy has begun to serve as a corrective to the increasingly extravagant claims made ever since Charles Homer Haskins for the novelty of the so-called "Renaissance of the Twelfth Century" (a twelfth century that began circa 1050).[10]

Thus, bit by bit, the image, created in the eleventh century and perpetuated into the twentieth, is being discarded. And yet even scholars convinced of the deep continuities uniting the ninth and twelfth centuries are cognizant of fundamental differences separating these periods. Major changes in social structure, exercise of power, and cultural production did take place which, if not so abrupt as to deserve the term *revolution* (and in fairness to them, metaphors apart, Bloch, Duby, Southern, and even Poly and Bournazel, never described the changes they charted in such simplistic terms), were nevertheless profound. In the following chapters, we shall indeed see evidence of change and discontinuity in all three regions examined.

Thus arguments about continuity and change, apart from forcing scholars to reexamine their premises, seldom add much that is positive to historical debate. All too often they degenerate into a kind of sterile semantic argument about the difference between revolution, mutation, transformation, and evolution. What is most interesting however is not primarily the rate of change itself or how such change should be quantified or classified, but why and how generations perceived discontinuity, and how these perceptions continued to influence the patterns of thought for a thousand years. Transformations that took centuries, starting at least in the second half of the ninth century, begin to be perceived in the later tenth and early eleventh centuries as having created a gulf between the two periods, a gulf that was as much psychic as physical. Over the fairly short period of roughly a century, from circa 950 to 1050, the evidence of this continuity had become unintelligible. Although surrounded by the material, social, political, and mental residue of this previous world, eleventh-century people were at a loss to understand the previous systems within which these elements had had coherence. Nevertheless, they sought to make sense of this inherited residue and to use it to form their own individual and corporate sense of identity. In their histories and chronicles, in liturgies, in patterns of landholding and inheritances, in the transmission of names within kindreds, in political and social alliances, they distorted the elements of their past by selecting some and forgetting others. Moreover, they placed them into new structures of meaning, transforming memories into legends and finally into myths—that is, into creative, exemplary, and hence repeatable models of past, present, and future. These myths were comprehensible within the new cultural systems in the process of being born. At the same time, these myths gave meaning, legitimacy, and form to these new systems.[11]

The focus of this book is on this perception of discontinuity and on the process of selection and creation of a past that embodies this perception, rather than on the details of social, political, and cultural transformation or even the specific content of memories of these changes. This process was not uniform across the former Carolingian world nor can one argue that it was always the result of an intentional program to create a useful past. It was, however, a political creation in the sense that individuals, groups, and leaders of secular and ecclesiastical institutions and parties sought to use memory as a tool of power. This could be a defensive mechanism to protect ancient traditions threatened by new realities, or it could be a mechanism of consolidation, by which these new realities could be either anchored in or absolved of a past. The circumstances within which memories were created or abandoned could be extremely local, or broadly societal. They could be the result of careful calculations or the by-product of other decisions. I am interested in this interplay of intentionality and serendipity, of remembering and of forgetting.

An Age of Forgetting

A focus on memory and the process by which people actually remembered and forgot around the turn of the millennium is particularly appropriate because in no region of Europe was this either a high point of formal historiography or of a keen interest in learned traditions of artificial memory. In southern Europe, where traditions of writing remained deeply rooted in the fabric of everyday life, this recording of the past was largely a piecemeal affair of notaries. As Chris Wickham and Thomas Bisson have argued for Italy and southern Francia, record keeping for legal and practical purposes did not lead to the elaboration of much formal historiography.[12] Elsewhere in France, while a historiographical tradition closely tied to the cult of Saint Benedict was developing at Fleury-sur-Loire, the historiographical traditions that would begin to coalesce into the royal chronicles of St. Denis were more than a century away.[13] In the empire, only the Chronicle of Thietmar of Merseburg continued something of the Carolingian and Ottonian historiographical tradition. Otherwise, fragmentary local chronicles, annals, and hagiographical texts formed the bulk of what can be considered historical writing.

Nor did intellectuals display any interest either in the classical tradition of memory techniques such as those found in the *Ad Herennium* or in elaborating new systems by which great amounts of information

might be stored for easy retrieval. As Mary Carruthers points out repeatedly in her study of medieval memory systems, such "arts of memory"
begin only in the twelfth century. To the extent to which *memoria* is
discussed at all, she argues, it appears not in the context of rhetoric or
homiletics but rather incidentally in the context of meditation and
prayer.[14] Janet Coleman likewise glides quickly from Bede to Anselm in
her masterful medieval memory theories.[15]

It would be a serious mistake, however, to suppose that the lack of
coherent historiographical traditions or treatises on the arts of memory
indicates that contemporaries gave little importance to memory. Quite
the opposite is true. The fifty years on either side of the millennium were
a period deeply concerned with memory and memories, but not in the
same way as their successors. This was, as we shall see, a period of important reorganization of traditions of all sorts. Archives were established or
restructured. Documents were collected and recopied, or as frequently
destroyed or invented. Families rethought their ties to distant ancestors
in light of new obligations. Ruling dynasties began to deal with the
problem of tidying up the often messy memory of their rise to power.
Local religious communities sought to interpret their relationship with
the Carolingian age and, more concretely, with their increasing burden
of memorial obligations for the dead, the heart of *memoria* in a technical
sense in this period.

This concern with *memoria* has largely escaped the notice of historians of memory for several reasons. First, in the tradition of Frances
Yates, historians such as Carruthers who have attempted histories of
memory in the Middle Ages are primarily interested in the means by
which specific written texts were memorized and transmitted. In other
words, their orientation has been that specific form of "educated memory" that looks both backward to the rhetorical training of antiquity and
forward to the homiletic tradition of the mendicant orders.

"Educated memory" flourished prior to the twelfth century but in a
very different sense. Technical *memoria* was essentially liturgical, and
the tools necessary to master it were not those of the rhetor but rather
those of the liturgist. The history of liturgical memory is intimately connected with the development of musical notation, an area of growing
scholarly interest and controversy. Prior to the ninth century, liturgical
music was transmitted entirely by oral means. Learning and performing
"from memory" was an enormously demanding skill requiring years of
study. Guido of Arezzo (ca. 990–1050), the music theorist in the
Roman curia, wrote that prior to his time it had taken ten years to learn
the antiphonary, however imperfectly (although he boasted that by
using his own method, which combined musical notation with a theoretical understanding, he was able to teach the same skills in one or at

the most two years).[16] However, the introduction of notation, which began to be frequent first in the Frankish world from the tenth century, by no means replaced memorization with reading musical scores. Notation still functioned more as aide-mémoire and perhaps for instruction. While a cantor might be reading from a score, choir monks were not "reading music" in their actual performance of the liturgy. Nor did notation indicate the complete performance as fully as a modern score. Rather it provided patterns upon which performers could improvise. This improvisation was quite different from modern, individualistic improvisation but probably meant variations according to learned and locally reinforced patterns, which remained oral.[17] Moreover, what was to be remembered in the early Middle Ages was not only texts, such as prayers and scripture discussed by Carruthers, but persons. As soon as one looks to liturgical memory, one finds an abundance of material and information, deeply and competently studied by a generation of German scholars.[18]

Not only must one look at other types of "educated memory" in the early Middle Ages, but one must understand this kind of memory as part of a much more diffuse field of "practical memory." Extraordinary feats of memorization—such as the ability to recite all the psalms or to learn all the liturgy necessary for the celebration of the monastic office throughout the year—thus are less the focus of this study than the complex process through which ordinary individuals order, understand, and retrieve all sorts of information that together provide the referential field within which to experience and evaluate their daily experiences and to prepare for the future.

The second reason that *memoria* around the millennium has been little investigated is that historians of memory have tended to dichotomize memory and written record, as though the two were mutually exclusive. Too many scholars assume that memory is oral and stands in opposition to the textual transmission and creation of the past. One can certainly use memory in this restricted sense, but to do so is to ignore the relationship between textual and oral transmission. For a society that conceived of memory primarily as a book, the distinction between what was actually written and what was not was blurred. If human and divine memory are books, then books form an essential physical extension of memory. Written records, personal recollections, and communal traditions share the same field, and *memoria* is the sum of them all.

The third reason that the study of memory in the tenth and eleventh centuries has been underappreciated is perhaps because historians are normally interested primarily in what is remembered, while this period was more concerned with the other vital component of memory—the ability to forget. Nietzsche described memory and its equally important opposite, forgetting, as "that malleable power of a person, a people, a culture, . . . to grow in new directions, to restructure and reconstitute what is past and foreign, to heal wounds, to replace what has been lost, and recast those molds which have been broken."[19] Precisely this power is most in evidence in the tenth and early eleventh centuries. Without too much exaggeration, one can characterize the decades around the first millennium as an age of forgetting, the mental clearing of the forest, if one will (another image used by Arnold of Regensburg), which made possible the great process of mental creation of the later eleventh and twelfth centuries.

Finally, millennial memory has been little studied because, as we have seen, historians have largely accepted this created past as an adequate reconstruction of these centuries. Unlike periods venerated for their creativity and innovation (like the ninth or the twelfth), writers and archivists of this period have not been credited with enough imagination or ability to invent a past. As a result, modern scholars continue to work from within the myths they have spun about their world.

Memory in Regional Context

The diverse regions of Europe that had been forcibly joined during the Frankish period did not share uniform traditions of culture, politics, or social order. Its unity came from a common inheritance of certain elements of late Roman provincial organization, an imposed religious and ecclesiastical system, and an aristocracy put in place by victorious Carolingian conquerors. It is the last, perhaps more than anything else, that gave Europe its cohesion in the ninth century, and the disintegration of this aristocracy was both cause and effect of the loss of cohesion in the tenth and eleventh.

In the tenth century, as the Carolingian veneer began to wear thin, very different forms of identity and continuity emerged. Heinrich Fichtenau has eloquently characterized the tenth century as a period during which men and women struggled to impose the inherited order of the old system on a world that increasingly resisted such anachronisms.[20] Thus concentration on the broad similarities of the post-Carolingian experience must not eliminate the very particular ways in which different social groups in various parts of Europe re-collected their pasts. As noted in the introduction, this study will focus primarily on three distinct regions: the old Neustrian heartland, which would become the core of an emerging France; the Piedmont and lower Rhône region, with its older ties to a Roman and Mediterranean past; and the Bavarian world with its very different institutions and traditions reaching back beyond the edge of memory to the late Roman world of Noricum and Raetia. Before entering the details of how these regions remembered and forgot their past, we need to review briefly the broad outlines of their own specific histories in the half millennium following the disappearance of Roman political structures. No reader should be fooled by these "canned histories"—they are highly selective and truncated versions of what the author deems necessary in order to follow the more specific discussions in subsequent chapters. They are in a sense "master narratives" which, even while providing a necessary background, mask much of what is most vital during this period. Much of what follows in subsequent chapters will not only complete but, to some extent, subvert these simplistic summaries. Readers who really know their histories of all three regions might wish to skip them entirely.

The Rhône

The Rhône watershed, with its littoral connecting Italy and Spain, and its fluvial connecting the interior of Gaul with the Mediterranean world, is the most ancient civilized region north and west of the Alps. The indigenous inhabitants, called collectively Ligurians by classical authors, inhabited both sides of the mountains and extended as far as the Rhône to the west, the Arno to the southeast, and north to the Durance. Marseille is a city perhaps older than Rome itself, having been founded by colonists from the Ionian city of Phocaea circa 600 B.C. Long an ally of Rome against Carthage and a protector of Roman sea routes and Alpine passes to Spain, the threat of Celtic enemies led to an appeal to Rome for assistance in 125 B.C., which in time brought the establishment of Roman control in the region between the Cévennes and the Alps. When later organized under Augustus after the conquests of the remainder of Gaul, the province of the Narbonensis became the *provincia* par excellence and has retained both its name, Provence, and its distinctly Italian air. Early on, full citizenship and Latin rights for cities such as Narbonne, Arles, and Marseille became the rule.

Although initially the Alps separated Provence from Italy for purposes of government, the ancient Ligurian cultural areas survived Roman political and cultural innovations. The Alps did not so much divide as unite the two sides of their slopes. A more fundamental division was the broad Rhône. In the fourth century, the region east of the Rhône along with the neighboring areas of Cisalpine Gaul were reorganized as part of the western Septem Provinciae and included the provinces of Narbonensis Secunda, the Viennensis, and the Alpes Maritimae and Cottiae.

Marseille took the losing side in the Civil Wars, siding with Pompey, and Caesar rescinded all of its political and commercial privileges. In its

Map 1. The Lower Rhône

place he developed the Greek city of Arles, well located on the Rhône just above its delta, into the foremost port in Gaul. Other cities, especially Vienne, the capital of the Septem Provinciae, competed with it, but Arles became the major commercial center, the residence of emperors, and in the fifth century the seat of the praetorian prefecture of the Gauls.

The prosperous cities of Provence early on acquired colonies of Eastern traders, including indigenous Greeks, Jews from at least the first century B.C., and Syrians. Within these communities appeared the first Christians, who by the early fourth century were sufficiently numerous to have organized churches headed by bishops. When the emperor Constantine convened a council of Western bishops to condemn the Donatists in 315, he chose Arles as the site, and representatives of sixteen Gallic churches attended. The ecclesiastical organization of the region followed closely the political, with Vienne and Arles disputing the position of metropolitan see.[21]

Provence was also the port of entry for Eastern monasticism into Gaul. In the early fifth century, Honoratus (later bishop of Arles) founded a monastic community on the island of Lérins off the coast of Provence. Around the same time, John Cassian founded two monasteries in Marseille modeled on those he had experienced in Egypt and Palestine—one, St. Victor, for men and the other for women. These institutions became the nuclei of a distinctive form of monasticism that spread through eastern Gaul and were centers for the education of ecclesiastical leaders through the lower Rhône as well as places of retirement for aristocrats during the turbulent fifth and sixth centuries.

The riches of Provence lured Visigothic raiders in 413, 426, 430, and 452 before being conquered by the Visigothic king Euric in the 470s. After his death in 483, all of Provence was held by the Burgundians briefly before being divided between the Burgundians north of the Durance and the Visigoths to the south. After Clovis's defeat of the Visigoths, Theoderic the Great annexed southern Provence into his Ostrogothic kingdom. The Franks acquired the northern portion of Provence when they conquered the Burgundians in 534 and the southern portions from the Ostrogoths two years later in return for their neutrality in the Goths' desperate efforts to resist Justinian's reconquest. Following the Lombard conquest of Italy, Lombard dukes led raids both through the Alpine passes and along the coast as far as the Rhône. In the 570s the Franks drove them back and extended the eastern boundaries of Provence by taking the valley of the Dora Ripuaria as far as Susa on the eastern slopes of Mount Cenis from the Lombards.[22]

Frankish interest in Provence focused on two areas. First, the Franks wished to control the strategic Alpine passes that connected the old Burgundian kingdom to Italy. Second, Frankish kings were eager to control the maritime commerce and thus the customs duties of the two principal ports, Arles and Marseille (the latter having recovered its importance in the course of the fourth and fifth centuries). As a result, at times Provence was divided between Merovingian kings, with one controlling Arles and the other Marseille, while at others it was united under a single northern ruler.

In keeping with their limited purposes in Provence, the Merovingians left intact its late Roman political organization as modified by the Burgundians and Ostrogoths. The royal representatives in Provence (as in lower Burgundy) were individuals termed *praefecti*, *rectores*, or, increasingly in the seventh century, *patricii*, assisted by judges, moneyers, and toll collectors. Municipal councils also continued to function at least into the seventh century. Most of the individuals filling these functions appear to have been drawn from the local aristocracy, although probably in the early seventh century some families from Frankish Burgundy established themselves in lower Provence, particularly in Marseille and Arles, marrying into the local elite and maintaining both local and super-regional spheres of interest.[23]

In the later seventh and early eighth centuries, the patricians managed to establish themselves as virtually autonomous rulers, in the manner of the dukes of other peripheral regions of the Frankish world. This brought them into conflict with Pippin II and his son Charles Martel. The penultimate patrician, Maurontus (termed *dux* in Frankish sources), allied himself with the Muslim Wali of Septimania in order to resist Charles Martel. However, in 737–38, with the assistance of other regional kindreds, Maurontus and his Muslim supporters were driven from Provence in a scorched-earth campaign that left upper Provence devastated for over a generation.

Following the death, sometime around 750, of the last patrician, Abbo, who owed his position to his support of Charles Martel, the Carolingians abolished the office and installed instead counts drawn from the north. However, the counts of Provence, established in Arles, were in many ways the successors of the patricians. They governed this vast area through their viscounts and their tribunals of Roman law judges. Typical of Carolingian *mainmise* elsewhere, their agents absorbed confiscated lay and ecclesiastical property into the fisc or redistributed it to their *vassi* and took direct control of the appointment of abbots in important regional monasteries such as St. Victor of Marseille and Novalesa, founded in the strategically vital Mount Cenis pass by Abbo.

The early Carolingians had no more direct interest in Provence than had their Merovingian predecessors. Their only visits to the region were in the course of their Italian expeditions, when the Alpine passes, especially the Mount Cenis and the St. Bernard, became vital invasion routes into the Lombard kingdom. In the course of the early ninth century, northern Provence, including the Viennois and the regions of southern Burgundy around Lyons, developed into a separate *ducatus*.[24] The entire region formed part of the inheritance of Lothar in the division of the empire by Louis the Pious, and Lothar seems to have drawn on support from the area of Vienne in his struggles against his father. Further south, the counts of Arles were largely on their own. In the middle of the ninth century, they were pursuing increasingly independent courses. In 845, Count Folcrad, termed "dux Arelatensis" by the *Annales Fuldenses* and "other Provençal counts" briefly revolted against the emperor.[25]

After Lothar's death in 855, his son Charles received a kingdom composed of the county of Arles and the region north of the Durance including the *ducatus* of Lyons and Vienne. The kingdom was an ephemeral political formation, largely dominated by the great magnates such as Girard of Roussilon, variously termed *marchio* and *dux*. After Charles's death in 863, his kingdom was disputed by his uncle Charles II (the Bald) and the former's brothers, Lothar II and Louis II, emperor and king of Italy. The long fight for the support of the Provençal aristocracy ended in the north in 870 in a victory for Charles the Bald, who installed his brother-in-law count Boso in Vienne. In 875, following the death of Louis II, Charles added the southern region, previously held by Louis, to Boso's control.[26]

Boso worked without cease to build his relations with Charles, with Italy, and with Pope John VIII. He also married Ermemgard, daughter of Louis II. After the deaths of Charles the Bald in 877 and his son Louis in 879, Boso was made king, the first non-Carolingian to claim the royal title. Boso was probably less interested in establishing a separate kingdom in Provence than in expanding his power in Italy and in challenging the surviving Carolingians, Carloman and Charles III (the Simple), both of whom were minors, for hegemony in all of western Francia and Italy. However, he met enormous opposition from supporters of the Carolingians on both sides of the Rhine and was unable to expand his claims beyond lower Burgundy and Provence, even losing the eastern portions of Provence to Charles the Fat and western portions to Carloman. Boso died a failure in 887. His wife fled with her son Louis to her uncle Charles the Fat who, in the absence of other legitimate adult Carolingians, had temporarily been recognized as king throughout the Frankish world. The childless Charles, approaching the end of his life, adopted Louis (less as the son of Boso than as the grandson of emperor Louis II). This act of adoption, as well as Charles's failing health and his inability to protect the kingdom, provoked a rebellion in favor of the Carolingian bastard Arnulf of Carinthia (see below), which led to Charles's deposition. Charles died shortly thereafter, but Arnulf agreed to the creation of a kingdom for Louis in lower Burgundy and Provence.

Louis's reign was longer than that of his father but equally ineffective. He sought to expand his kingdom south into Italy only to be captured and blinded by Berengar of Friuli in 905. He returned to Vienne and reigned for twenty more years, while his cousin Hugo of Arles, grandson of Lothar II, ruled as duke of Vienne and marquis of Provence.

As we shall see in chapter 6, Hugo, with his "Burgundian" supporters, sought to reconstitute the old Middle Kingdom of his great-grandfather, Lothar I, not only in lower Burgundy and Provence but in upper Burgundy, which since 888 had been a separate kingdom ruled by the Welfs Rudolf I and Rudolf II, and in Italy, where he was crowned king in 926. In Provence he and his supporters, probably with the assistance of Muslim adventurers who had established themselves in the Maritime Alps in the late ninth century, harried the indigenous aristocrats and seized control of key bishoprics such as Embrun, Arles, and Marseille in an attempt to merge Provence into his Italian kingdom. Although pressed by circumstances to abandon Provence to Rudolf II in 933, Hugo did not abandon his ties to the region and, when forced from Italy in 946, returned to Provence where he died the following year.[27]

The violence and political confusion of the first decades of the tenth century left Provence under the nominal authority of the kings of Burgundy but actually under the autonomous control of the various strongmen, many originally established in the entourages of Louis the Blind or Hugh of Arles. These opportunists managed to create local ties and to play the various parties off against each other for their local advantage. Chief among these were the new counts of Arles—Boso (942–966) and his sons Rombald (965–1008) and William II (the Liberator; 970–993), who dominated lower Provence and Arduin, and the marquis of Turin, whose family had come into the Alps from the west and who took control of the passes between Maurienne and Turin.[28] By uniting in 972 to expel the Saracens from Provence, the counts of Arles and the marquis of Turin solidified their positions as de facto autonomous rulers of their regions. Their dependence on the kings of Burgundy Provence or of Italy were merely nominal. By the beginning of the eleventh century, the ancient region of Provence and Cisalpine Gaul was well on the way to becoming small, fragmented lordships, dominated by an aristocracy whose sphere of interest was increasingly local and whose ties to the more international traditions of their ancestors increasingly unimportant.

Neustria

The nascent France of the early eleventh century corresponds but poorly with the ancient boundaries of Roman Gaul. The heart of the kingdom, the royal domains, cut across the Roman provinces of Belgica II, Lugdunensis II, Lugdunensis Senonia, and Aquitanica I. In fact, the region between the Loire and the Rhine had undergone a series of social, cultural, and political transformations from late antiquity to the new millennium. The result was a richly layered palimpsest whose future, in the eleventh century, was still impossible to read.[29]

The kingdom of Syagrius, taken over in the late fifth century by the Roman commander in Belgica Secunda, the Frankish king Clovis, was more a residual than a formal political entity. Grants to Burgundian and Gothic commanders and their subsequent expansions had reduced Roman Gaul to an isolated northern region protected by a multiethnic army dominated by Franks long under the influence of Roman legal and

Map 2. Neustria

military tradition. The establishment of Clovis as ruler of this region, and his adoption of the orthodox faith of the indigenous Gallo-Roman aristocracy, created the base for an amalgamation of barbarian and Roman society between the Loire and Rhine and for an expansion of Frankish military and political power south to the Pyrenees and east beyond the Rhine to the Enns.

In the heartland the Frankish kings and their associates continued the process of assimilation into what remained of Roman culture while working closely with what remained of the Roman provincial administration, and both were considerable. The *civitates* of northern Gaul continued a vigorous if somewhat reduced life, especially in their public roles as centers of justice and administration and, increasingly, of religious organization under their bishops. Titles and legal documents continued to be registered in the *gesta municipalia*, in some places well into the eighth century. Tax obligations continued to be assigned and collected for the fisc. Bishops, selected from leading members of senatorial families, exercised along with royal counts the powers of Roman magistrates they had enjoyed since the time of Constantine.

The divisions of the lands ruled by Clovis among his sons respected the traditional divisions of late Gallic dioceses, and each son ruled from an ancient *civitas*: Paris, Reims, Orleans, and Soissons. By the end of the seventh century, three great Frankish kingdoms had emerged from the interplay of regional aristocracies and royal succession and intrigue: Austrasia, Burgundy, and Neustria. The first was in large part the old Rhenish Frankish kingdom around Cologne, the second the old Burgundian kingdom to which had been added portions of Aquitaine. Neustria, the most western region and the traditional base of Clovis, became the center of the most powerful Merovingian kingdom. Under Dagobert I, it formed the center as well of a united Francia.

The concentration of vast fiscal lands in the region, its ancient Roman administrative and episcopal cities, and its monasteries—both the ancient institutions such as St. Martin of Tours and Marmoutier in the south and new foundations such as St. Denis, Corbie, and Chelles, founded or patronized by Dagobert, his successors, and their wives—made Neustria the prize in the Frankish world. This prize was violently disputed in the second half of the seventh century, first among aristocratic factions within Neustria and then, increasingly, between the Neustrians and the Austrasian Franks, led by the Pippinids. By the end of the century, the Pippinids had seized control of the region, its monasteries, and its Merovingian monarchs. Pippin II, and even more his son Charles Martel, brought about a major change in the power structure of Neustria by placing their kin and Austrasian supporters in important positions throughout the region, especially as abbots and bishops, thus breaking the power of the old Neustrian aristocracy. The central institution in this project was St. Denis, which had enjoyed the special patronage of the later Merovingians and which now became the central religious and political power base of the Pippinid family in the West.

Under Charles's sons, the united Frankish realm was subdivided in a way that sought to destroy the traditional distinctions between Neustria and Austrasia in favor of a unified Francia between the Rhine and the Seine. Repeatedly in the later eighth and early ninth centuries, Pippin and then Charlemagne (Charles the Great) filled important comitial and episcopal posts with their Austrasian supporters, further unifying the aristocratic society of East and West. This unity survived less than a century, however. In the divisions of the Frankish world that followed the death of Louis the Pious, his son Charles the Bald ultimately received the portion that corresponds roughly to the Neustria of the seventh century. By recognizing the rights of the aristocracy in his kingdom, Charles won their support and established what would become a fundamental relationship between the West Frankish king and his supporters: kings and aristocrats were partners in public power, with the latter enjoying inheritable control over their *honores* or public functions and the right to participate in the election of their king.

Under pressure to protect his kingdom from Vikings and Britons to the west, east, and north—and from brother Louis the German in the east—as well as to make good his claims to Aquitaine, Charles confirmed a series of great aristocrats, most of them from northern Francia, in positions of extraordinary power along a band stretching from Flanders to Toulouse. The most important of these was Robert the Strong, who obtained the counties of Anjou, Touraine, Blois, and Orleans as well as the lay abbacies of Marmoutier and St. Martin of Tours. These grants, beginning in the 850s, laid the foundation for Robert's family, later known as the Capetians, to replace that of Charles on the West Frankish throne.

The power of Robert's kin in the center of old Neustria grew rapidly under Charles and his ineffectual successors, particularly owing to the former's ability to organize effective resistance to the Vikings. After the death of Charles's grandson Carloman in 884, a delegation of the kingdom's aristocracy invited the East Frankish king Charles the Fat to assume the crown, which he did until shortly before his death in 888. During these four years, Charles increased the power and authority of Robert's successor Eudes, who largely ruled in his place. The year 888 marked a crucial moment in western Francia as it did in Provence, Burgundy, and elsewhere in the Frankish world. Following the death of Charles the Fat, Eudes was elected king of the West Franks. This non-Carolingian recognized the suzerainty of the illegitimate East Frankish Carolingian Arnulf and thus in a sense continued the fiction of Carolingian dynastic prerogative. But the audacity of the election and Eudes's undisguised efforts to work his position to the advantage of his family indicated a major change in the nature of the kingdom, which was hotly opposed by defenders of the Carolingian tradition, especially by Archbishop Fulk of Reims. Fulk and his allies managed to arrange for the Carolingian Charles III (the Simple) to succeed Eudes, but at a great cost. In return for Eudes's cooperation, Charles had to accept Robertinian control of the region centered around Paris, including the position of Eudes's brother as virtually autonomous marquis of Neustria and authority over the resources of royal monasteries such as St. Denis, St. Germain des Prés, and Fleury. Charles granted the same recognition of autonomy conceded the Robertinians to other powerful aristocratic families holding positions of counts in the kingdom. A few years later, in 911, Charles recognized the Viking chieftain Rollo's control of the lower Seine and, in the same year, the legitimacy of the non-Carolingian Conrad as king of the East Franks. Charles's acceptance of severe limits both to royal power within his kingdom and to claims without became the blueprint for future West Frankish monarchs.

The heirs to this program were the Robertinians. By attempting to recoup in Lorraine the authority he had abandoned in the West, Charles ended by alienating the aristocracies of both regions, solicited the aid of the Viking Rögnvald against them, and in 922 was defeated and imprisoned by a coalition led by Robert of Neustria.

From 922 on, the Robertinians controlled the fate of the West, whether directly as kings, as brothers-in-law of kings, or as power brokers for fatally weakened Carolingians. As "Dukes of the Franks," they recalled in their power and their title the Carolingians in the last decades of the Merovingian dynasty. Within their domains guaranteed by Charles the Simple they ruled without royal intervention. Outside, they created marriage alliances with the East Frankish Ottonians for assistance against the remaining Carolingians and their supporters. This alliance set the stage for the election of Hugh Capet in 987 and the destruction, if rather messy, of the Carolingian pretender Charles of Lorraine the following year.

The royal demesne at the heart of the new dynasty's authority lay between Orleans and Paris, with centers of royal power north of the Loire around Orleans, in the area of Paris and St. Denis, and around Compiègne and Senlis. Within this circumscribed area, the kings were effective and powerful lords by the standards of the time. However, the same recognition of rights, reaching back to Charles the Bald, which had made possible their rise, had created similar principalities throughout the kingdom. By the beginning of the eleventh century, the counts of Toulouse, Blois, and Anjou, and the dukes of Aquitaine, Normandy, and Flanders, enjoyed similar powers and some no doubt nourished ambitions for still more. The Capetian kings held certain major advantages, to be sure, including control of major episcopal sees and royal monasteries. However, they were in many respects but one princely family among many.

Bavaria

In the eleventh century, Bavaria was already an ancient and expanding region with a complex, layered tradition of social, cultural, and political heterogeneity and rupture. Much of Bavaria had been included in the Roman provinces of Noricum and Raetia, in which a Roman political and military presence had continued until the 480s.[30] Gradually, over the next centuries, within the region roughly bordered by the river Lech

Map 3. Bavaria

in the west, the Enns in the east, the southern slopes of the Alps in the south, and a vaguely defined line north of Regensburg corresponding to the modern Palatinate, the indigenous Romanized population merged with Alemanni and Germanic migrants from what is today Bohemia. Under pressure from the Franks to the northwest and Goths to the south, who both sought to fill the political vacuum left by the Roman withdrawal, this population fused into a new entity that called itself the Bavarians.[31]

The heterogeneous nature of Bavarian society continued well into the ninth century, although from at least the end of the sixth it was nominally part of the Frankish empire. Its hereditary dukes, the Agilolfings, were a family variously described as Frankish, Alemannic, and Lombard. Indeed, they were closely interrelated with Lombard kings and, from the mid-seventh century, ruled Bavaria in a regal manner. In addition to the

Agilolfings, Bavarian law recognized five other principal *genealogiae* (or clans) with a wergild double that of other freemen. The majority of the society included a still broader group of *nobiles*, and then a variety of simple free and unfree, some apparently holding a status that had evolved from the position of their ancestors as inhabitants of the former imperial fisc.

The center of ducal power was Regensburg, a former Roman *castellum* on the Danube whose ancient fortifications continued to provide the Agilolfings protection. Other Roman early centers, especially Salzburg and Passau, survived as much reduced population centers through the fifth and sixth centuries and emerged in the late seventh as centers of ecclesiastical organization. Indigenous Christianity also survived, primarily in these old Roman areas, and archaeological evidence shows that pilgrimage sites such as Lorch continued as cult sites through the sixth and seventh centuries.[32]

The Christian communities of the Alpine regions in the fifth and sixth centuries had been dependent on the Italian ecclesiastical provinces of Milan and Aquileia. Little is known about Bavarian religion in the subsequent century, but by the eighth the Agilolfing dukes, especially Theodo (ca. 680–717), promoted a reorientation to the north, but within the context of an independent Bavaria.[33] In 716 Theodo obtained papal permission to establish an ecclesiastical province independent of Frankish influence composed of four dioceses. These were to correspond to a quadripartite division of the duchy itself among the duke's heirs, who were to be established in Regensburg, Freising, Passau, and Salzburg.[34]

Although the division of the duchy did not materialize, the four dioceses did, with the assistance of western bishops who had been previously invited or welcomed by the Agilolfings. The first may have been Bishop Erhard of Regensburg, who according to Gottfried Mayr may have arrived in Bavaria from the Vosges region in the late seventh century.[35] Duke Theodo invited Bishop Rupert of Worms, an important Frankish aristocrat, to Bavaria and granted him Salzburg. Emmeram, an Aquitanian who arrived in Bavaria on his way to preach to the Avars, was welcomed in Regensburg and retained there as its bishop, perhaps because Theodo intended to make Regensburg the metropolitan see of Bavaria. However, the Aquitanian ran afoul of the ducal family, allegedly for having impregnated the duke's daughter. Theodo's son executed him, thus creating an important Bavarian martyr whose cult was preserved in the monastery in Regensburg of which he became the titular patron, while Salzburg eventually became the metropolitan see. Corbinian, possibly of Gallic and Celtic background from near Melun, came to Bavaria from Rome and established the see of Freising. Passau too had a bishop consecrated in Rome, Vivilo, who arrived in Passau sometime before 739.

The regal prerogatives taken by Theodo and his successors in the seventh century were possible because of the extended period of grave political crisis in Francia. Beginning in the 720s, after having established his power in Neustria and Austrasia, Charles Martel and his successors fought to bring Bavaria under their control. At the same time, Bavarian influence spread east past the Enns and down the Danube at the expense of the Avars. Carinthia in particular came under Bavarian hegemony. The last significant period of Bavarian independence occurred under its last duke, Tassilo (749–788), who conducted himself as a king rather than as a duke. He entered a marriage alliance with the Lombard king Desiderius, ordered Bavarian church councils, sponsored missionaries to the Carinthians, and negotiated with the Avars. These clear indications of monarchal pretensions disturbed not only the Carolingians in the West but, apparently, Bavarian nobles with Frankish ties and interests who felt threatened at home by the increasing ducal power. In 787 Charlemagne intervened, met little Bavarian resistance, deposed his cousin Tassilo on trumped-up charges, banished him for the rest of his life to a monastery on the lower Seine, and took firm control of Bavaria.

Charlemagne confiscated the extensive Agilolfing lands into the fisc, not always sparing ecclesiastical lands donated by or with the permission of the earlier dukes, whose confirmations he declared invalid. However, few other Bavarian magnates lost positions or wealth. Carolingian Bavaria retained its territorial integrity while growing at the expense of the Slavic principalities to the east. Nor was its tradition of political autonomy forgotten. From 814 it was a subkingdom, ruled from 817 to 876 by Louis the German, the second son of Louis the Pious, who came to rule most of the eastern portions of the Carolingian world. From 856 he established his son Carloman on the Pannonian frontier, thus preparing for him to assume control of Bavaria after Louis's death. Carloman died in 880 and was succeeded by his brother Louis the Younger, who died two years later. Briefly, between 882/84–888, Charles the Fat, the third son of Louis the German, ruled a once more united Carolingian kingdom by default as the sole surviving adult, legitimate Carolingian.

Louis the German divided much of his time between Frankfurt and Regensburg, the two centers of his power. Carloman favored Regensburg and the nearby royal palace at Otting. Among eastern towns only Regensburg and Aachen had palaces and residences within the city that were owned by monasteries, bishops, and aristocrats. These urban residences gave Regensburg an especially distinctive importance both as a royal center and as a quasi capital for lay and ecclesiastical magnates of Bavaria able to support a thriving merchant community. Still, frequent royal presence did not mean royal control. The Bavarian aristocracy, particularly in the East, was largely autonomous, with a power base in inherited land, new lordships in the Slavic east, military followers, and the ability to form coalitions of similar-minded aristocrats that kings could oppose only with great difficulty.

By 887 Charles the Fat was in poor health, had failed dismally to drive Viking raiders out of western Francia, and, in an effort to secure his succession, had adopted the non-Carolingian Louis of Provence as his presumed heir. A group of Bavarian and Slavic nobles, rallying around the illegitimate son of Carloman, Arnulf (known as Arnulf of Carinthia, 887–899), forced Charles into retirement (he died six months later) and established Arnulf as king. As we have seen in Provence and western Francia, across Europe new non-Carolingian dynasties were appearing: the Robertinian Eudes (Odo) in western Francia, the Welf Rudolf in the "Middle Kingdom" (Burgundy), Louis, son of Boso, in Provence, and the Unrochinger Berengar of Friuli in Lombardy. However, as the *Anglo-Saxon Chronicle* reported, at least initially the new kings looked to Arnulf as a sort of overlord because he alone was a descendant of the Carolingians on the paternal side.[36]

Arnulf's successes in defeating Viking raiders on the Dyle near Louvain in 891 and in supporting Berengar against Wido of Spoleto, as well as his ability to restrain noble factions in Saxony, Alemannia, and Thuringia, justified the wisdom of his succession. At home in Bavaria, however, he had difficulty controlling his nobles or protecting his favorites, particularly toward the end of his reign after he had suffered a stroke.

In his dealings with those beyond the Frankish kingdom, Arnulf initiated a new and ominous policy. In his 892 campaign against the Slavic Moravian kingdom, which had developed in the vacuum left by the collapse of the Avar empire, Arnulf employed a new steppe people, the Magyars, who as early as 863 had begun occasional raids into eastern Francia and who began to settle the Carpathian basin in 896. Arnulf may even have encouraged them to initiate their first major raid into Italy in 899, the year of his death.

Like his father, Arnulf was more successful in producing competent bastards than legitimate sons. The former, Zwentibold and Ratold, were mature men who received positions, respectively, as king of Lotharingia and subking of Italy. His only legitimate son, Louis the Child, was six years old at his father's death and, although acknowledged as his legitimate successor, was never able to assert his authority before his premature death at eighteen.

During the political vacuum of Louis's short reign, Bavaria was profoundly affected by the ravages of Magyar raids, which demonstrated the impotence of the king. Initial resistance was directed by Liutpold, margrave of Bavaria and a kinsman (presumably by marriage) of Louis. However, in 907 Liutpold attempted to engage the Magyars near the border of their own territory at Bratislava (Preßburg). The Bavarians were defeated and Liutpold killed. For the next six years, Magyars raided with impunity throughout Bavaria and the rest of the East Frankish kingdom. Liutpold's son Arnulf (the "Bad," 907–937) of Bavaria took not only his father's place at the head of the Bavarian resistance but also, implicitly, that of the *roi fainéant* Louis the Child. In 908 he was addressing in his charters all the "bishops, counts and princes of this kingdom," calling himself "By divine ordination duke of the Bavarians and the adjacent lands," a title almost royal in its formulation, recalling intentionally the older Bavarian duchy of the Agilolfings.[37]

Arnulf's claims were but the most explicit of the newly self-assertive leaders of the so-called "More recent Tribal Duchies" who sought to fill the vacuum of military and political leadership east and west of the Rhine. In Bavaria, Arnulf not only led armies but called councils and assumed protection of monastic lands, which he, like other regional magnates across Europe, occasionally confiscated to reward his supporters. In the shifting field of East Frankish politics, Arnulf had to find help where he could. After the death of Louis the Child in 911, Conrad I was elected king and sought to ally himself with Arnulf and other southern magnates by marrying Arnulf's mother Kunigunde. A joint expedition against the Magyars brought an important victory in 913. Soon, however, Conrad attempted to bring Bavaria under royal control, and the result was protracted war against his stepson. Temporarily, Arnulf was driven to seek asylum with his Magyar enemies but returned to fight Conrad, who was fatally wounded during an expedition against the Bavarian duke.

Following Conrad's death, Arnulf's power in Bavaria was such that an assembly of magnates elected him king (although whether this was understood as king of the East Franks or simply of Bavaria is unclear). Henry I, elected at Fritzlar in 919, invaded Bavaria but could not defeat Arnulf, who fortified himself within the walls of Regensburg. Ultimately, he submitted nominally to Henry, but Arnulf continued to rule Bavaria as an autonomous subkingdom until his death in 937, holding synods in Regensburg and Dingolfing, making a separate peace with the Magyars in 927, and extending Bavarian influence into Bohemia. In 935 he was even able to designate his son Eberhard as his successor, apparently with royal approval.

The autonomy Bavaria enjoyed under Henry, who had sought support from the dukes largely as a senior partner rather than as a sovereign, ended with the ascension of his son Otto I (936–973). In 938 Otto found an excuse to invade Bavaria and, after an initial reversal, managed to expel Eberhard and replace him with Arnulf's brother Berthold, who had been and remained loyal to the Saxon king. In the same year, he arranged the marriage of his brother Henry with Arnulf's daughter and betrothed his sister to Duke Berthold. Along with this marriage policy Otto ended ducal control over the Bavarian church. No further Bavarian synods were called by the dukes, and the king took control of episcopal appointments. The absorption of the duchy into the Saxon family's control was completed in 947 when Berthold died and was replaced by his brother-in-law Henry, although in some respects the latter acted more as an independence-minded Liutpoldinger than a Saxon.

Bavarian discontent united with a widespread disapproval of the influence Duke Henry exerted over his royal brother and led in 953 to open rebellion. Otto's son Liudolf of Swabia and his son-in-law Conrad of Lotharingia, fomented the revolt and were soon joined by the Liutpolding Arnulf, count palatine of Bavaria and brother of the deposed Eberhard, who with Liudolf drove Henry from Bavaria and seized his treasury at Regensburg. The revolt spread to Saxony and Thuringia and was made more serious by the intervention of the Magyars, possibly at the invitation or at least with the approval of Liudolf and Conrad, who quickly joined with them. This outside threat hastened the collapse of the revolt, and Liudolf retreated to Regensburg where he was eventually captured after a long siege.

The effects of this revolt and subsequent suppression were in the short term devastating for Bavaria. Arnulf was killed in the siege of Regensburg, Archbishop Herold of Salzburg, who had joined the revolt, was blinded, and Bavaria was ravaged both by the actions of the opposing armies and those of the Magyars.

However, after the Lechfeld, the Magyars ceased to pose a threat to the duchy. Duke Henry regained his position, which became de facto hereditary at his death in 955 when his minor son Henry (the Quarrelsome, 985–95; r. 995–78) succeeded him under the regency of his Liutpolding mother Judith. Although Henry lost his duchy following his revolt in 974 against Otto II after the death of the latter's father, he obtained its restoration in 985 by Otto III.

Throughout the latter tenth century, the Liutpoldings continued to be the key Bavarian family. After Henry lost Bavaria, which was given to Otto of Swabia, the Liutpolding Henry, son of duke Berthold, received the newly created duchy of Carinthia while another member of this powerful clan, count Liutpold of the Nordgau, received a march in the East, the future Austria. When Otto of Swabia died in 983, Henry of Carinthia succeeded him even though he too had rebelled against Otto II in 978.

Other kindreds, connected both to the royal family and to the Liutpoldings, were also major players in Bavarian political struggles of the tenth and early eleventh centuries, alternately supporting or rebelling against the king in order to enhance their families' positions. After

1002, when Duke Henry the Quarrelsome's son Henry IV of Bavaria (Emperor Henry II) secured the royal succession, the king passed over the Babenberger Henry of Schweinfurt, margrave in the Nordgau, and made his brother-in-law Henry of Luxembourg duke. This reneging on a quasi promise brought Henry of Schweinfurt and his Bavarian supporters into revolt. Duke Adalbero of Carinthia revolted in 1019 and Duke Conrad of Bavaria, deposed in 1053, was joined by the duke of Carinthia and the bishop of Regensburg in an attempt to replace Henry III with Conrad. As serious as these rebellions were (especially since the Carinthians in particular could at times look to the neighboring Hungarians and Slavs for assistance), beginning with Henry II the kings were able to maintain better control over the duchy of Bavaria as a whole than over more northern duchies where their rule was less direct.

The memories actively creating pasts for these three regions—Provence, Neustria, and Bavaria—will provide the touchstones of this investigation. However, in addition, the book will exploit a wider documentary base, stretching from Saxony to Italy but returning to these three regions as laboratories of memory creation. In so doing, it will attempt to place them in a broader context but will not forget that all history is in a sense local history. Generalizations about European history always risk degenerating into what John Freed has recently termed "Common Market History," a tendency to homogenize the rich diversities of experience into a bland and ultimately false synthesis.[38] Individual men and women, often faced with very specific problems and needs arising from their immediate circumstances, made the decisions that determined what of the past was to survive and what was to be discarded or buried with reverence.

As I have said before, these studies will be less concerned with the memories of trained rememberers than with those of more ordinary men and women burdened with the task of preserving and creating the past. Nor are they primarily the memories of kings and princes, although these inevitably and appropriately have their place in the following pages. Rather I am interested in the memories of lesser mortals, of the lay sister of Bishop Walthard of Magdeburg, entrusted by her dying brother with his memorial foundation; of a Bavarian monk, troubled by weak eyes and a fear of death, recording the memory of Saint Emmeram in fulfillment of a vow; and in the memory of an aged peasant woman who was wont to sit each afternoon in the dying sun of her Alpine village and tell her neighbors tales of long ago.

This book makes no claim to present a comprehensive view of any of the topics it explores. Nor does it pretend to exhaust the possibilities of analysis of memory and oblivion in any of the regions it treats. The very idea that such a comprehensive study might be possible is inimical to my understanding of the nature of history. Since Herodotus, history has been not a neatly packaged, "definitive" pronouncement on a particular problem, comprehensibly and exhaustively presented, but rather a series of investigations. I present these investigations then as a series of interrelated meditations on the twin problems of remembering and forgetting. It is my hope that they will help to elucidate some aspects of the topic and, more importantly, that they will offer ways of examining remembering both in the Middle Ages and in other times and places. They are only examples, steps into an infinite. Augustine judged it rightly: "Great is the force of memory, enormously great, my God, a chamber vast and infinite. Who has ever sounded its depths?"[39]

II

MEN, WOMEN, AND FAMILY MEMORY

SHORTLY BEFORE HIS DEATH in 864, Duke Eberhard of Friuli prepared the testamentary division of his property.[1] This included the division of his lands, arms, treasures, and books among his four sons and three daughters. The remarkable list of books that had formed his library has rightly drawn the attention of scholars interested in the extent of literacy among the Carolingian aristocracy.[2] As vital as this question undoubtedly is, however, we cannot forget that the primary issue in the testament was the division of his real property, lands inherited from his family, known to scholars as the Unrochinger for the most important name in the family "onomastic stock," *Unroch*, as well as that acquired in service to the Carolingians, including his father-in-law Louis the Pious.

Eberhard was one of the most successful members of what was truly an "imperial aristocracy" in the ninth century, that group of powerful families closely allied to the Carolingians who rose along with the descendants of Charles Martel to dominate vast portions of Western Europe. As Karl Ferdinand Werner has shown, this great family originated in the region of Mainz but, through their cooperation with the Carolingians, by the ninth century held positions of power and influence from Carinthia to Brittany and from Flanders to Italy.[3] Eberhard's brother Berengar was duke in Septimania, and he himself became duke of Friuli. He married a Carolingian princess, and his own son Berengar achieved the ultimate goal of any aristocrat: he was elected king of Italy and, ultimately, emperor.

The vast sweep of Eberhard's lands and interests is obvious in the testament. To his eldest son Unroch he left properties in Lombardy and Alemannia. Berengar received properties near Annappe and in the area between Liège and Dinant in modern Belgium. Adalard inherited around Lille, and Rodulf in the Pas de Calais, Antwerp, and Kempenland. His three daughters, Engeldrud, Judith, and Heiliwich received smaller bequests in the Low Countries.

The Unrochinger were extraordinary only in the heights to which they had risen. They were by no means unique in their pan-European holdings and interests. They were but one of many families whose interests and wealth were spread across the empire and who thus had as great a stake in its preservation as did the Carolingians themselves.

One sees a similar breadth of outlook in the families of Bernhard of Septimania and his wife Dhuoda, who composed around 843 a manual of advice for her son William.[4] If the geographical breadth of Eberhard's world is evident in his testament, so too is the social breadth of Dhuoda's in her manual, described by Pierre Riché as "a sort of spiritual and moral testament."[5] Dhuoda, like her husband, came from an Austrasian family whose origins in the region of the Moselle of present Luxembourg must have seemed far from Uzès, on the border between Provence and Septimania, where she penned her text. Still, she urged her son to remember his *genealogia*—that is, those kin living and dead particularly tied to William. These included maternal kin from the north as well as ancestors and aunts and uncles spread across the Carolingian world.[6] Through her book of advice and spiritual guidance, Dhuoda sought to insure that her son would preserve the *memoria*, that is, the formal, liturgical memory, of this broad and important kindred throughout his life.

The widespread interests of families such as Eberhard and Dhuoda had been made possible by the expansion of the Frankish world, and the disintegration of the latter would fragment the former just as fully. Already Eberhard sensed this impending fate since in his testament he specifies that the division he made in his will should be implemented:

> unless any king of the Lombards or of the Franks or of the Alemanni, (May it not be so! and I do not believe it will happen) should violently without cause alienate from any of the above named brothers the property we have granted him in this division, then we wish that they should divide the remaining property equally among themselves.[7]

Such confiscations and conflicts were of course precisely what did happen in the following decades, as the Carolingian realm fragmented into separate kingdoms and these in turn fragmented further into local, largely autonomous principalities. The history of this political disintegration is well known and has been often rehearsed. What has been less studied is the effect of this disintegration on family and regional consciousness. In the middle of the ninth century, men like Eberhard and women like Dhuoda still retained the broad horizons of a Europe that stretched from the Tiber to the Scheldt. They knew their place in this world, moving between estates north and south, maintaining relations with far-flung kin, and educating their children in the tradition of internationalism that was their heritage. Their world disappeared as their children and grandchildren found that the formulas of political, social, and cultural agendas appropriate for the ninth century no longer resonated fully in the worlds of the tenth and eleventh. The political turmoil of the last decades of Carolingian rule forced members of these great clans to make hard choices, to throw their energies and entrust their fates to the issues of specific regions, saving there what they could and abandoning their other, more remote lands and alliances.

Despite his inheritance in Annappe and the Condre, Eberhard's son Berengar cast his lot firmly with Italy. St. Giulia of Brescia, where Berengar's daughter Berta was abbess, rather than Cysoing, became the religious institution responsible for preserving Berengar's *memoria*. Others of Eberhard's descendants rooted themselves in the Ostrevant around the family monastery of Cysoing, which preserved their *memoria* and, as an integral part of it, Eberhard's testament. Dhuoda's family, too, failed to maintain the European tradition of which she was a part. Her beloved William died in the civil wars that engulfed the later ninth century. Her son Bernard Plantevelue (Hairyfeet) managed to survive by creating a power base in the Midi. His son William the Pious (d. 918) controlled Auvergne, Berry, the Mâconnais, the March of Gothia, and the Limousin. However, William's successors, his nephews William (d. 926) and Acfred (d. 927), sons of the count of Carcassone, were not their uncle's equals either in breadth or in ability. Instead, they were locally oriented and connected aristocrats who saw this vast assemblage disintegrate until by the time of Acfred's death he controlled only the Auvergne.[8]

So it went across Europe. From the imperial aristocracy emerged the local aristocracies of post-Carolingian Europe, each family deeply embedded in the particular regions that now formed their power bases. New times demanded new strategies, and as horizontal connections with distant but influential kinsmen became less important, the victors in the power struggles of the ninth century began to emphasize autonomous, vertically oriented ties between father and son on the model of the Carolingian royal family. These houses or lineages, descended from the great aristocracy of the ninth century, formed the core of the later medieval nobility. This continuity has led historians to argue that continuity, rather than a social revolution, characterized the transition from the Carolingian aristocracy to the French and German nobility.[9]

But what a gulf separated Eberhard and Dhuoda from their successors. Although the patient reconstruction of family histories by modern scholars can demonstrate this descent, many twelfth-century aristocrats knew little of their ancestry. A few families, such as the Welfs or in France those of the counts of Flanders, Vermandois, and Champagne, were proud of their origins in the Carolingian world, but most ignored it entirely. Families in the Midi and Bavaria looked behind the Carolingian age to largely mythical origins in the world of Late Antiquity. Elsewhere, as in Alemannia and much of western France, aristocrats claimed descent from wily adventurers of the tenth century, men of no illustrious ancestry who, through cunning and martial skill, rose to power and prestige.[10]

Actually, whatever the legends, the ancestral past was greatly foreshortened. The great family of the Welfs, for example, who in the twelfth century formed the most powerful noble family in the empire, remembered their ancestry from the Carolingian period but in a confused manner. Although the family first achieved prominence through the marriage of Judith, the daughter of Welf and Heilwig, to Louis the Pious, by the early twelfth century the family recalled none of this glorious past that had established them as the first family of the empire. Instead, the *Genealogia Welforum*[11] traced the family's origins to an anachronistic and improbable account that they had begun with Eticho and Henry "of the golden Plow," whose daughter Hildegard married Louis the Stammerer.[12] Others remembered even less. As Count Fulk le Réchin of Anjou explained around 1097, he knew little about his ancestors, for he did not know where they were buried.[13]

Thus if continuity characterized the biological relationships between ninth and twelfth centuries, discontinuity characterized the mental relationships of this same period. In this chapter, we shall examine some of the ways in which family memory was preserved and transformed during this period, paying attention to those in society particularly charged with remembering, and how changes in these roles brought about changes in that which would be and could be remembered. Our first subject is memory specialists—women, at the start of our period, but in some regions increasingly challenged by reformed male monks.

The Memory of Women

"The Memory of Women" must be understood in two different senses. The first is the active role of women remembering, preserving, and transmitting the past. Women had a privileged role in the vital process of preserving and, through the very act of preservation, structuring and molding the past for families, regions, and institutions. Moreover, there were aspects of memory that are particularly characteristic of women, and the form of female memory owes something to the particular social, political, and cultural position of women in the societies of the eleventh century.

The second and equally complex issue is the place of women in individual and group memories. The role of women as rememberers is directly connected to the manner in which women were themselves remembered in the variety of transmitted *memoria* of the eleventh century. The place of women in the carefully selected, restructured, and present-minded discourse that forms what we know of medieval memory depended on the attitudes of male authors toward this memorial role.

The two topics—women who remember and the women who are remembered—are interrelated yet distinct. In neither case is the subject women per se, but rather the elaboration of mental categories, quite probably shared by male and female authors, viewed as female. These constructed categories do not necessarily correspond to actual social roles. As we shall see, there is a very clear difference between the image of the role of women in remembering and the image that emerges from documents of practice. Instead, they betray specific ideological traditions as well as pressing political agendas of their authors, agendas pursued within different matrices of political power. However, in time, when these specific circumstances ceased to have immediacy, these images remained, confusing subsequent attempts to understand women and memory in the eleventh century.

The memory of women can be most clearly observed in family *memoria*, especially the responsibility for mourning and remembering the dead. In his account of the death and burial of Archbishop Walthard of Magdeburg in 1012, Thietmar terms only the service conducted in the church before the burial his *memoria*,[14] but this liturgical action was but one part of an extended *memoria* that began with the final illness and continued through liturgical and nonliturgical celebrations for the deceased.[15] The ritual begins with the dying person on his deathbed, seeking pardon and attempting to make amends for his past misdeeds. A layman might be accepted into a monastic community so that he could die a monk. At the moment of death, he might be placed on sackcloth spread on the ground in the monastic tradition. After death, the body is washed and prepared for burial, carried to the church where the liturgy is performed, and then transported to the tomb for actual burial.

All of this occurs in public to the accompaniment of cries and wailing. As Archbishop Walthard lay dying, Duke Jaromir of Bohemia stood by crying while Thietmar himself had to leave the room for sorrow.[16] The agony of Count Odo of Tours was accompanied by the "mourning of vassals, the outcry of domestics, and the frequent exclamations of women."[17]

This mourning continues as the dying person enters his final agony, a moment of great drama since at the last moment he might see those fiends come to carry off his soul. Archbishop Walthard looked suddenly to his left: "I do not know what he saw to his left; he energetically protected himself with a sign of the holy cross made with his right hand, turned away his body and face, contorted his face as if he were going to cry, and then quickly relaxed into a smile."[18]

A young monk at St. Emmeram around the same time was not so lucky. Although unable to say what he saw, his gesticulations left no doubt in the minds of those praying at his bedside. Arnold, who was a close friend of the dying man, described the scene:

> When we, having lifted him from his bed, had placed him on the floor of his cell, he seemed to push against someone with his arms and then turning sharply and gazing to his left he shrank back in horror from the face of the enemy so that his eyes rolled back and his head was averted and thrown back fatally, as I might describe the gesture, so that he almost drove out those standing by. And so that it might be clear how much the faith of Christ is worth where there is merit and how much it is lacking where there is mortal sin, he attempted to extend his right hand, with effort, wishing to make the sign of salvation, but he was unable to do so, and he suddenly shook with a convulsion and was covered with a pallor, he stiffened, and thus he breathed his last.[19]

The brothers standing by the dying monk were so horrified by what they had witnessed that their singing of psalms was changed to mourning. "Who would not have wept?" Arnold asks, in the face of so horrible a sight. Indeed, years later, he could "hardly write these things and hand them over to memory [memoriaeque tradiderim] without sighs and weeping."

The mourning and weeping continued through the celebration of the funeral and the journey to the grave. Thietmar described the manner in which Walthard's funeral cortege was met by the archbishop's weeping *familia*, the clergy, and a great multitude of Jews and orphans. He, too, asks, but in a very different vein, "Who could have refrained from weeping?" The funeral cortege of the West Frankish Carolingian Lothar in 986 was likewise composed of weeping clerics and laity. Even the singers could hardly perform their funeral dirge for their own weeping.[20]

Of these four death scenes, two are deaths of clerics presumably taking place in the sole company of men and only one of the other two explicitly mentions the role of women in this mourning. And yet women seem to have had an even more central role in the *memoria* of their families, both at the time of death and thereafter, than these texts would suggest. Their expected role in public mourning is shown most clearly in a series of illuminations from the Sacramentary of Bishop Warmundus of Ivrea completed around the year one thousand and justly recognized by Jean-Claude Schmitt as an extremely precious document for understanding mourning and burial gestures.[21] Although aside from the Virgin and the Empress Helen, women are rare in the manuscript as a whole, mourning women are prominent in eight of the ten illustrations of the *Ordo in agenda mortuorum*. The iconographic freedom of these scenes and the presentation of the characters in contemporary dress suggest that these scenes are taken from actual burial practices for the laity. In the first (plate 1), as the ill man lies penitent on his deathbed, a woman sits at his head, her left hand on his pillow, her right holding her cheek in a sign of sorrow.[22] In plate 2, the dying man is placed naked on a haircloth which lies on the floor while a woman leaning over him beats her breast and tears at her clothing.[23] In plate 3, the man breathes forth his soul in the presence of clerics and laity. A woman, her hair disheveled, reaches for him and must be forcibly restrained.[24] In plate 4, the naked body is seated in a chair and washed by two men.[25] In plate 5, the body, which has been wrapped in a shroud, is placed in a coffin and covered with a cloth, while a woman tears at her disheveled hair.[26] In plate 6, the funeral cortege moves toward the church. Both the pallbearers and those members of the *familia* accompanying the coffin cry out, but the featured figure is a woman, her arms raised and her mouth open in lamentation.[27] The scene in plate 7 is in a church. While the priest reads the liturgy, mourners continue to cry out and the woman throws herself on the coffin.[28] Plate 8 shows the procession to the cemetery. Once more the pallbearers and crowd lament while the woman, her hair disheveled, strikes her breast.[29] In plate 9, gravediggers prepare the tomb and the sarcophagus.[30] The final scene (plate 10) shows the burial. As the priest, accompanied by the clergy, blesses the cadaver, which has been lifted from the coffin, the woman, her hair in disarray, reaches out for the body and must be forcibly restrained by a layman.[31]

These striking images present, more clearly than any text, the central role of the female mourner in the series of rites that mark death and burial. She appears in eight of the ten scenes, and in the sixth she is the central figure. In comparison, the clergy appear to be peripheral to the scenes and are drawn as smaller figures. The woman's mourning gestures and disheveled hair, her rending of hair or clothing, her uplifted hands and attempts to throw herself on the body—all of this is presented with enormous care and precision. If one considers the entirety of the *Ordo in agenda mortuorum* as presented in the sacramentary's iconography, the clergy plays only a supporting role in the drama of the *memoria*, in which the grieving woman is central.

This centrality was not limited to the public mourning that took place at the time of death. Rather women were central to the more lasting tradition of *memoria* within which the dead were kept present for the living. However, the imperial origins of Warmund's sacramentary are significant. The image of women as rememberers and women remembered differs considerably in the sources from the East and those from the West in the early eleventh century. In the former, women are as central as is the distraught mourner in the sacramentary. In the latter, they are almost invisible.

Plate 1. The woman watches at the deathbed (fol. 191r).

Plate 2. The woman mourns the dying man (fol. 193r).

Plate 3. The woman is restrained while the man breathes
out his soul (fol. 195v).

Plate 4. The corpse is washed (fol. 198v).

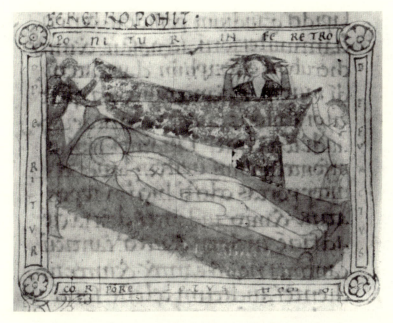

Plate 5. The woman tears her hair as the body is placed
in a coffin (fol. 199v).

Plate 6. The woman laments as the cortege approaches the church (fol. 200v).

Plate 7. The woman throws herself on the coffin (fol. 201v).

Plate 8. The woman again laments as the cortege approaches
the cemetery (fol. 203v).

Plate 9. Gravediggers prepare the tomb (fol. 205r).

Plate 10. The woman attempts to throw herself onto the coffin
as it is lowered into the tomb (fol. 206v).

One can begin to recognize the differences by examining two texts, each probably written around the same year (1002) and each describing the last days of an empress. The first is Odilo of Cluny's (994–1049) *Epitaphium Adalheidae imperatricis* and the second *Vita Mahthildis Reginae*. The first, written by the great abbot of Cluny, presents what one might call the Cluniac, or perhaps the reformed monastic model of the memory of women. The second, written probably by an abbess or canoness of Neuhausen, presents a radically different image of women and memory. Patrick Corbet has shown that each text is the careful product of a highly reflected rhetorical tradition, molding the memories of the two women to a particular program. Thus they are not simply descriptive but rather normative. That is, they propose radically opposed ways of understanding the relationship between the living and the dead and the role of men and women in this relationship.[32]

Odilo relates that, while the empress Adelaide was staying in Geneva after the death of her son Otto II, she made donations for the benefit of his soul to various monasteries, including Monte Cassino, Cluny, and St. Martin of Tours. So that the monks might remember Otto, she addressed the following words to the monk of St. Martin of Tours, to whom she entrusted the task:

> I implore you, my dearest one, I implore you to address the holy priest thus: "Receive, priest of God, as a sign of my veneration, these small presents that Adelaide, servant of the servants of God, who is herself a sinner but by the grace of God empress sends you. Receive a part of the cloak of my only son the Emperor Otto and pray for him to Christ, Him whom you clothed in the person of a poor man with a cloak cut in two."
>
> The day on which she was going to leave this location [Orbe, in the canton of Vaud in Switzerland], in one and the same hour, she left, in the presence of the sinners who we are, a perfect example of humility and she showed without arrogance but with humility, that she was blessed with the spirit of prophesy. There was present a monk [Odilo] who, although unworthy, was called abbot, and for whom she had a certain respect. She turned her eyes toward him and looked at him. Both began to cry abundantly. I wish to say that in this she did more than if she has cured many ill people. She humbly seized his rough clothing, pressed them on her holy eyes and on her serene face, kissed them, and said to him: "Remember me, my son, in your contemplation and know that I will never again see you with these eyes. I confide my soul to the prayers of the brothers for when I will have abandoned mortal things." Then she took the path by which she arrived in the place where, in virtue of divine dispensation, she had decided to prepare a tomb for herself.[33]

On first view, the twin images of Adelaide, both as Odilo remembers her and of her involvement in the remembering of others, seem unexceptional. The *Epitaphium*[34] appears a straightforward glorification of the empress, as Karl Leyser wrote, "presenting her as the exemplar of cardinal Cluniac virtues—*discretio* and *caritas*."[35] Corbet concluded that Odilo had constructed a sort of mirror of princes, which aimed neither to present a specifically female form of spirituality nor to solidify dynastic obligations. Rather it was probably, as Joachim Wollasch suggested, an attempt on the part of Cluny to insert itself into the empire through the monastery of Selz am Rhein, founded as her burial place by the empress and directed by a professed Cluniac. Cluny claimed that the monastery enjoyed freedom from the Ottonian *Reichsklöster* system, a claim never admitted by the emperors.

The *Epitaphium* does more, however, than simply promote Cluniac claims within the empire. It presents a Cluniac reading of Adelaide's role in imperial memory. These two passages are key to the image Odilo constructs of Adelaide and her role in the *memoria* of her family and indeed in what might be called the French model of female remembrance. Adelaide is shown as the model friend of Cluny and other male monasteries, showering them with gifts and begging them for their prayers. On the anniversaries of the deaths of her friends and family, she gives charity to the poor and to monks. Her words of wisdom quoted above come not from herself but rather from the *prophetiae spiritus*.

However, this image of Adelaide and her role as rememberer must be juxtaposed with another image of the death of an empress, this one by an anonymous hagiographer writing in all probability during the same years as Odilo. This is the *Vita Mahthildis Reginae*, also carefully studied by Corbet. Here we see a very different kind of female remembrance, one that is much more direct, more active, more focused on women:

> Then, she called to her granddaughter Matilda, the daughter of Emperor Otto [Otto I], greeted her with the warning that she should be pious and humble, prudent and careful and that she should care for the flock committed to her care and that she should seldom go out of the monastery lest she should be impeded by secular cares from the service of Christ. She placed in her hand a *computarium*, in which were written the names of the dead princes; she commended to her the soul of her lord king Henry [Henry I], she also commended to her her own soul and those of all the faithful whose memory she has collected.[36]

The description of the dying empress giving a calendar to her namesake is drawn directly from the *Vita Mahthildis Reginae antiquior* (composed ca. 974).[37] In both versions, Mathilda is active, direct. Those standing around her weep but not the empress herself. Mathilda is entirely in control of herself and of the others, as she has been through her life. She has long prayed for the dead along with the canonesses; she does not leave this to others. The *Vita Mahthildis Reginae* goes still further to emphasize the direct role of the empress within the sphere of family *memoria*.[38] Adelaide's first act upon the death of her son Otto had been to ask a cleric, the priest Adeldach, to say a mass for him.[39] Later she continues a weekly memorial on Saturdays, three celebrations each year on the octave, tricesimus, and the day of his death. These celebrations take place at Quedlinburg, but the empress is present and participates in them herself. She has guarded the family necrology, which she now passes to her granddaughter, who has inherited her responsibilities along with her name. These include not only the liturgical *memoria* but also the direction of the religious community.

One might suppose that the different images are the result simply of different women, that they are transparent views into the lives of two different people. Alternatively, one might suggest that because the *Vita Mahthildis Reginae* is drawn from an earlier text, what one sees here is a change over time. But neither hypothesis sufficiently explains the differences between the two images. That the spirituality of the two may have been quite different is entirely possible. What concerns us here, however, is that different authors within different cultural traditions around the year one thousand chose to present them as very different figures.

The clearest evidence that the difference is less in the "reality" of the two women than in the way they are portrayed by the different authors comes from another image of Adelaide written by Odilo's contemporary, Bishop Thietmar of Merseburg (975–1018). He too depicts her as consumed by concern for her family's memory. However, while Odilo's Adelaide acts through monks, Thietmar's Adelaide takes a more active role herself:

> How much the empress Adelaide was intent upon securing in words and deeds the liberation of the soul of her lord to the end of her days cannot be described. For whatever honors or worldly advancement came to her she never ascribed to her own merit but rather to Christ saying, in David's words of praise, "Lord, give glory not to us but to your name."[40]

Thietmar does not specify exactly what actions Adelaide took to secure the salvation of Otto, but neither does he mention her appealing to monastic communities for their intercession on behalf of her late husband. Through Thietmar's *Chronicon* as well as in other late tenth- and eleventh-century imperial texts, we do not see women simply making donations to male communities of monks to pray for their husbands and families. Rather, not only empresses but other German women take direct, active roles in praying for the memory of their families, especially for their men. Women in fact seem to have been specifically expected to look to family *memoria* as a primary obligation, even when sons, brothers, or fathers survived. This role included individual prayers, fasts, and penances undertaken by the women themselves, not just donations to religious houses. Countess Liudgard, the widow of Margrave Werner, had throughout her life offered continuous prayers, fasts in the cold, and acts of charity for her husband rather than for herself.[41] When Duke Ernst of Swabia, having been shot with an arrow in a hunting accident, realized that he was dying, he asked a bystander to "commend my soul to all the faithful who are not here and exhort my wife that she might preserve her honor and that she might not forget mine."[42]

Women made donations for the souls of their families, of course, and were even apparently the designated persons to do so even if they were not the closest heirs. As Archbishop Walthard of Magdeburg lay dying, he called his lay sister to him and reminded her of her promise, if she should be his heir, to give his property at Olvenstedt to St. Maurice, even though he had living brothers who would normally have been his closer heirs.[43] However, such donations were less typically to male institutions such as Cluny but rather to nunneries, where women and many family members would pray for the deceased. After the death of Count Gero in 980, for example, his sister Tetta and his wife Aethela endowed the nunnery at Walsleben for this purpose.[44] Although the nunnery had been founded by Gero himself in 979, the year before his death, Thietmar erroneously ascribed the foundation to the two women, perhaps because such an initiative fit better his model of how liturgical *memoria* were established. The great female institutions of Saxony, such as Quedlinburg and Gandersheim, were but the greatest of dozens of female institutions founded in the second half of the tenth and the first half of the eleventh centuries.[45]

As Leyser has suggested, the role of women was to be the "custodian of men's life and soul."[46] This meant a much more active role than simply making bequests to monasteries. Women's good works and prayers were to secure the successes of their menfolk in this life, and they were also responsible for the welfare of their men's souls in the next.[47] As Corbet points out, men did not play the same role for women. Otto the Great, for example did not pray for the soul of his wife Edith.[48]

This image of the woman as intercessor, as rememberer, is almost entirely absent in French sources of the same period. One looks in vain for women acting in this manner, say, in Rodulfus Glaber or in Ademar of Chabannes. In the West, memory is presented as a specialized practice of men, primarily reformed monks, who remember on behalf of families. Women have a role in memory, but that role is passive rather than active: the past may be remembered through women, women by whom land and office may be transmitted. These women are but markers, indicating filiation of property; they are not actively involved in the process of remembering that property. Women who are active transmit not familial or religious glory but heresy, discord, and confusion. The generally positive valuation of women in the empire has no parallel in French texts.

Heretics, wicked queens, or seducers seem to be the primary female roles, and even then they are relatively minor characters in French chronicles. The archetype is Constance, wife of Robert the Pious, who, as we have seen, introduced novel and dangerous fashions into the royal court and was connected by implication with the heresy that is uncovered in Orléans in the close entourage of the king and queen.[49] Apart from Odorannus of Sens, also implicated in the heresy and who, as the recipient of the queen's commission to fabricate a new reliquary for the remains of Saint Savinianus, praised her both for her charity and her dutiful attention to the monks of St. Pierre-le-Vif, Constance is generally presented as a vicious and dangerous figure.[50] Helgaud of Fleury, in his *Epitoma vitae regis Rotberti*, depicts her as a despoiler of the golden altar decorations given the monastery of Saint-Aignan.[51] This is no casual allusion but, as Jean-Pierre Poly has shown, part of Helgaud's carefully developed and reworked polemic intended to depict the queen as enemy of her husband's lineage. Helgaud revised the account of the alienation in the earliest redaction of the *Epitoma*, which attributed the alienation to her greed and gave a longer and more detailed description of how she removed the gold, gave seven pounds to the monks to repair the monastery's roofs, and distributed the remaining eight pounds to others (presumably to pay for her war against her son).[52] Her alien origins and negative influence on her husband are likewise emphasized by Helgaud's depiction of Constance, "swollen by anger, swearing on the soul of her father."[53] This blasphemy is the inversion of how one's soul ought to be remembered.

There is a relationship between the role of women as rememberers and how women are remembered in the two traditions. In his analysis of the women of the Saxon aristocracy, Leyser suggested that the prominent role they play in the histories and panegyrics of Ottonian and early eleventh-century authors is due to the high mortality of aristocratic men and the relatively favorable treatment of female heirs in customary law, both of which left considerable amounts of land in the hands of women and which encouraged the foundation of numerous religious houses for women (at least thirty-six between 919 and 1024). Women, he suggests, appear more predominantly in imperial historiography because they were privileged in the East. Thus, according to his line of reasoning, whether or not the hagiographical texts accurately reflect the individual personalities, they do reflect social and demographic reality. If it could be shown that in the West women did not take as active a role in society as in the East, that they did not tend to survive their husbands, or that they did not enjoy control over property to the extent that Saxon women did, then this argument would have considerable merit. However, it is not at all clear that this was the case.

In 1962 David Herlihy studied charters of land donations involving lay principals: 20,000 charters from Italy, 20,000 from southern France, 11,000 from Germany, 5,000 from northern France, and 5,000 from Spain.[54]

The following chart summarizing the results indicates the percentages of charters in which women appear as the principal donors:

TABLE 1
Percentages of Charters in which Women
are Principal Donors

Region	10th	11th	12th
Italy	11%	13%	9%
S. France	13%	11%	9%
N. France	11%	8%	9%
Germany	8%	15%	12%

Herlihy's purpose in compiling this data was to illuminate women as landholders. He thought that these statistics, along with the appearance of matronymics, indicated the relative importance of women as owners or managers of land in different regions. One may question whether these figures support this hypothesis, but they do indicate the involvement of women as primary donors. For my purpose, the statistics suggest rather something else: the relative uniformity of women as principal donors across both time and space.

Apparently during the tenth century, the period during which women in the empire were remembered as being the most active and powerful, their involvement in donations was a bit less than in the West. In the eleventh century, when the texts remembering them were written, their involvement was perhaps a bit more frequent, but given the crudeness of the statistics, it would be hard to argue that women in the West had significantly less control over their property.

Penny Gold's study of donations in Anjou confirms the general outline provided by Herlihy. Her work, as she pointed out, finds stability of women's participation from 1000 to 1249. Some 11.9 percent of donations and sales were made by female alienators, and roughly half of all alienations had at least one woman in the consenting role. The pattern of participation varies according to the life cycle of the woman: unmarried daughters were similar to unmarried sons but appear only half as frequently; wives appear frequently as consenter with husband, but seldom is a husband consenter with his wife. Only in widowhood do women become similar to men in the transfer of property.[55]

Widowhood was, however, an important period of life for most women in France just as it was in the empire. In France, Robert Hajdu has estimated that 62.4 percent of married women in the twelfth century (the earliest period for which we have anything resembling statistics) outlived their husbands and that the average length of widowhood was nineteen and a half years.[56] As in the empire, women had considerable periods during which they could exercise important control over property and look to the *memoria* of their husbands.

Given this demographic similarity and the similar control women exercised over property, it is not surprising to find that in the tenth century France knew forceful, active women on the Ottonian model. In fact, the most important *were* Ottonian women. If one looks carefully, one sees that there were women in the West who played roles quite parallel to those of Mathilda and the other Saxon women about whom so much has been written. The most obvious is Gerberga, daughter of Henry I and Mathilda and thus sister to Otto I. Gerberga married first Gilbert of Lotharingia, then (ca. 939) King Louis IV. Like her mother, she was an active participant in public affairs and was a great help to her husband and a major figure in the kingdom during her son Lothar's minority. She appears as an intermediary in Louis's diplomas, and two royal diplomas indicate that they were prepared in her presence. She accompanied her husband on military expeditions to Aquitaine in 944 and Burgundy in 946. While Louis was held prisoner by Hugh the Great's vassal Theobald in 945–46, she used her relationship with her brother Otto to seek aid. After Louis's death, she continued to play a key role on behalf of her son Lothar.[57]

Likewise Emma, the daughter of Empress Adelaide and her first husband Lothar of Italy, attempted the same sort of public political role but with less success. Although presented negatively by Richer, her forceful role is evident both in her efforts on behalf of her husband and in her attempts to play a part similar to that of her mother-in-law with her son Louis V after Lothar's death.[58]

But even if women's life expectancies east and west of the Rhine were roughly similar, even if their control of property was similar, and even if individual royal and aristocratic women operated in similar spheres, one might still argue that the extraordinary number of foundations of female institutions in the East indicates a major difference in the role of women in the empire. Actually, this difference, too, is to some extent more apparent than real. If thirty-six such houses were founded between 919 and 1024, this indicates less a greater importance in female religious life in the East than the total lack of such institutions in the more recently conquered and converted lands east of the Rhine. Such foundations were not made in the West for the simple reason that there was no need: they were already there, in great number and varying importance, and had been, in many cases, since the seventh century.[59] The extremely poor documentation on many of these institutions across the centuries makes statistical analysis and comparison impossible. However they were numerous throughout most of France. Jean Verdon lists over twenty-seven "principal" monasteries in the north in the tenth and eleventh centuries and even more in the Midi. The spectrum of women's monasteries ranged from great, royal monasteries such as Chelles, Notre-Dame de Laon, Hasnon, Faremoutiers, and Notre Dame de Soissons to simple family foundations housing a few women. Again, one sees parallels with the foundations in the East where, alongside a few great royal houses such as Quedlinburg and Gandersheim, the majority of the institutions were small communities founded on family estates. True, across their long history many of these western institutions disappeared and others were converted to male monasteries, but old foundations were reestablished and even some male institutions were given over to women. Like the arguments concerning the longevity of Saxon women or their control of property, the arguments concerning the number of female religious foundations must be reconsidered.

Given similar demographic profiles, similar exercise of control over real property, and similar public roles for women on both sides of the Rhine in the tenth century, one might reasonably expect to see in the French historiography and hagiography of the eleventh century an image of women playing a role similar to that of women in the empire. This is emphatically not the case, however. First, while female monasteries certainly existed in France, they never enjoyed the high status and recognition that houses in Germany received from male authors. Nor did they produce women writers on a par with Hrothswitha of Gandersheim. Second, memorial texts of France, especially chronicles and histories roughly contemporary with imperial ones—that is, the late tenth and eleventh centuries—present a radically different image of women from that in the empire. One looks in vain for a positive image of a woman in Rodulfus Glaber and Ademar of Chabannes. Gerberga and Emma, for example, hardly appear in the historical memory of the early eleventh century. For Rodulfus, they are simply the sources of male heirs. He does not even mention Emma's relationship to Otto I.

The images of the role of women in the two societies as reflected in eleventh-century historiography thus cannot be explained by a difference in their social condition, actual access to property, or public involvement. Rather the varying images of tenth-century women created by authors of the eleventh century result neither entirely from events, inheritance law, or mortality tables but come also from differing ideologies closely tied to different power relationships within the two regions and the perceived roles of women within the traditions of liturgical *memoria*.

Part of the explanation for the French model may be closely tied to the formation of lineages there, while in the empire families were still organized in more traditional *Sippe* or clans. Women are capable of being the persons responsible for family memory only if they are part of the family. But around the turn of the century, northern French women seem more like temporary guests in their husbands' homes than full family members. Weakly attached, they were not considered to be competent to guard the family's memory in liturgical *memoria*. As Georges Duby suggested, "The matrimonial bond was thus dissolved very easily in the French court, in a region less retarded than the Germany of Saint Henry."[60] Actually, this appeal to the "archaic" nature of the Germanic world, reminiscent of Karl Bosl and other German historians, is probably not entirely accurate and is in any case unnecessary. The ambivalent position of women within the husband's family could just as easily have been a survival of Roman tradition, in which the wife was not part of the family of her husband or children. Thus, the French rather than the German tradition might be termed "backward," if such labels must be used at all. Be that as it may, in the French system the woman was seen not as an active member of the family but as a foreigner, important because she brought alliances and riches, but also dangerous because she might bring something more: alien novelty.

Much in this kin-based argument recommends itself, but it is not sufficient, particularly since the so-called French model was not so much French as monastic. Who should be responsible for the *memoria* of the family? The answer given in the West was offered not coincidentally by reformed monks such as Odilo and Rodulfus Glaber. Not women, but men—or better reformed monks, angels in Cluniac ideology—can best guard both the liturgical commemoration of the dead and the narrative, formal memory of the past, a memory in which women are present only in a passive manner. In the following century the contrast between Cluny's efficacy and the unreliability of even well-intentioned women in the care of the dead was underlined in Peter the Venerable's *De miraculis*. By juxtaposing the unfaithfulness of women in carrying out their obligations of preserving the *memoria* of the dead and the faithfulness and efficacy of Cluniac intervention, he portrays the latter as the appropriate trustee of *memoria*. In one story Peter tells of the spirit of a dead mercenary who appears to his former lord to entreat him to obtain from the lord's wife eight solidi that were owed him and to spend these for his soul. Rather than spending the money on masses as she had been instructed, the woman had kept the money, thinking that no one but the dead man could know of the debt. The same spirit goes on to report that King Alfonso, by giving directly to Cluny, had avoided such a prolonged torture. He too had been in torment but had quickly obtained release through the prayers of the Cluniac monks.[61] In a second story Peter tells of a miner trapped for almost a year in a collapsed mine, but who is sustained by the weekly offering of wax and bread that his wife, believing him dead, makes to a priest for masses for his soul. Each week a spirit brings him bread and light. Still, on one week, preoccupied with other business, the woman forgets her husband, with the result that he is gravely tormented by hunger and darkness during that time.[62] The implication was clear: women, by their fickle and unreliable nature, were weak vessels in which to entrust something as important as one's salvation.

However, as the research of Joachim Wollasch, Maria Hillebrandt, Franz Neiske, and Dietrich Poeck in Germany and of Barbara Rosenwein, Constance Bouchard, and others in North America has shown, women played a principal role in the foundation of Cluniac monasteries, in the reform of other houses, and in the redirection of charity for the souls of their husbands, sons, and themselves. Even in patriarchal families where office and power were inherited in the male line, women played an important behind-the-scenes role in deciding where a family would make its gifts. Nuns were relatively uncommon, but lay women might lead husbands to make donations to monasteries they had never patronized but to which they had had relations before their marriage. For example, Agnes, daughter of Otto-William of Burgundy, married William V of Aquitaine, and this marked the beginning of her husband's generosity toward Cluny. Agnes also made donations to Cluny in her own name. In Burgundy, Ermengard, of the family of the counts of Chalon who had founded Paray, married the lord of Bourbon but on her death left her dower property to Paray for the good of her own soul.[63] Even the much-maligned Constance is described by abbot Albert of Micy in a letter to Pope John XVIII as having "donated much property to God and to the saints she venerates at the above-mentioned monastery [of Micy] for her salvation and for the redemption of the souls of her husband and of her deceased sons."[64]

Thus, east and west, women appear in documents of practice as playing decisive roles in *memoria*, either directly as in the empire, or indirectly as donors and selectors of the appropriate intercessors for their memory and that of their husbands' families. Such female roles were emphasized, perhaps even exaggerated in the empire, while they were forgotten in the reformed monastic memory of these women and their families. They disappear from narrative histories, unless, like Constance, they were retained as negative examples of the dangers of female inter-ference. In the Cluniac model of women—the most perfect example being Odilo's treatment of Adelaide—the woman is the passive, emo-tional supplicator. In his characterization, he proclaims that by her tears of supplication, she did more than if she had worked miraculous cures. Her passivity is more prized than the active power of a wonder worker. Her role is clear: she petitions. The representation of Adelaide is simul-taneously a representation of Odilo and of the role of Cluny in remem-bering: Odilo remembers. And yet this artificial construction of the memory of the role of the empress within the memorial tradition dis-torts her actual role in the memory of the dead, including that of Odilo himself. As Gerd Althoff has shown, the name of Abbot Odilo appears in the necrologies that depend on the royal Saxon necrology conserved at Quedlinburg and elsewhere by imperial canonesses.[65] If Odilo pre-served the *memoria* of Adelaide, he forgets to tell us that she did the same for the *memoria* of Odilo.

More is at stake in these differing elaborations of women's role in memory than competition between monks and canonesses. Implicit in the two traditions is an attitude toward central authority and legitimate exercise of power. In the empire, imperial memory was entrusted to women, women who were both part of the family and who led their lives in institutions closely connected with the imperial house. This model was diffused through society, with aristocratic families establishing and maintaining similar institutions for their own *memoria*. Similar institu-tions existed in the West, but they were de-emphasized by authors who claimed not only a privileged and more effective role in memory but also an autonomous political basis. Reformed monasticism claimed to stand outside of domination by king or family.

One might stop here, but there is another dimension of the memory of women yet to be explored. Thus far we have actually considered only the role of women in liturgical memory. Did they have a more general role in the preservation of memory, tied to but not entirely subsumed under this liturgical role? Evidence is scarce but intriguing. Women may have been entrusted not only with liturgical remembrance but with other kinds of more secular memorial foundations. The tenth-century *Vita Sanctae Odiliae* recounts the story of a young man who gives the saint three saplings. He tells her to plant them "so that you will be re-membered in posterity."[66] How often such simple memorials as trees planted by women may have served memorial functions cannot be known.

Nor do we know much about other kinds of memories women were expected to hold. And yet the *Chronicle of Novalesa*, written around

1048, suggests the possibility that women were assumed to possess a vast reservoir of lore, a reservoir of which our sources say virtually nothing.[67] In this monastery, recently reestablished after a century of abandonment, the anonymous chronicler painstakingly attempted to collect the scattered fragments of the memory of his institution, fragments he wrote onto scraps of parchment scavenged from the floor of the scriptorium or cut from the margins of books. Among these fragments of the past, we have the image of an aged woman, no less a construction than the Adelaide of Odilo or the Mathilda of the *Vita Mahthildis Reginae*. This image is what might be called (with some caution) a folkloric construction of female memory.

> After the last pagan invasion to take place before the reconstruction of the place, the location of the tomb of this above-mentioned Walter was entirely unknown (as were others) by the local inhabitants. There was at that time a widow, Petronilla by name, living in the town of Susa who, it was said, because of her great age, walked all bent over and whose eyes were almost entirely darkened. This woman had a son named Maurunus, whom the pagans had taken away as a captive by force from the above-mentioned town along with others. It was said that he remained with them in their land for more than thirty years. Afterward, having received permission from his own lord, he returned to his own home where he found his mother, now worn out by old age, as we said above, and accustomed to sit each day in the warmth of sun on a very large stone that lay near the city. The men with the women of the city came to this woman inquiring of her the ancient traditions [*de antiquitate*] of the place, and she used to tell them many things, especially about the monastery of Novalesa. She told them many unheard-of things that she had seen or that she had heard from her parents, especially about the number of abbots and the destructions that had been caused by the pagans. One day she was taken by some men to the place where she showed them the tomb of Walter, which previously had been unknown, just as she had heard from those who were born before her ancestors, since formerly no woman dared to go near that place. She also indicated how many wells there had formerly been in that place. For the neighbors claimed that this woman had lived almost two hundred years.[68]

Petronilla was ancient, and although blessed with second sight, she was physically blind. Her son had lived many years among the Saracens, who had finally allowed him to return home. She knew where were buried the saints of the monastery although women had never been allowed to visit the monastic site. And she knew the locations of the underground waters, the springs of the area. One can imagine what Rodulfus Glaber might have made of an Italian woman with contacts among the Saracens

Plate 11. Women at baptism (fol. 61v).

(pagans par excellence) who knew the secrets of the underworld. Here, however, she is presented positively because she knows the sacred burial place of Novalesa's saints.

The text presents a triple fiction. First, the Walter in the text is none other than the hero of the *Waltharius*, long sections of which were copied directly into the Novalesian *Chronicon* with the explanation that in his old age the epic hero became a *conversus* in Novalesa. Second, Petronilla's age is indeed great, almost two hundred years, a necessary fiction if she is to bridge the gap between the past and the present of the monastery. Third, she should not know where Walter was buried because, according to the chronicle, women were in past times forbidden to enter the monastery precincts. However, as Gisella Wataghin-Cantino and Chiara Lambert, the archaeologists who have excavated Novalesa, have found, one of the earliest and most privileged burials in the Carolingian church was that of a woman.[69]

Within this triple fiction, Petronilla plays a role that was perhaps very widely assigned to women in eleventh-century society and one against which the reform monks fought: women watched over the dead, they were the bridges between the living and the dead. One sees a similar case in Thietmar of Merseburg's *Chronicon*. He tells how his cousin Brigida alone was able to explain to him the meaning of a ghostly apparition in a churchyard at Walsleben and a similar occurrence at Magdeburg.[70] Women, responsible for mourning the dead and for the transmission of life from one generation to another (the only other group of lay women portrayed in the Sacramentary of Warmund are godmothers preparing to receive their godchildren from the baptismal font: plate 11),[71] and as the partner more likely to survive the spouse and thus to be in a position to preserve and transmit the past to the future, may have had a generally recognized role as those who best knew the dead and who could keep their memory alive. If so, the silence of the male reformed tradition about women's role may indicate an active desire to forget. Women were the primary rivals of the reformed monastic tradition in the domain of memory. If they were the bridges of memory, it was perhaps essential to destroy these bridges, these women, even at the cost of the loss of part of the past. They were thus forgotten, silenced, not in the practice, but in the image, of the memory of women in the eleventh century.

Family Memory and Naming

One effect of removing memory from the women of the family and entrusting it to professional rememberers could be a loss of continuity with older family traditions, as indicated most forcefully in the transformation of the onomastic stock of large portions of western Europe where male Benedictine monasteries and not women were entrusted with family memory. The relationship is not necessarily directly causal but nonetheless striking. In the Germanic regions of Europe, the name pool declines gradually from the tenth to the twelfth and thirteenth centuries.[72] In the West, as in Provence, a remarkable rupture takes place in the last quarter of the tenth century.

In 847 Robert, the vicarius of Count Adalbert of Provence, held a public court to consider a complaint raised by the advocate of Bishop-Abbot Alboinus of St. Victor of Marseille concerning rights to the duties collected from a nearby villa. Present were some forty-six persons "including échevins and judges, both Roman and Salic."[73] Of those present one-third bore names not recorded in Provençal charters of the later ninth, tenth or early eleventh centuries: these included biblical names such as Joseph, Aaron, Jonathan, Jacob; Germanic names like Wildemaris, Ansulf, and Guinifred; and Latin names such as Gaudentius. Another third appear only in the ninth and tenth centuries but disappear from the region before the 990s. Only the remaining third—including such names as Adalbertus, Theudbert, Benedict, Robert, and Geraldus—would continue through the eleventh century. In general, this group of names is diverse (only one name repeats) and on the whole doomed: most will disappear for centuries, and those that will continue will not be among the most common Provençal names in the eleventh century.

In 1038 Count Josfred of Provence invested Viscount Fulco of Marseille with property near Toulon so that he might donate it in turn to St. Victor of Marseille.[74] Present were twenty-eight clerics and laymen, largely the kinsmen and *fideles* of the count and the viscount. The name pool could hardly be in sharper contrast with that of the previous document. Only one name repeats in both—Adalbertus, certainly one of the most common names in all of Europe. But this is hardly surprising: fully half of the names are new in the tenth century and two do not appear before the eleventh. The names are much more widely shared, and the networks through which they overlap are complex: a mother and son share the name Stephen; a father and a son share William; the viscount's son bears the name of his father's lord, Josfred. This contrasts with the ninth-century document in which only one name repeated in this large assembly. The most common of all Provençal names in the eleventh century, Pons, is carried by three of the persons present but by no one at the ninth-century assembly.[75] This comparison demonstrates clearly the radical differences between the onomastic worlds of the ninth and eleventh centuries.

These two individual cases highlight a general pattern in roughly three thousand Provençal names from the ninth, tenth, and early eleventh centuries. In the Rhône valley we can follow a complex transformation of naming traditions within the period of roughly 850 to 1050: First, there is a great constriction in the total pool of names used from generation to generation. Second, with this constriction, certain names become increasingly common. Third, while some names disappear, others emerge and become overwhelmingly frequent.

In the evaluation of 2,853 names in charters between 850 and 1049 we find a total of 862 (or 30 percent) unique names. However, examined over the entire period, we see a definite progression from many unique names in the earlier period to a progressive contraction in the naming pool until the end of the tenth century and then a slight expansion in the early eleventh. It is not, however, simply an expansion of old names but rather the introduction of names new in the tenth century (see table 2). We see a similar pattern if we examine specific cartularies from the region, such as those of the cathedrals of Apt and Arles (see table 3).

George Beech has discovered similar transformations in the names of persons from the Poitou between the ninth and the twelfth centuries.[76] He found a total of 1,300 different names, of which 460 appear with

TABLE 2	
Percentage of Unique Names in Provençal Charters	
850–900	74%
900–950	68%
950–1000	33%
1000–1050	50%

TABLE 3		
Percentage of Unique Names in Arles and Apt Charters		
Date	*Arles*	*Apt*
850–900	93%	92%
900–950	76%	85%
950–1000	53%	46%
1010–1050	63%	89%

some regularity. However, he found that the greatest variety of names achieved its apogee between 925 and 950, after which the number of different names fell without cease until the end of the twelfth century. Bernadette Barrière has observed a similar pattern for the Limousin: in the tenth century she finds sixty different names per hundred persons, while at the start of the twelfth century only thirty.[77] Similar declines appear in other regions of France: at Agde, a decline from 78 names per 100 in the tenth century to 16.5 per 100 in the thirteenth; in Burgundy, a decline from 47 to 29 per 100.[78] Other regions do not indicate such extreme declines, although the evidence is difficult to compare because of the scarcity of tenth-century data.[79]

Just why this took place is not yet fully understood. Among the possible factors are certainly: the expansion of the practice of baptismal sponsors giving their godchildren their own names; the tendency of vassals to name their children for their lords (who may also have been their godparents); changing traditions of inheritance and marriage that made it less likely that some sons would produce offspring and thus transmit their own names; the growth of dynasties and with them the increasing importance of a few key names for the consciousness of group identity.[80] Nor were these changes uniform across Europe. Although Monique Bourin speaks of "l'Europe Chrétienne des noms" and of "l'Europe de l'encellulement,"[81] as we have seen above the constriction of the name pool was not as rapid or as dramatic in Germanic regions in the tenth and early eleventh centuries.[82] Nor did a marked increase of Christian names appear in the Germanic regions of Europe prior to the later twelfth century. The rhythm observed in the West was not universal.

Whatever the merits of these and other causal explanations (and some do not seem to fit the Provençal situation very well), the effects are clear enough. The size of the onomastic network within which one can be at home with his memories of past persons contracted. With the loss of common names and the transformation of kinds of names, then those persons and events associated with the lost labels too are likely to become lost. On the other hand, as we shall see later, with the constriction of the number of names, individuals bearing the same name tended to become conflated.

The process of selection by which these names were preserved or disappeared is striking and relates directly to the broader question of individual and group identity. Names were preserved in two manners: The first and most direct was through the reuse of names within families. We see examples of this in the text from 1038 discussed above as well as in the family of the viscounts of Marseille. Count Josfredus (Joufré) was the son of William III (992–1019) and grandson of Count William II (the Liberator, 970–993). This family was descended from a count Roubaud (Rodbald) and his son Boso, who had first appeared in Provence in the entourage of Hugh of Italy in the first half of the ninth century. The family's origins are argued by Poly to have been from the Toulousan; they may have been from lower Burgundy or both.[83] In any case they established the names Josfred, William, and Bertran that became, in the course of the eleventh century, the primary names in the comitial family.[84] The viscountal family of Marseille had descended from a Viennois family of Count Theutbald, whose son Arlulf had been active in Provence in the entourage of Hugh of Arles and who had been granted a large amount of land by King Conrad near Trets in 951.[85] His descendants came to control both the episcopacy and the viscounty of Marseille throughout the eleventh century. However, the names Fulk and Pons and Aicard for the viscounts and Honoratus or Pons had not appeared in the Viennois family tradition, nor do the "founders" names, Arlulf and Theutbald, long continue in the Marseilles family (although they survive among distant cousins).

The second means by which names were preserved was through the role of monastic institutions in preserving, transmitting, and forming this memory. Bishop Poncius remembered his ancestors through St. Victor. This is no coincidence. As Joachim Wollasch, Karl Schmid, and their colleagues have demonstrated, the preservation of *memoria*—and in particular the *memoria* of dead patrons—was a primary social role for monastic communities.[86] They served as the locus of memory for the family. However, how this monastic preservation of memory selected and preserved the past was a function of the needs and interests of the monastery, not simply that of the family.

These interests began with the establishment of the family as patrons of the monastery and seldom looked farther back than this period. In the case of the viscounts of Marseille, this is clear: from the period before the incorporation of the family into the patronage of St. Victor, nothing is retained of the family's past. In the case of the counts of Provence, this particular institutionalization of memory begins in 1019 with the burial of William III at the monastery of Montmajour.

The institutionalization of memory through liturgical commemoration and the preservation of charters of donation or quitclaims seldom reaches back more than a generation. Prayers, as I have argued elsewhere, were exchanged for land, and this exchange created and preserved the memory of the dead.[87] But prayers for specific persons in Provence seldom go beyond the generation of one's parents. In some sixty specific mentions of individuals in *pro animis* formulae from the region in the tenth century, only one donation mentions grandparents by name, in contrast to thirty-five that mention fathers and thirty-one mentioning mothers.[88] This failure to preserve in archival texts the names of the preceding generation may in part explain why, while the history of the counts from the preceding generation of William II the Liberator is fairly clear, his father Boso and his grandfather Rodbald remained in his day almost entirely obscure. They had in their day looked to preserve their *memoria*, but in Cluny, not in Provence. Similarly, one should not be surprised that the viscounts of Marseilles show no evidence of knowing that they descended from count Theutbald. His *memoria* had been preserved elsewhere, especially at Romans, but not in Provence.[89]

The most detailed evidence both of the role of monasteries in the institutionalization of onomastic and thus familial memory and the effects of monastic interests in the form in which this memory is preserved comes from the cartulary of Lérins. Sometime around 1125 a notice of the acquisition of property at Vallauris, an important domain in the diocese of Antibes, was entered into the cartulary of Lérins.[90] The document explains in detail how, over a century and a half, the monastery acquired the property that had originally been granted to Rodoard, one of the followers of William the Liberator in 961. In a penetrating analysis, Poly has used the text to demonstrate the inheritance practices of the Provençal aristocracy and the process by which great estates of the tenth century progressively fell into the hands of the church.[91] Poly terms the document a "genealogy" of the house of Antibes Grasse, the earliest genealogical text from Provence.[92] Indeed, it does provide information on five generations of the descendants of Rodoard and discusses the marriages and inheritance of nineteen of his descendants and their spouses.

Rodoard divided the estate among his three children—Gaucerannus, Guillelmus Gruta, and Oda—the first receiving one half of the property, the latter two one-quarter each. Gaucerannus and Guillelmus also divided another fief at Vallauris, again with Gaucerannus receiving one-half and William one-fourth. Gaucerannus later received the other half of the *episcopatus* of Antibes from the count. His sons William Gaucerannus and Aldebertus, bishop of Grasse, divided his estate after his death. Aldebertus sold, with the *laudatio* of his son William "the Lombard," his half of the estate at Vallauris to Lérins except for one manse, which he gave to his daughter.

Oda's share, which had constituted her dowry, passed first to her three children, a son Petrus Signerius, and two unnamed daughters who married, respectively, Aldearius of Maganosc and William of Clermont. Petrus's share passed to his son William, who donated it to Lérins when he and his son entered the monastic community. Aldearius' son Audibert and his grandsons, Fulk, Petrus Crispus, and Isnard, donated their portion of the property to Lérins as did the grandsons of William of Clermont, Isnardus, his son Ramund, and Isnardus' cousins Bertran and Petrus.

The portion of Rodoard's second son, Guillelmus Gruta, also eventually came into the possession of the monastery. His daughter Accelena and her husband Beraldus of Mougins gave portions of the estate to Lérins. The remaining part of Guillelmus Gruta's share passed to his son Petrus de Opia and then to unnamed "milites" from Sartoux (commune of Cannes, arr. of Grasse, Alpes Maritimes), who gave it to Lérins.

The major difficulty in acquiring this entire estate rose when the grandson of Bishop Audibert, William the Lombard's son Fulk of Grasse, began a protracted conflict with the monks to obtain their recognition that Fulk held some rights to the property. It was this conflict that led to the preparation of the brief notice,[93] and the conflict ended only when Fulk had renounced his claims in favor of the monastery.

As Poly pointed out, this is hardly a genealogy in any normal sense.[94] Only individuals who shared in the progressive dismemberment of the estate of Vallauris or its ultimate reunification were present. Thus the senior branch of the family, the descendants of Gaucerannus, were quickly forgotten and the descendants of William and Oda are followed in much detail. If this text is a genealogy at all, then, it is a genealogy of land, in which the descendants of Rodoard play only a supporting role.

For our purposes, the document is illuminating because it demonstrates so clearly how monasteries such as Lérins and Montmajour could serve as repositories of family memory, but only on their own terms. Rodoard's descendants are remembered, but only to the extent that they had entered relationships with the monks which, sealed by exchanges of property, had given rise to written evidence that could later be reused. The notice draws on a series of charters and, quite possibly, necrological notices[95] extending back to the late tenth century when around 990 Guillelmus Gruta entered the monastery, presumably on his deathbed, and donated property to his community.[96] The whole notice is composed of paraphrases or verbatim excerpts from previous charters, a number of which were copied into the cartulary.[97] Here as elsewhere, the record of family reaches back but one generation: Guillelmus

Gruta's father Rodoard but not the latter's ancestors are remembered at Lérins. His geographical and social origins matter not at all because the monastery was interested rather in the origins of his property and because, like much of the land held in the tenth century, he had acquired it from the count of Provence following the expulsion of the Saracens. Land kept memory alive, both through the periodic donations from the estate of this tenth-century "founder" of the family and through the periodic conflicts with his successors. For those persons not related to these monastic memorial institutions by ties of land, there were no tags, no points of reference, by which to remember them. Thus more distant ancestors and their names disappeared from the region and from the name pool.

So it was that by the eleventh century the semantic tags of familiar names to which to attach the past had been transformed. Small wonder then that the memories transmitted with these tags were restructured, attached to a few familiar names from the past, and radically simplified.

Aristocratic Oblivion

This double loss of continuity of burial place and of onomastic continuity brings us back to the observation of Count Fulk le Réchin that he knew little about his ancestors because he did not know where they were buried. When Fulk considered his ancestry, he looked back to find in the past that which he was in the present—that is, a continuity in office and in land that was qualitatively the same as his own. He sought himself in the past. But only a past that was structurally and geographically continuous with his present could afford him this. The epitaph of Count William II of Angoulême recorded by Ademar of Chabannes echoes the importance of this physical continuity. Count William died 6 April 1028 shortly after his return from a pilgrimage to Jerusalem and was buried in the basilica of St. Eparchus before the altar of St. Denis. The epitaph, engraved on a lead tablet placed at his head, reads, "Here lies the beloved lord William count of Angoulême, who died in the same year as his return from Jerusalem, the eighth of the ides of April, on the hosanna vigil in the year of the incarnation 1028, and all of his ancestry lies in the church of Saint Eparchus."[98]

Just as monasteries determined to safeguard the bodies of Fulk's ancestry as well as those of William until the resurrection, so too did the monks preserve their *memoria*, a *memoria* at once liturgical and social. But this *memoria*, unlike that which might have been preserved by sisters, widows, or daughters, was disjointed, alienated from the family it served. As at Lérins, preservation was possible, but it was a service provided in the matter and according to the conditions outlined by the monastic institution. It had to be ever renewed through continued bonds of gifts and exchanges uniting the laity and the monks.[99] Ancestry before these bonds was uncertain, and continuity should the relationship between monastery and family be broken was precarious. The loss of a family's monastery could mean more than the loss of wealth or power: as we shall see in subsequent chapters, it could mean familial amnesia as well.

In conclusion, the rapidly changing families of the tenth and eleventh centuries looked to two means of preserving their *memoria*. First came the members of the family itself, principally the women, who were enjoined to mourn the dead, pray for the departed, and to keep the *memoria* of their men alive. Memory was likewise maintained within the family by the practice of name-giving. Who specifically chose names for children we do not know, but names passed through families as did land as part of the inheritance and identity of the kindred. The second means of preserving family memory was through the Church, particularly through monks and nuns.

In practice, canonesses, reformed monks, and lay women worked together in varying combinations to this end. However, for political and ideological reasons, reformed monks in the West, in the midst of a power struggle within a weakened monarchy, presented themselves as superior to women as guardians of *memoria* while portraying women as dangerous threats to social and political stability unless they accepted a passive role both in commemoration and in public life in general. In the East, a different power relationship between secular authority, both imperial and ducal, reduced the political influence of reformed monasticism, with the result that women maintained the traditional role of "custodian of men's life and soul."

When commemoration was removed from the family to the monastery, then the memory of the dead was continued but on monastic terms, terms that transformed and truncated the access of lay families to their past.

III

ARCHIVAL MEMORY AND THE

DESTRUCTION OF THE PAST

ACROSS EUROPE archival memory—that is, the preservation of charters and diplomas—underwent a profound transformation between the ninth and eleventh centuries, a transformation that determined what records of the past future generations might access and, to a considerable extent, how they might interpret these records. A full understanding of what an early medieval archive might have looked like can be drawn from the only institution founded in the early Middle Ages, the monastery of St. Gall, where the contents of the archive slowly formed over the eighth and ninth centuries and have survived virtually intact—some 839 original charters from before the year 920, by far the largest such collection in all Europe.[1] Still, as Rosamond McKitterick has pointed out, St. Gall's collection was not the largest archive of the early Middle Ages. In the East, Fulda, Lorsch, and Reichenau easily had more charters than St. Gall, and one can only with great difficulty form an impression of the original state of the archives of the older West Frankish monasteries such as St. Denis, St. Martin of Tours, Corbie, and the like. Episcopal sees, too, had rich archives, only tantalizing fragments of which remain. Finally, documents that originally formed part of lay archives have survived in ecclesiastical archives with enough frequency to demonstrate that archival collections were not the exclusive domain of the Church.

The St. Gall collection is not only unique in that most of it survives but also in that the documents survive as original charters. Elsewhere, most of what survives from the period before the year one thousand does so not as originals but in copies or summaries. It is the process of making these copies, and the effects on the nature of archival memory of the change from individual *cartae* to *libelli* or whole books, that forms the subject of this chapter.

The vocabulary used to describe these collections in medieval Latin as well as in modern studies in English, French, and German is varied, inconsistent, and confusing.[2] I shall use the term "cartularies" to describe what are often in German termed *Kopialbücher*—that is, integral copies of documents, usually in the first person (e.g., "I, *X*, give . . .") and referred to as the subjective form, written into rolls or gathered quires (*libelli*)—although, as we shall see, such collections often contain other material as well. I shall use the term *Traditionsbuch* (pl., *Traditionsbücher*) to refer to books or separate *libelli* containing primarily summary notices of transactions, usually in the third person ("*X* gave . . .") and termed objective, although some contain scattered integral copies of tradition notices and even first person notices as well. Modern editors often use the term *Traditionsbuch* to refer to both.[3]

Not all copies of early charters are preserved in cartularies or *Traditionsbücher*. Other documents are preserved in various mixed forms of texts. Many copies or summaries of charters survive because they were inserted into narrative texts such as histories or *gesta abbatum* or *gesta episcoporum*. In some cases, modern editors have wavered between describing such texts as chronicles or cartularies, using at times the term "chronique cartulaire." As we shall see, the line between such documents and ordinary "cartularies" is very unclear, even more so than is usually assumed. Another form in which documents are preserved is in later confirmations termed *pancartes*. Finally, portions of early private and royal charters are preserved in summary or in extensive excerpts within hagiographic and other narrative texts.

These types of extant documents probably do not do full justice to the range of early medieval recording of charters. Important institutions probably kept a variety of different types of records, some overlapping, for different purposes. Fragments and hints of these can be found in surviving capitularies and, possibly, in blocks of material copied later into cartularies or *Traditionsbücher*.

Certainly much of the loss of original archives can be attributed to successive man-made catastrophes, beginning with the internal wars of the eighth century, following through the Viking, Saracen, and Magyar invasions of the ninth and tenth, the crises of the Wars of Religion, the French Revolution, and the furious destructions of the two world wars in the twentieth century, not to mention the chance fires and natural disasters of the past thousand years. However, it appears that much of the archival riches of the early Middle Ages simply disappeared as a result of neglect or intentional destruction. Moreover, this process was well under way by the twelfth century. Many institutions preserved their cartularies and *Traditionsbücher* with more care than they did their originals. In subsequent centuries, originals were progressively less consulted when copies were available, and the former were allowed to deteriorate or disappear. Further, the creation of the latter may have led directly to the destruction of the former. Frequently, when twelfth-century historians or cartulary compilers sought to recover the past of their institutions, the only record of earlier charters existed in copies or summaries of the ninth or tenth centuries.

Traditionally, diplomatists have given low priority to the study of cartularies as such, using them primarily to reconstruct texts of lost originals with little regard to the nature, function, and history of this genre. Examination of their contents focuses on the identification of genuine, forged, or interpolated texts which, properly categorized by the techniques of diplomatics, can then be exploited as though they were originals. When editing cartularies, most nineteenth- and twentieth-century editors have ignored the organization of the cartularies themselves, attempting instead to present all the charters and documents of a given institution in a chronological order regardless of provenance and organization in the cartularies or tradition books themselves.[4] In other words, most scholarly attention has focused on eliminating the cartulary itself in order to provide transparent windows into the original archives of an institution.[5] This process was considered legitimate because the cartulary was considered a self-evident attempt to preserve the contents of the institution's archives. In the words of Émile Lesne, "Each cartulary is a witness to the state of a church's archives at the time that it was written."[6] Because of such assumptions about the unproblematic nature of these collections, the history of cartularies and similar collections has yet to be written.

And yet such a history is badly needed. Neither the existence nor the purpose of such collections is self-explanatory. When one considers the question of archival preservation and transmission from the modern perspective of legal evidence, it seems appropriate that originals, not copies, should be preserved with the greatest care. As legal instruments for the defense of property rights, originals had some claim throughout much of Europe; copies, before the creation of public notaries and the means of authentication associated with *pancarte* confirmations, had none. While records of Carolingian *placita* occasionally mention the use of both private charters and, more frequently, royal diplomas, as evidence in legal disputes,[7] one never hears of copies carrying such evidentiary weight. Nor were copies of charters the most obvious form of administrative record since, unlike other forms of administrative documentation, they rarely indicate revenues or even provide precise descriptions of the properties.

If cartularies did not guarantee title, if they did not provide adequate descriptions of properties, if they did not record revenues and obligations, why then were these copies made? What was the meaning of a cartulary? These are important questions because, rather than being "a witness to the state of a church's archives at the time that it was written," each cartulary is the result of a process of neglect, selection, transformation, and suppression. The strategies and intentions of copyists (one might better say, of authors) determined what documents would be preserved through copying or summarizing and how these copies and summaries would be made. This process of selection and emendation, which had already begun by the eighth century, determined what access to the past would be available to future generations. Unless we understand the circumstances that gave rise to these collections and their transformation in the course of the ninth through eleventh centuries, we cannot understand their role in preserving and creating the past.

The history of this genre has been much disputed, in part because the heterogeneous origins and purposes of these collections do not allow for simplistic explanations. Moreover, any comprehensive explanation for the appearance of cartularies must explain not only their appearance in the eastern regions of Francia in the 820s but also their total absence in the West before the tenth century.

Between Management and Memory

Much of the early debate on the origins of cartularies focused on their administrative, political, or legal roles. More recently and fruitfully, scholars have begun to recognize their memorial and historical significance. Early in this century Alfons Dopsch suggested that the appearance of these charter collections was related to the reforms of Benedict of Aniane begun in 817.[8] His suggestion was based on the observation that the earliest *Traditionsbücher* (meaning for Dopsch both what we are terming cartularies and *Traditionsbücher*) come from this period.

In a series of studies on imperial estates, Wolfgang Metz argued that cartularies emerged not from a tradition of religious reform per se but rather from royal concerns about monastic and imperial estates.[9] In particular, he suggested that the elaboration of the cartulary of Fulda,[10] one of the earliest cartularies (composed in 828), was intimately connected to the reform of that monastery by Hrabanus Maurus following the disastrous abbacy of Ratgar (802–817) and must be understood in relationship with other types of estate inventories and capitulary directives demanding inventories of royal benefices and imperial monasteries.[11] The most important of these is the *Brevium Exempla*, a fragmentary inventory of ecclesiastical property which contains two lists of *traditiones* to the Alsatian monastery of Wissembourg.[12]

Metz argued that the Fulda cartulary, like other forms of property inventories such as the list of properties for Fulda *ad usum fratrum nostrorum* prepared under the administration of Hrabanus Maurus and preserved in the twelfth-century *Codex Eberhardi*,[13] shows the influence of the *Brevium Exempla*, which he took to be a model intended to standardize reports of royal property. Certainly, the section of the *Brevium Exempla* taken from Wissembourg's list of *precaria* and *beneficia* in the

Wormsgau presents certain affinities with the cartulary of Fulda as well as other ninth-century cartularies such as those of Mondsee, Passau, and Regensburg. The properties are organized by *Gau* (county), indicate the donor or recipient, and specify the conditions of tenure. The first section of the *Brevium* to contain tradition notices specifies such notices "de illis clericis et laicis, qui illorum proprietates donaverunt ad monasterium . . . et e contra receperunt ad usum fructuarium." Such records, because of the continuing relationship between the institution and the donor as "precarialist," were of direct, practical importance at least until the latter's death. The next section, "de beneficiariis qui de eodem monasterio beneficium habere videntur," since it records theoretically temporary benefices, likewise serves practical needs.

Walter Goffart has suggested another possible connection between the origins of *Traditionsbücher*, cartularies, and royal reforms. In his study of the Le Mans forgeries, he speculated that the formation of such records may have resulted from changing royal policies concerning the disposition of church lands not directly needed for the support of the monks or canons.[14] He argued that, between 743 and 819, Carolingian rulers dealt with property that had been donated to churches but subsequently confiscated, whether by the king or by others, at their own discretion. Lands necessary for the community might be restored but other "superfluous" property would be granted to rent-paying lay tenants. After 819 the emperor renounced his right to distribute ecclesiastical property acquired subsequently although the earlier divisions of property continued to be administered as before. The effects of this policy may not have greatly altered the situation, but it may have made ecclesiastical institutions more aware of the need to record the origins of property and the nature of precarial holdings and benefices so that, as they fell vacant, the more recent ones at least could be redistributed by the Church and not by the king.

A number of difficulties make all these hypotheses untenable. The first is that the earliest tradition notices, the *Notitia Arnonis* (788–790) and the *Breves Notitiae* (798–800) of Salzburg, while not cartularies in the sense that we are using here, antedate the programs described by Dopsch, Metz, and Goffart by a generation.[15] Even if later policies may have influenced such collections, they cannot be used to explain their origins. As Heinrich Fichtenau, following the suggestions of Alain de Boüard, has observed, the *notitia* of the eighth century stand in a long tradition that reaches directly back to the *gesta municipalia* of the late Roman city.[16] The forms of notices prepared before urban magistrates shade directly into those prepared before the bishop.

Moreover, one must ask why, if the elaboration of these collections was a response either to the reforms of Aachen or imperial policy in general, similar collections were not made in the western half of the empire.

Not only are there no extant fragments of such collections but no prefatory comments by later compilers of western cartularies suggest that they are working from previous collections similar to those from the East. Some collections of documents were made with specific, ad hoc purposes in the defense of legal claims such as that prepared by the monks of St. Calais for Pope Nicholas I in the mid-ninth century or the series of papal bulls and royal diplomas prefaced by the charter of Bishop Berthefridus which makes up the earliest "cartulary" of Corbie.[17] However, these collections are quite different from those made in the East. Finally, one must wonder why the earliest cartularies contain many types of documents in addition to sales, donations, *precaria*, and *praestaria*, those documents most closely related to internal administrative concerns.

A much more fruitful approach to understanding these texts began with Fichtenau who, in his path-breaking *Urkundenwesen in Österreich*, recognized that, from the start, charters were never created for purely legal or administrative purposes. More recently, Peter Johanek has wisely redirected the discussion away from legal to commemorative functions of such documents.[18] In a recent historiographical study of *Traditionsbücher* largely summarizing Fichtenau and Johanek, Stephan Molitor has pointed out that these collections of tradition notices served simultaneously three functions: legal, historical, and sacral.[19] This is equally true of cartularies. As they developed in the ninth through eleventh centuries, cartularies protected not simply property rights both vis-à-vis tenants and royal authorities, but they also protected the memory of benefactors and that of the deeds of abbots and bishops. Moreover, these memorial roles greatly affected the form of these collections as well as the principles of inclusion and exclusion of their contents. This memory, a fundamental element in the institutional memory and thus in self-perception and identity, goes far to explain both the forms that cartularies and related documents assumed and the critical choices of inclusion, exclusion, and adjustment of the documents preserved in these cartularies.

Still, these general observations do not explain the particular appearance, and then disappearance, of cartularies in certain regions, nor do they explain the contents and organization of these collections. This chapter will suggest a general outline of the origins and development of these particular types of serial records in both the eastern and western regions of the Carolingian and post-Carolingian world. In essence, I will argue that the impetus to summarize and then copy the contents of land charters arose first in Bavaria and Alsace where the nature of the Carolingian *mainmise* in the late eight century at the expense of the local dukes created problems for institutions needing to defend their traditions in the fullest sense of the term against royal pretensions.[20] These concerns led to the preparation of dossiers of charters (probably bundles of originals particularly in need of protection) and to the elaboration of historically and geographically constructed summaries of donations prepared between the 780s and the death of Charlemagne. Later, during the reign of Louis the German, these dossiers and tradition *notitiae* were copied along with other charters into cartularies. Initially, some of these were intended primarily for administrative purposes, others more to preserve the *memoria* of benefactors than to serve narrow legal or administrative ends. Most of the administratively motivated compilations were one-time affairs, not continuing programs. Where subsequent cartularies did appear, they were much more connected to their memorial than to administrative concerns. Moreover, these later compilations shaded rapidly into the older tradition of retrospective, summary notices of transactions, *Traditionsbücher*, rather than copies of charters.

In the West, where the Carolingian rise to power had taken a different course, such copies or summaries were never compiled. Instead, original charters were preserved in institutions' archives. Occasionally, ad hoc dossiers of specific charters were copied, but these were intended as partial defense against rival institutions or local magnates, not title vis-à-vis the king. East and west, cartularies and *Traditionsbücher* were reborn in the tenth and eleventh centuries as part of the concern for reforming the past in light of present needs.

One can best begin to understand the origins of cartularies by abandoning preconceived notions and examining the evidence of the earliest cartularies, their formal characteristics and their contents, and then following the transformation of charter collections in subsequent centuries.

Carolingian Cartularies

Cartularies—that is, integral copies of charters relating to a particular religious institution—develop from three different but complementary traditions, each appearing for the first time during the first half of the ninth century. Some, such as that of Fulda (which was prepared in 828) and those of Regensburg, Mondsee, Passau, and Wissembourg, were collections designed primarily to assist the internal administration of episcopal and monastic estates. They were part of a complex and intensive system of estate management and reorganization. However, they were never exclusively intended for such practical purposes and drew both content and form from earlier compilations. At the same time, another kind of cartulary, typified by that of Freising, appeared which was more suited to a memorial than an administrative role. Finally, some collections were made in the course of pursuing specific claims. In various combinations and in fits and starts, all these traditions would continue through the eleventh century and beyond.

The prehistory of cartularies must begin with summary tradition notices, which both antedate cartularies and, in the East, would outlive them. Here Salzburg led the way, with the *Notitia Arnonis* (788–790) and the *Breves Notitiae* (798–800), prepared under the direction of Bishop Arn and combining both chronological and topographical organization.[21] Their core and model was the still earlier *Libellus Virgilii*, Bishop Virgil's defense of his church's rights to the Maximilianszelle in the Pongau and around Otting in the Chiemgau.[22] Virgil was Irish, and his decision to use a written account of property as a defense may have been drawn from insular tradition. In any case, as Herwig Wolfram has pointed out, these and other Bavarian *breves* are less concerned with recording the income of property than recording their titles to property.[23] The threat to the stability of previous donations was real: in his diploma of 791 confirming earlier ducal donations made to Kremsmünster (which must have drawn on a preliminary *schedula*, similar to parts of the *Notitia Arnonis*), Charlemagne specifically stated that donations made by Tassilo were not by this simple fact secure.[24] Thus as we shall see, in Bavarian collections such as those of Passau and Regensburg, one finds summaries of traditions from the Bavarian dukes and their contemporaries just as we do in the Salzburg material. However, these collections do much more than simply record land titles. Like the *Breves Notitiae* and the *Notitia Arnonis*, they are at once enumerations of properties and histories establishing the past of their institution within the wider domain of sacred history.

These *notitiae* were not drawn up exclusively from memory. At a preliminary stage charters must have been gathered into dossiers from which the details of the *traditiones* were extracted. Similar dossiers must have been collected in other Bavarian churches such as Freising and Passau. Although there is no reason to think that they were copied into cartularies or *Traditionsbücher* in the late eighth or early ninth centuries, they formed important parts of institutions' archival collections. As we shall see, some of them found their way into the ninth-century cartularies.

We can perhaps form a more nuanced picture of the concerns that led to the elaboration of cartularies as well as of the transition from these early *Traditionsbücher* if we examine in some detail the form and contents of the earliest extant cartularies.

The Fulda cartulary originally consisted of a collection of roughly two thousand private acts written into fifteen separate booklets, each containing acts relative to a specific region or Gau.[25] Within all but that of the Wormsgau, the charters are arranged chronologically by abbot. At

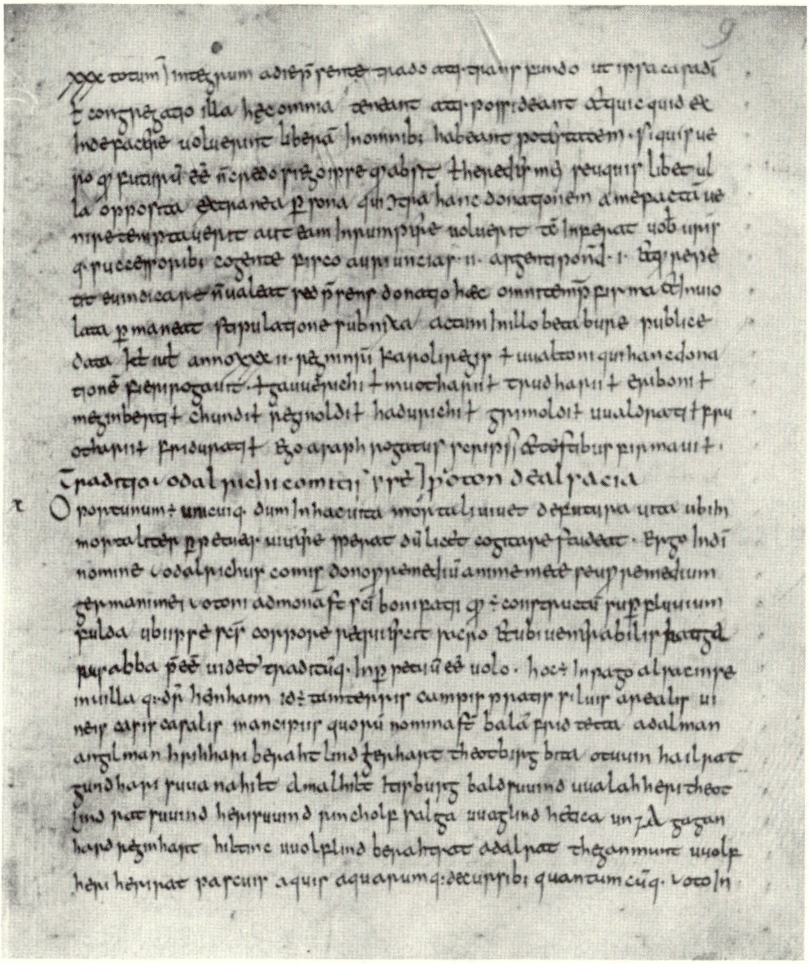

Plate 12. An unadorned, administrative document (the Fulda Kopialbuch, Hessisches Staatsarchiv, Marburg, K 424 fol. 6).

some time before the middle of the twelfth century, these fifteen book-lets were combined into eight or ten volumes. Today only eighty-seven leaves of this cartulary are extant (see plate 12).[26] The remainder of the cartulary can be reconstructed from the twelfth-century copy of Fulda charters known as the *Codex Eberhardi* and from the copy made by the sixteenth-century humanist Johannes Pistorius the Younger. The cartu-lary contained primarily charters of donation and *precaria*.[27] In addi-tion, sales, three exchanges, and two *praestaria* (that is, returns by the abbot of donations of which the donors will have life use)[28] originally included in the cartulary, have survived in the *Codex Eberhardi*. In sum, the Fulda cartulary was a series of *libelli* organized geographically and then, within most regions, chronologically. This geographic organization and the preponderance of donations and *precaria* suggests that the cartulary had a practical purpose, that of maintaining records of land rights within the various Gaue where Fulda had acquired property.

A fragment of a Regensburg cartulary now preserved in Munich[29] as part of the St. Emmeram *Traditionsbuch* is only slightly later than that of Fulda. All that survives from the cartulary is a *ternio* containing copies of twelve charters from 739–822 probably made during the episcopacy of Bishop Baturich (817–847), a former monk at Fulda who may have had personal experience of Fulda's cartulary.[30] This fragmentary collection contains primarily charters from 760, near the end of the episcopacy of Bishop Gawibald (736–761) to 814. Too little remains of this fragment to be able to determine the organization with any certainty. However, like that of Fulda they are not in chronological order but are generally arranged geographically. Charters one through five and ten and eleven concern property near Mallersdorf southeast of Regensburg. Charter six is a donation at Wolkering five kilometers south of Regensburg between the city and Mallersdorf. The order of charters seven, eight, and nine is not readily apparent since they concern, respectively, an island (Opinesaldaha) and donations in Upper and Lower Austria. The final charter, no. 21, is a fragment that may date from after 822.

The earliest portion of the Mondsee cartulary consists of fifty-two leaves[31] containing 138 charters, the latest from 854.[32] The first page bears the rubric in capitals: *Incipit liber traditionum*. Like the Fulda cartulary, the organization is topographical. However, this organization is more advanced than that at Fulda since within each Gau charters are further organized by location. Thus the cartulary is divided into six geographical regions.[33] The first section begins with the rubric "[ ] homines tradiderunt ad istum sanctum locum quod dicitur Matahgauue." Each subsection begins with the rubric, "Incipiunt capitula de pago . . ." In the left margins are indications of the specific locations within the Gau. Although the charters are integral copies in subjective form rather than objective tradition notices, the witness lists are entirely omitted, with only occasionally the mention "testes multi." The organization and the omission of witness lists both point to the purpose of the cartulary for the internal administration of the properties of the monastery.

The oldest Passau cartulary, like those considered above, also dates from the middle of the ninth century, possibly begun under the episcopacy of Bishop Reginhar (818–838) or his successor Hartwich (840–866).[34] The oldest portions are again ordered by Gau.[35] At the top of fol. 1 is the title: "Cartae de traditionibus ad sanctum Stephanum de Rotahkouue." On fol. 23 one finds "Cartae de traditionibus ad sanctum

Stephanum de Matahkauue." The cartulary was continued until the beginning of the tenth century with fols. 11–16 (Rottachgau) and fols. 17–22 (Traungau) added in this later period. The nature of the pieces contained in the oldest portion of the cartulary is more diverse than in the other, previously discussed cartularies. They contain not only copies of donations, *precaria*, and *praestaria* (no. 56), but also notices of earlier traditions (nos. 2 and 50), notices of royal *placita* (nos. 50 and 54), and even fragments of documents that may have no relationship to Passau.[36]

The contents of the Passau cartulary show the complexity of the archival materials from which it was assembled, materials that have more in common with the Salzburg collections than with the *Brevium Exempla*. The latter called for the recording of *precaria*, *praestaria*, and benefices. Cartularies such as that of Passau record some of these to be sure, but not exclusively. Only twenty-six out of a total of fifty-four donations are either precarial or benefices. The remainder record simple donations. In addition, this collection, fragmentary as it is, contains a variety of other sorts of documents hardly of a practical, immediate use in the administration of property. It would appear then that the compiler worked from various sorts of documents, possibly already arranged by rough geographical order in the archive, but of a heterogeneous nature. These include a *placitum* of *missi dominici* guaranteeing the free status of a woman from 800–804 (no. 50), a *placitum* establishing the servile status of a group of peasants (no. 54), a notice of oaths concerning property usurped by one Gisalhartus drawn up ca. 818–838, and a series of objective tradition notices.[37]

The common thread in most of these documents, some reaching back almost a century, indicates a variety of concerns arising from the early years of the incorporation of Bavaria into the Carolingian sphere. Of primary concern were the rights to property donated in the time of the independent Bavarian dukes, and most of the documents either concerned that period or the early reign of Charlemagne. Of the fifty-eight documents, eight certainly and two more probably date from the period before 788. Nine date from 788–89 and five from 788–800. Only four documents in the original portion of the codex can be surely dated from after 814, and three of these actually concern donations or circumstances of the earlier period. One records oaths about the status of property in the time of Charlemagne (no. 73), another concerns a benefice originally given ca. 800 (no. 74), and a third is the renewal of an earlier donation (no. 70). All the other donations, *precaria*, and *praestaria* from the period after 814 were entered in the early tenth century.

It would appear then that the scribe was not working simply from the archives of the monastery, attempting to transcribe donations, *precaria*, and *praestaria* for the purposes of administrative control. Still less was he interested in copying all the charters of the cathedral establishing land rights. And although he was working as late as the 830s or 840s, he showed little interest in recording post-814 donations, benefices, or *precaria*. Rather he had before him, either in original or in copy, a collection of documents that pertained to the crucial transition period from Agilolfing to Carolingian rule, which he copied, along with a few select documents that, although posterior, related to this earlier period. In this it resembles, to some extent, the sort of dossier from which Arno of Salzburg composed the *Notitia Arnonis* and the *Breves Notitiae*. Like these earlier Salzburg texts, the primary concern of the compiler appears to have been less the enumeration of incomes or properties for purposes of administration than the establishment of rights to property, rights possibly thrown into question by the transition from Agilolfing to Carolingian control.

Moreover, the notice on fols. 28v–29r in the Passau collection, reminiscent of the beginning of the *Breves Notitiae*, begins with something of a brief history of the foundation of the church of Passau, which presumably took place in 739 ("Incipit scientia qui scire valeat in quo tempore edificata erat ecclesia ista in tempore duci Paiauuariorum [Otilo]"), and continues as a brief account of the consecration and deposition of relics. This historical narrative corresponds to the historical narrative portions of the *Breves Notitiae*.[38] It then describes early donations by Cotafrid and his wife Kepahilt at the time of the veiling of their daughter Cotalind and another donation by one Folchraat. However, these tradition notices do not specify the properties donated or their locations, only the names of the *servi* and *ancillae* who worked them. The series of at least nine charters from 788–89 can be seen in part as the confirmation of earlier donations, now made under Charlemagne, as in no. 31 in which the Priest Perhari explicitly says that he had given a villa "sub tempore Tassiloni principi" and now "per tempore Caroli regi et cum sua licentia" renews it. For one such donation, that of Irminsuuid made on her deathbed ca. 789–791, the confirmation by Charlemagne is still extant.[39] This too reminds one of the Salzburg *notitia* made "una cum consensu et licentia domni Karoli."[40] Other donations may well have been forced surrenders of property to the bishopric of Passau by Charles's vanquished Bavarian opponents.

Both the content of the Passau collection—that is, materials relating to the transition from Agilolfing to Carolingian rule—and the date of the termination of the dossier from which it was copied (ca. 814) suggest that its elaboration may have been a response to circumstances in the early reign of Louis the Pious. One finds evidence for such concerns outside Bavaria as well. At this same time, the St. Gall charters were first organized into a collection.[41] Both may relate to the program of confirmations of earlier diplomas by Louis the Pious during the first years of his reign.

In conclusion, the heterogeneity of the materials in the Passau cartulary, including documents that seem to relate to property over which, by the mid-ninth century, Passau had no apparent control, suggests that the cartulary records a tradition, but one aimed at remembering and thus, perhaps, recuperating, not simply administering. This collection appears thus in its inception less an instrument of administrative or even legal control in a narrow sense but rather of recollecting (in a literal sense) the traditions about the church of Passau, its relics, its lands, its dependents, and its patrons.

The cartulary of Freising, which may antedate that of Fulda, was prepared by the deacon Cozroh for Bishop Hitto (811–835).[42] This collection, consisting today of 404 folia, differs fundamentally from the other cartularies in its principle of organization. It is structured chronologically, with the charters grouped by episcopal reign. Within this general chronological order, there appears to be no principle of geographical or chronological subdivision except in the charters of Hitto that are in roughly chronological order. Cozroh's grouping of material seems essentially based on the existing divisions in the cathedral's archives between *cartae* that Cozroh terms *traditiones* and *notitiae*.[43] The possibility of exploiting the collection for administrative or evidentiary purposes is made possible only by the elaboration of a table of contents compiled after the manuscript was completed, in part by Cozroh and in part by others. The manuscript begins with (incomplete) lists of the charters of each bishop's reign. Fifteen charters from the period of Bishop Joseph appear under the rubric "IN NOMINE DOMINI. INCIPIUNT CAPITULA" (see plate 13). The following folio begins with the rubric: "INCIPIUNT CAPITULA DE TEMPORIBUS HEREDIS [Arbeo] EPISCOPI" and lists eighty-two charters. Two hundred charters are listed for the reign of Atto, and 280 for Hitto. The collection includes acts of donation, exchange, tradition notices, notices of *placita*, and judgments. Most of these titles identify the charter or tradition notice by donor and by location ("Traditio x ad y"), thus making it possible, in theory, to locate specific acts by the name of the principal or by the specific location. However, others identified the document only by the name of the principals: "Cltescalch et Ermanlind," "Uuitagauuo reddidit," "Cotescal et Ermanlind," while some documents were omitted altogether in the table of contents. Nothing in this suggests a collection organized with an eye primarily for practical consultation for administrative or legal purposes.

We have a much clearer understanding of the Freising cartulary since its author, Cozroh, explained its inception in a preface. He placed the

IN NOMINE DNI NRI IH

XPIOE TEMPORIB; GENE RAN
OICIRI CULMINC IURIS SUBLI
MATI HATIONIS EPI INCIPIUN
OIVERSAS IRRVPTIONES PIRCOI
ICE PER ACTIS MOOOOMASCIE
MARINE MOPRIGISING IS
TRAOITIOOGOTCOZI AORICHARES
husu ETFOLMOTI FRISSUI·

Detradmone quamfecir deorcoz adricha
res husum tradidit eni addomu scie
marie terrirorium folmoti frissui eoqd
ipse folmot defunctuso testum partem
terrirorii folmoti frissui proprea qd iam dic
tuf folmot adhuc uiuenf ipsu terrirorium
tradidit inman frissui· ut ipse iam dictum
terrirorium tradidisse addomu scie marie
semp uirginif prosedempcione animae sue·
hoc pactu irteru accessit iam dictus deorcoz
& tradidit de sua herediiate testua parte in
omnib; quicquid depropriaherediiate insu
pradicto loco adrichates husum habuit· eo
modo utambas partes habete licuisse addier
suor· post obrum uo illius firm cuomni Irre

composition of a cartulary within a broad range of renewals undertaken by Bishop Hitto upon his arrival in Freising.[44] Cozroh described the elaboration of a charter collection in the context of other text-oriented projects initiated by Hitto. First, Hitto restored the cathedral's copies of sacred scripture and sought out whatever was missing to complete whatever texts of sacred scripture could not be found. Second, he completed the church's collection of "cantelenis et omnium divinarum documentorum officiis," (that is, the liturgical texts of the cathedral). In addition, he had them decorated with works of precious metal and artful decorations. Finally, he ordered copied the records of those who had enriched the church with donations for the redemption of their souls. Cozroh emphasized first the importance of preserving the *memoria* of these patrons: "so that the memory of those who had enriched this house with their property and had made it their heirs might remain in perpetuity, or whatever they had handed over and given for the salvation of their souls to this house."[45] He went on to say that records of donations had been lost through carelessness as well as through the wickedness of both outsiders and "false brothers," because there were many who desired to alienate the property of the church and against whom Hitto had constantly to strive. To facilitate the consultation of these records of donations, the bishop therefore ordered Cozroh to copy "rationabiliter" "whatever he found written in each charter and confirmed by certain testimony" into a single volume. This was to include both the donations in the time of his predecessors and in the time of Hitto's own reign. Cozroh was further enjoined neither to add to nor to diminish what he found in the originals, correcting only scribal errors. The advantage of this copy, Corzoh explained, was that the charters would be more accessible to those who wished to read them because they were organized rationally.

Thus at its inception, the collection ordered by Hitto had a triple purpose. First was the necessity to record the *memoria* of benefactors, a vital obligation closely related to the liturgical commemoration of the living and the dead and thus linked to the liturgical reforms also undertaken by Hitto. Just as the liturgical texts had to be repaired, completed, and ornamented, the memory of those for whom liturgies were to be celebrated had to be protected and reformed. In this sense, the *volumen* prepared by Cozroh belongs to the same class of texts as necrologies and *libri vitae* and is intended for the same purpose.[46]

However, in addition to preserving the *memoria* of the patrons and donors, Hitto wished to preserve the written record of *testimonia* and *confirmationes* that were being purloined by those who desired to obtain the property of the church. Cozroh did not explain exactly how copies of that "singulis cartulis exaratum certisque testimoniis confirmatum" would thwart such attempts, and one should not conclude that the cartulary was intended to be—or indeed would have been accepted as—valid evidence before a Bavarian court. However, the *memoria* that was to be preserved was not only that of the donors but also that of the *traditiones* and *condonationes* themselves, in light of their significance in establishing truth against both outsiders and brethren who threatened the church of Christ by alienating that which belonged to it by law. Finally, the "rational" organization of the charters was temporal, thus making the collection at once a record of rights and a history of the early bishops. The original collection contained charters from the episcopates of Bishops Joseph, Arbeo, Atto, and Hitto. It was continued by Cozroh to 848 and by others through the episcopacy of Erchanbert (836–854). Within each episcopate only the charters of Hitto follow a chronological order.

This early collection should be seen in conjunction with the *Gesta episcoporum* of Freising. When, in 1187, a *Gesta episcoporum Frisingensium* was composed, the author simply inserted those sections of Cozroh's charter collection into it as the exclusive source of information about the earliest bishops.[47] In fact, Cozroh's collection is itself a *gesta episcoporum*. As Michel Sot has emphasized, like charter collections, *gesta episcoporum* and *abbatum* share an interest in clarifying and preserving the history of church property: "*Gesta* are additionally and, sometimes, primarily a history of inherited lands."[48] Distinctions between cartularies and *gesta episcoporum* or *abbatum* are somewhat artificial. As Sot points out, many authors of *gesta* relied heavily on their institutions' archives, either summarizing diplomas and charters obtained during the reign of each abbot or bishop and appending them to the end of the account of each ruler (as at Le Mans) or integrating whole documents into their narrative. The extreme example of the latter is the *Gesta abbatum S. Bertini Sithiensium*, which is so nearly a series of documents that it was first edited by Guérard as the *Cartulaire de l'abbaye de Saint-Bertin* and then the short connecting comments were later published by Holder-Egger as the *Gesta Abbatum*.

Such collections of traditions pertaining to the crucial transition from ducal to royal control may not have been limited to Bavaria. Alemannic and Alsatian monasteries likewise were actively recording their *traditiones*, their *memoria*, in similar forms. The Wissembourg cartulary dates from the middle of the ninth century, most probably between 855 and 860.[49] It contains 275 charters, the most recent document being from 855. Again, the order is by Gau. Fols. 1–55 concern Alsace and fols. 56–83 the Saargau and Seillegau. The former is preceded by a table of contents labeled "Hec sunt nomina que renouata sunt de pago Alisacinse." Just as the Bavarian collections paid special attention to Agilolfing donations, these documents are generally organized according to the most important donations from the ducal family of the Etichonen and then by miscellaneous donations in northern Alsace from lesser family groups or by place. The editors have found less order in the Saargau and Seillegau charters, perhaps because these are largely much older and thus the family groups were less familiar to the copyists. The contents of the cartulary are largely limited to sales, donations, *precaria*, and *praestaria*. However, it also includes related documents such as the decision of a judgment in favor of the monastery (from ca. 785), which follows the copy of the original *praestaria*.[50]

The editors of the cartulary suggested that it was never intended to be a comprehensive copy of all Wissembourg charters. Of 125 places in Alsace and 63 from the Saar- und Seillegau, the later so-called "Edelinsche Urbar," or manorial account, contains only two dozen, an indication that the properties recorded in the cartulary may have been recorded specifically because they were being redistributed as either fiefs or *precaria* and thus particularly likely to be lost to the monastery. The specific properties included in the cartulary, according to the editors, were outside the direct administration of the monastery. The very precariousness of monastic control over these particular lands may explain their inclusion in a separate codex. They further suggest that another charter collection preserving documents related to the properties still effectively administered by the monastery may have existed at one time, but if it did, it is now lost.[51]

The Wissembourg cartulary may not be the only example of an Alsatian collection. The now lost cartulary of Honau in Alsace written in 1079 contained some one thousand acts dating from the foundation of this Irish monastery until the time of Charlemagne.[52] It is impossible to determine whether this section of the cartulary was copied from an earlier cartulary, but the number and unity of the charters from the earlier period suggests that it, too, might reflect concerns to preserve the traditions of the institution, which passed from Echtonid to Carolingian control.

No comparable collections from the western portions of the Carolingian empire exist from the ninth century, nor are there hints in later texts that such collections did once exist but have disappeared. Not that collections and reorganizations of charters were not made in the West during this time. At the Breton monastery of Redon, for example, Wendy Davies has been able to determine that during the abbacy of Ritcant (867–871) the charters of the abbey were reorganized.[53] First, all documents directly relating to Redon were collected together in rough chronological order. Then other documents were put haphazardly into a second collection. Finally, charters beginning with Ritcant's own

abbacy were organized chronologically into a third collection. However, Davies observes that "there is no need to suppose that this archival
activity involved a massive act of copying and recopying: it may simply
have been a process of organizing in bundles and endorsing where
necessary."[54]

Organization of originals rather than copying seems to have been the
norm in the West. Charles the Bald had specifically enjoined the ecclesiastical institutions of his realm to preserve the originals of royal and
papal privileges, and in general this seems to have been the practice for
private charters as well.[55] A primary exception was when, in pursuit of
specific legal claims, copies of select documents pertaining to a specific
issue were made. The monks of St. Calais, for example, assembled a collection of charters in 863 which they transmitted to Pope Nicholas I to
obtain his confirmation of his privilege for their monastery.[56] However,
this collection, like the collections assembled by the Le Mans forger(s),
differs fundamentally from the East Frankish ones. They are ad hoc dossiers, drawn up in defense of specific claims for a specific case. They appear to have been copied from the institution's archives or forged for the
occasion, not copied as part of a continuing administrative program.

The Transformation of Cartularies

The form of cartulary as administrative instrument does not seem to
have continued through the tenth century. The practice of making integral copies of acts gradually disappeared in the East to be replaced by
summary notices (*Traditionsnotizen*). In part, but only in part, this process may be explained by the disappearance of private charters. As we
have seen, already in the ninth century *Traditionsnotizen* existed alongside cartularies and were at times copied into them. Moreover, some
charters were summarized into *Traditionsnotizen* while others were copied in their entirety. Rather than positing a transition from cartulary to
Traditionsbuch, it might be better to see two traditions, both existing
since the early ninth century, but one (the cartulary) disappearing in the
course of the tenth. Thus the transition must have been related not only
to the forms of documents produced in the process of conveyance but
also according to the needs and interests of those preserving their
memory.

This change can best be followed in Regensburg where, in spite of
modern losses, fragments of a continuous archival tradition survive from
the ninth to eleventh centuries. Already in the nineteenth century Berthold Bretholz argued that, unlike some Bavarian cathedrals and monasteries that seem to have kept their traditions and charters on an irregular

basis, there is no reason to think that the lacunae in the Regensburg traditions from the ninth through the eleventh centuries are the result of anything but modern losses.[57] Unfortunately, these losses were severe, but while only portions remain of the ninth- and tenth-century materials, we can reconstruct what the whole would have looked like.

As we have already seen, the oldest portion of St. Emmeram's collection is the first *ternio* of a cartulary containing the earliest material from the time of Bishop Gawibald (739–761), prepared under the episcopacy of Baturich around 822.[58] The second is the so-called *Traditionsbuch* of Anamot.[59] It is today bound with a miscellaneous collection of various eleventh-century hands containing documents from 800 to 1021. Anamot's actual volume begins on fol. 70 and was dedicated to Bishop Ambricho (+891). The original dedication and ornamentation of the collection indicates the extent to which this volume, like that of Freising, was dedicated to preserving the *memoria* of the bishop. Originally, the volume began with a fourteen-line verse dedication praising the bishop (now fol. 70v) and calling the reader's attention to a picture of Ambricho that followed.[60] The dedicatory verses and picture were followed by a register of 108 documents, in turn followed by a dedication to the bishop. This dedication, like that to Bishop Hitto of Freising, emphasizes the elaboration of the collection of "scedas traditionum atque concambiorum necnon et commarcarum" within the broader interests of Ambricho in the preservation of books and the discharge of the liturgy.[61] Ambricho died before the collection was complete, and his name was then erased from this dedication (except for the first letter), as the collection was apparently to be rededicated to his successor Aspert (891–894). However, Aspert too may have died before it was finished, and the second dedication was not completed. The collection is divided into two books, each with a contemporary register. Although some of these documents retain the first person, the vast majority are already tradition notices, written in the third person and describing actions completed in the past.

There is a third fragment of another collection by Anamot that consists of a double sheet of parchment containing the last three charters of the first book. It was probably a copy of the extant collection. The survival of this fragment suggests that at Regensburg, as elsewhere, multiple copies of the institution's traditions were deemed necessary.

Finally three fragments of a *Traditionsbuch* survive from the period of Bishop Tuto (894–930). They are similar in size and form to the other early books, suggesting that they were prepared within the framework of a continuing tradition of such collections.

In 975 Bishop Wolfgang separated the monastery from the cathedral and installed its first independent abbot, Ramwold. A new series of tradition books began with Ramwold, a series concerning only the property of the monastery.[62] These traditions follow roughly chronological order and are now contained in Munich St. Emmeram KL Lit. 5 1/2. The manuscript contains 195 leaves with around nine hundred traditions from 975 (the year that Abbot Ramwold took office as first independent abbot) until 1235 (the year of Abbot Berthold II's death).[63] The portions written in the late tenth century corresponds to the need of the newly independent monastery to establish a *Traditionsbuch* for the property exclusively in the possession of the monastery. These were obviously written and reformed after the events they record since the first eighteen have initials that follow alphabetically.[64] Bretholz concluded that the codex was prepared during the life of the abbot, but that it was prepared from time to time and not as events occurred.

The subsequent entries of Ramwold's successors were done in more chronological order. From the abbacy of Wolfram (1001–1006) only two entries survive (103–104). This was a troubled time when Bishop Gebhard I (995–1023) and the canons attempted to bring the monastery back under their control and deposed Wolfram. Much more material survives from Abbot Richolf/Richold (1006–1028).[65] Here, however, entries are not clearly separated by abbots, and there seem to be more scribes. This might suggest that these were direct entries, but the use of the term "bonae memoriae" by the names of abbots in some shows that these are only later compilations. After fol. 75 chaos begins, with notices written in a variety of hands in no discernible order. This apparent confusion may be related to the long period of unrest and uncertainty in the monastery, as conflicts with the bishops and the claims and counterclaims of abbots and anti-abbots lasted into the middle of the twelfth century.

In conclusion we can see that between ca. 822 and 1021, first charters and then, increasingly, notices of traditions were regularly copied into books. These included donations, exchanges, and donations of *servi* (*censuales*). Royal, imperial, and papal diplomas did not normally appear here. They were kept in originals or in other types of copybooks.

Western Cartularies

As we have seen, cartularies containing copies of private charters may have been unknown in western Francia in the ninth century. Although long excerpts from charters found their way into narrative texts such as *gesta abbatum*, collections of charters tended to remain just that—collections of originals—unless, for specific reasons, some were copied in the course of particular disputes. The earliest cartulary from outside eastern Francia comes not from the continent but from England. Around the turn of the millennium Bishop Wulfstan I of Worcester had prepared a cartulary of the bishopric's charters and leases organized, as in the earlier Frankish cartularies on the Fulda model, by geographical location.[66] At the end of the eleventh century this cartulary was recopied by Hemming as part of the efforts by Bishop Wulfstan II to preserve the archives of the church. Wulfstan II had the earlier cartulary as well as original deeds and leases copied into Worcester's great Offa Bible. Portions of the original cartulary as well as that of Hemming survive today in BL Cotton Tiberius A. XIII. The earlier cartulary contains charters[67] and leases[68] grouped by shires and contains documents from Worcestershire, Winchcombeshire. Oxfordshire, Gloucestershire, and Warwickshire.[69] The list of leases is particularly interesting because it shows clear evidence of having been a practical record of lessees updated periodically. Ker has shown that nine of the leases, from the years of Oswald's episcopate, form a run, each concluding with the name of the original lessee and of his heirs, and in one case, that of his heir's heir. These Old English notes are in the main hand of the manuscript, and the wording indicates that this is a contemporary record: the original lessee is spoken of in the past tense and the current holder in the present. In addition, a second hand has noted in the margin the names of the original lessee and his heir. In some twenty cases a later annotator added to the marginal notation, tracing the holdings even further.[70]

The practical value of the collection is elucidated by a letter of Bishop Oswald's in which he explained for the benefit of his successors that, by order of King Edgar and with the sanction of the Witan and the testimony of the nobles of the realm, the lands that were held at lease were to be restored to the control of the church of Worcester after a period of two to three lives. Each leaseholder was bound by the terms of his charter, copies of which were kept in the cathedral's deed box.[71] Thus, like the copies of Carolingian *precaria* and *praestaria* recorded in cartularies of Fulda, Mondsee, Wissembourg, and elsewhere, these copies of leases were practical records needed for control and administration of church property.

Unfortunately, this early cartulary is unique in England, and it is thus impossible to determine whether it represents an innovation introduced from the Continent as part of the reforms of the tenth century (a response to the need for income to pay Danegeld) or a common, ancient practice in Anglo-Saxon England. M. K. Lawson has suggested that general ecclesiastical insecurity may have led to the compilation of a similar cartulary at Glastonbury around the same time,[72] but it is quite probable that the lost cartulary of Glastonbury dated only from the end of the eleventh or beginning of the twelfth centuries. Other efforts similar to those of Wulfstan II to establish title may suggest that such collections were not common before the end of the eleventh century.[73] And yet one must note that the earliest continental collections, the *Libelli Virgilii*, the *Breves Notitiae*, and the cartulary of Fulda, all have insular roots. The first two were prepared by or for an Irish bishop; the last is written in a Continental insular hand. Perhaps the Worcester cartulary of Wulfstan I represents the end of a long insular tradition. We will probably never know.

The later Worcester cartulary prepared by Hemming is much closer to the western continental tradition than the earlier eastern practice. Here one finds not only copies of charters but narrative accounts of alienations of Worcester property, the history of the see, and the efforts that he and Bishop Wulfstan II undertook to recover the property, including the statement that the testimony had been sworn before the Domesday commissioners and entered "in authentica regis cartula." Emma Mason has argued that the particular circumstances that led to the composition of this cartulary were concerns about the pluralism of York and Worcester and Wulfstan's desire to delineate clearly between lands and revenues of the bishopric and those specifically dedicated to the monastic *mensa*.[74] Finally, unlike the earlier cartulary, Hemming's was apparently not revised and updated. It was a commemorative, historical volume, not a working administrative tool.[75]

The western continental cartularies that begin to appear after the middle of the tenth century more closely resemble Hemming's cartulary than that of Wulfstan I or the earlier, East Frankish collections of Fulda, Passau, Mondsee, and other eastern institutions with their geographical organization and administrative role. They tended, like that of Freising and like the contemporaneous *Traditionsbücher*, to emphasize the memorial role of the documents over their administrative or legal possibilities. The earliest extant is that of St. Bertin called Folquinus, written around 962 and known as the *Gesta abbatum S. Bertini Sithiensium*. Folquin explained his purpose for creating this narrative "chronicle cartulary":

> We have heaped up a codex of little pieces of parchment in the body of one book so that, if by chance anyone should be desirous of investigating the possessions of this place, he might have recourse to it; here he is able to find the number and the names properly joined together under the heading of the year of the birth of the lord or the time of each king, as far as it was possible for us, but not all, because many were neglected by our predecessors, in part through the burning of books, in part destroyed by age.[76]

What books if any might have been destroyed is unclear. At the same time, he twice describes his work as a *gesta abbatum* of St. Bertin.[77] Thus he announced that the purpose of copying the monastery's charters was to enable the user to find the number and the names of the donors to the monastery and that the order would be chronological. He also indicates that the collection was incomplete, but as complete as he was able to make it in the middle of the tenth century. Moreover, unless one takes the suggestion that some charters were lost through the "librorum incensione," there is no suggestion that he was drawing upon or is aware of earlier cartularies or collections. If any volume had contained charters, it might have been a volume of royal and papal privileges such as the Corbie collection now in Berlin.[78] He seems to have been working from originals or apparent originals. We are at the beginning of cartulary formation at St. Bertin, but a cartulary intimately connected to a chronological vision of his institution and its abbots, not simply an administrative or legal document.

A century later, the monk Paul of St. Père of Chartres found himself in the same situation, creating a "libellus" from the privileges found in the archives of his monastery.[79] He too proposed to collect them "per ordinem," this order being again essentially chronological. Paul entitled the first two books respectively the *Liber Aganonis* and the *Liber Ragenfredi*, after the abbots from whose reigns the charters they contained came. He did not claim to have copied all the charters of the monastery but, in the case of those of Abbot Arnulf, only those that contained "useful" information.[80] However, like Folquin, he did not limit himself to a collection of charters but included all that he had learned about his institution from texts or oral accounts.[81] Here one finds fragments of polyptichs, brief biographies of abbots and patrons, a famous account of the heresy at Orléans, and material Paul has learned "priscorum relatione."[82] Both cartularies are thus "tradition books" in the fullest sense of the term, selecting, gathering, organizing, and thus creating a past for their institutions.

This commemorative, historical concern is common not only to "chronicle cartularies" but even to many western cartularies of the eleventh century that seem more simple collections of charters. This is even true of cartularies that included preexisting collections of documents. Constance Bouchard, the editor of the twelfth-century cartulary of Flavigny, for example, has argued that this cartulary probably recopied one dating from ca. 1020, making it the first known Burgundian cartulary.[83] This earlier cartulary, she argues, included groupings of documents dating from different periods of Flavigny's history. The groups themselves (some of which were already in chronological order) were further arranged chronologically in the cartulary, thus creating a document organized by periods in the house's history.[84]

The most important example of commemorative cartularies is that of Cluny. The earliest cartularies from Cluny (the so-called cartularies A and B, now BN nouv. acq lat. 1497–1498), were written in the eleventh and twelfth centuries. The first, written in the abbacies of Odilo (994–1049) and Hugh (1049–1109), contains documents from the reigns of abbots Berno, Odo, and Maiolus. Here, as in the chronicle-cartularies of St. Père and St. Bertin (and indeed, in the cartulary of Freising), the charters are arranged in broadly chronological order by abbot—although within that general organization Dominique Iogna-Prat, who has submitted the early cartularies to an intensive and penetrating examination, discerns both a chronological and a geographical order.[85] Cartulary B contains documents from the abbacies Odilo, Hugh, and Pons—that is, into the second decade of the twelfth century. Within these collections, the documents are apparently arranged by type of property. Thus, while the second completes the first, its organization indicates that the concept of the collection evolved over the decades during which the charters of Cluny were being collected, organized, and transcribed. It is the initial form and purpose of Cartulary A that concerns us here.

The collection was begun during the abbacy of Odilo and at his instigation, and the oldest portion of the cartulary, two bifolia (now fols. 7–10), date from his abbacy, probably ca. 1030.[86] At a later date, probably in the second half of the eleventh century, these two bifolds were inserted into a *quaternio*,[87] and two charters from Berno's abbacy were copied onto fol. 10 with other charters of his abbacy, continuing to fol. 36v. The next section begins with a "Prefatio temporibus domni Oddonis abbatis" (fol. 37r), followed by charters from Odo's abbacy which start with two charters of Bishop Berno of Macon (fols. 37r–38r). The sections containing the charters from abbacies of Ayardus (beginning fol. 84r) and Maiolus (164r sqq) differ from the those of Cluny's first two abbots in that they lack prefaces.

On the first four folia of the new *quaternio* a contemporary hand recorded a series of annalistic notices, the so-called *Venerabilium abbatum cluniacensium Chronologia*.[88] Since the same hand that entered dates to 1251 also wrote the entries up to 1088, one can reasonably suggest the former date as the probable moment when this portion of the manuscript at least received its present form. At approximately the same time, another quire of two bifolia and a single leaf was added before the *quaternio* (today fols. B to F) on which were written a catalogue of the charters of Berno's time.

Drawing attention to the twelfth-century catalogue of Cluny's library,[89] Iogna-Prat has suggested that the item described there as "a *volumen* in which is contained who was the founder of this place, and who was the first abbot, or who [was] after him, how long he lived, and the charters of those things which in the time of each were given to that place, and a *hymnarius* with canticles and psalms, some customs [*consue-*

tudines] and some prayers of the martylrology" may refer to the original portions of Cartulary A.[90] This may be the case, and one can compare this combined concern for charters and liturgical texts with the similar combination in Cozroh's description of Bishop Hitto's concern for liturgical manuscripts and records of donations. However, if for a time these materials were combined, it is unlikely that this was the original intention.

The original intention of the collection of Berno's and Odo's charters is made clear from their respective prefaces.[91] The first presents the rationale of the entire collection. All the *donationes* made to the monastery by the just in past times were to be collected into one *volumen*, with those of each abbot in its own *libellus*.[92] Probably, the individual *libelli* were initially maintained separately so that additional material could be added as it was found and organized. This seems to have been done, explaining in part the confusing paleographic and codicological state of the cartulary. The undertaking is termed a *narratio*, with its beginning containing the *tempus et gesta* of Abbot Berno "and in what manner he, enriched by the most excellent prince William, ennobled [Cluny] with his own allod which is called La Frette."[93] Thus the author of the cartulary conceives of this *libellus* as the *Gesta Bernonis*. But these *gesta* are essentially the acquisitions and donations of land made by, to, of, and through the efforts of the abbot. The preface begins with a mention of the donation of La Frette perhaps because, as Barbara Rosenwein has pointed out, this property, left to Cluny by Berno in his testament, held a special place in Cluniac *memoria*.[94]

Similarly, the preface to Odo's charters refers to the "series primi libri aureum tempus et lucida gesta domni . . . Bernonis." Then, after a brief account of Odo's life, it concludes by announcing that the collection of charters makes it possible for one who wishes to learn "how many and how various were the properties acquired for the use of the monks through the industry of that aforementioned father."[95]

The cartulary, then, was conceived of not as a copy of the monastery's archive, and still less as an aid to administering the monastery's estates, but rather as a *gesta abbatum* like that of St. Bertin. In keeping with this principle, the cartulary contains few charters that do not directly concern transactions between Cluny and other parties. Although the extant charters of Cluny include documents that antedated acquisition of land by the monastery and that entered the archives when Cluny acquired the concerned properties, normally these were not copied into the cartulary but rather preserved as originals in the Cluniac archives. While these charters may have provided valuable evidence for administrative and legal aspects of estate management, they had no place in the history of the abbots.

The Cluniac cartulary does not introduce the kinds of commentaries and digressions characteristic of St. Bertin and St. Père but, like them, it is not simply a literal transcription of the charters. Their editor, Alexandre Bruel, found that copyists of the earliest portions of the cartulary introduced much greater changes into their text than did their successors in the twelfth and thirteenth centuries.[96] These were of six different kinds: (1) simple corrections of barbarisms and errors of Latin; (2) changes from direct to indirect discourse or vice versa (for example, in BN or. 23 one reads, "Hanc igitur donat Gyrardus et uxor sua Suficia," while the cartulary A of Mayeul 436, cccclxvii, writes "Ego Cirardus et Sufisia uxor mea"); (3) simple abridgements; (4) minor expansions, in some charters, for the purpose of clarification (for example, a donation that originally read simply "Deo et sancto Iohanni" adds "et ecclesiae Cauarriacensi quae ad Cluniacum spectat"); and (5) when charters were later confirmed by royal diplomas, notice of the confirmation is sometimes added at the end.

But the most interesting kind of change is (6) a series of additions that indicate the extent to which the cartulary was not simply an "accurate" copy of the originals. While Cozroh had taken pains to explain that in his copy he had neither added nor subtracted anything "nisi scriptoris vitio aliquid depravatum repperisset," that is, except for correcting scribal errors, Bruel found a variety of changes of a rhetorical nature. Some very laconic originals were given a preamble to add solemnity. Others were given an elaborate penal clause at the end. In still others one can see that there is a general development throughout the text. Bruel's predecessor Bernard had thought that these differences indicated that these acts had been chirographs, only one portion of which exists today. Bruel doubted that such double acts had ever existed. Rather he argued that the monks of the eleventh century were shocked not only by the barbarisms but also by the rhetorical style of the short notices of early donations that they had before them. They felt called upon to augment and amplify them in order to impress their contemporaries with solemn formulas of piety and threats of punishment. Such changes are far from forgeries in any sense. Rather they continued the tradition, already evident in the charters of St. Gall, of expanding laconic sketches of transactions in accordance with rhetorical and religious patterns.

This attitude reflects a very different attitude toward the scribe's task than that of Cozroh or of twelfth-century copyists. The cartulary was not simply a collection, it was a *narratio*, and as such had to be reworked in conformity to that which was fitting for the later eleventh century. We have seen a similar preoccupation at Regensburg, where the *arengas* of the document in the late tenth-century *Traditionsbuch* were so composed that each begins with a word whose initial letter is in alphabetical order. Like the cartulary chronicles of St. Bertin and St. Père, the cartulary of Cluny served first the *memoria* of the abbots, a *memoria* that had to be presented in a seemly manner.[97]

Such revisions and reworkings of the past were not forgeries. However, forgeries were certainly common in the eleventh century, particularly in dossiers of documents compiled in the course of specific disputes. As we have seen, this sort of collection already existed in the West in the ninth century at Le Mans and St. Calais. Such forgeries raise still other sorts of questions concerning the nature of archival memory since they often included a double process of creation and destruction. The genuine originals that served as the forger's models were often destroyed to cover his tracks. Thus the increasing importance of archives and their intense use in the eleventh century paradoxically explains the destruction of some of these great collections. The most outstanding example is that of St. Denis.[98]

Silencing the Past: The Last Merovingian Papyrus

The archives of St. Denis have preserved by far the greatest number of extant Merovingian diplomas as well as private acts from northern Europe written on papyrus. As Henri Leclercq said, "If we did not possess the diplomas of the monastery of St. Denis historical science would suffer some lacunae, but the science of diplomatics would be decapitated."[99] Recently the extraordinarily rich Sandionysian archives from the Merovingian period have been seen as evidence that St. Denis played a special role in the production and preservation of royal charters.[100] This may or may not be the case; perhaps we are seduced by our sources since we know that other institutions possessed thousands of early charters, now almost entirely lost. In any case, what has survived of the St. Denis papyri has less to do with what may have been deposited there in the seventh century than it does with the decisions about the usefulness of this archive in the eleventh. An examination of these documents presents an opportunity to understand how the past was preserved, transformed, and discarded in the eleventh century. In particular, we can observe the process by which a rich archive, reaching back to the dawn of institutional archival formation, was systematically pillaged and destroyed in order to build from its fragments a more useful and appropriate past.

Because of the importance of historical and pseudohistorical writing at St. Denis in the ninth century and because of its central role in promoting a royal ideology and a radical new aesthetics beginning in the twelfth, historians tend to assume that its significance was uniformly high during the intervening period. In fact, this is hardly the case. As Thomas Waldman has pointed out, between the death of Charles III (the Simple) and the accession of Louis VI in 1108, one sees a decrease in royal attention and favor toward St. Denis.[101] The last Carolingians seem to have had no particular relationship with the abbey, and while the Robertinians acquired the position of lay abbot and used the institution as a major foundation of their power in the north, their involvement weakened rather than strengthened the monastery's independence. Monastic lands were alienated in favor of their supporters, they invited first Maiolus and then Odilo of Cluny to reform the spiritual life, and they used the monastery for episcopal synods (not always in accord with the monks' wishes).[102] The vibrant intellectual life of the monastery, as evidenced by the activities of its scriptorium, also diminished. Donatella Nebbiai-Dalla Guarda has been able to identify few manuscripts produced at St. Denis in the late ninth through early eleventh centuries.[103] Most of these are patristic and liturgical texts, and little of this production suggests a great interest in history. Of these, only the *Vita et acta S. Dionysii*,[104] the *Praeceptum Dagoberti regis*,[105] and the *Privilegia ecclesiae Sancti Dionysii*[106] suggest a concern with the past. The importance of St. Denis as a center of historiographical production would only return toward the end of the eleventh century through the influence of the historical school of Fleury.[107] These earlier texts indicate not so much a concern with interpreting and creating a comprehensive view of the past as preserving specific aspects of its relationship with royal and episcopal powers. This was, however, vitally important since, as the monastery gradually began to reemerge as a center of royal favor in the eleventh century, the precise issue was what these previous and thus proper relationships had been. In a diploma of 1005–1006 Robert the Pious confirmed for St. Denis those *consuetudines* that it had previously enjoyed.[108] In a subsequent diploma of 1008, Robert spoke of the restoration of the *libertas* and *dignitas* lost since the time of Charles the Simple by him and his father.[109] But what exactly were these *consuetudines*? In what did the *libertas* and *dignitas* consist? These questions, at once concrete and complex, were the kinds of practical historical issues concerning the monastery.

Chief among these issues, and one that had appeared already in 994, was the relationship between the monastery and the episcopacy.[110] The most burning aspect of this issue was the dispute with the bishop of Paris over the monastery's independence, as it claimed to enjoy the right of immunity from the bishop, the right to demand the consecration of oil, chrism, altars, blessings, and ordinations from the bishop at any time, and the right of direct appeal to Rome. This conflict, which continued through the first half of the eleventh century, was terminated by a bull of Alexander II in 1065 and a diploma of Philip I in 1068, each confirming the rights of the abbey. According to the act of Philip, the conflict had been brought before the magnates of the realm in the royal presence. The abbey had presented *decreta* of Dagobert, Clovis, Thierry, Childeric, Pippin, Charlemagne, Louis the Pious, and Charles the Bald as well as a *privilegium* of Bishop Landry of Paris and *privilegia* of the Roman pontiffs.[111] With royal permission, the case was brought to Alexander II. The latter explained in two small bulls, one directed to King Philip and to Count B., the other to the archbishop of Rheims, that the case had been brought before him twice. He invited the parties to appear before him in an ecclesiastical assembly. There, after having heard both sides, he had decided in favor of St. Denis. This decision, made according to Léon Levillain at the Lateran Council of 1065, was contained in the bull of that date and cited the bulls of Alexander's predecessors Zachary, Stephen II, Leo III, Nicholas I, and Leo IX as well as the privileges of the bishops made at the time of Charles the Bald. Philip then reinforced the papal decision by his diploma, which confirmed the privileges of his predecessors.

As is often the case, the community of St. Denis had built its case on a series of genuine, forged, and interpolated papal and royal documents. The nature of these documents, brilliantly and painstakingly clarified by Levillain, makes it clear that St. Denis had enjoyed originally a much more limited immunity granted by Clovis II and Bishop Landry. Levillain's detective work shows how the monks first made a (now lost) draft of the forged and interpolated documents, then produced two sets of copies. One was a "cartulary" consisting of thirteen bulls and diplomas plus the acts of the Council of Soissons and a list of bishops of the monastery of St. Denis. This copy, the *Privilegia ecclesiae Sancti Dionysii*, was completed around 1061 and was almost certainly the collection sent to Rome for examination by the pope and the synod.[112] Shortly after it was completed, it was bound together with the addition of the decretal of Gregory I (*De monachorum libertate*, the *Relevatio S. Stephani* describing a vision he experienced of St. Denis),[113] a diploma of Charlemagne for St. Denis, and the three bulls of Alexander II.

The second set of forgeries, also copied from the draft, consisted of pseudo-originals of the documents in the first portion of the cartulary, written on parchment and papyrus. Although copied with less attention to the details of the content than were the cartulary copies, it is these copies that most concern us because they give us a glimpse into the state of the Dionysian archives in the eleventh century, its contents, organization, and the skills of the monks who maintained and ultimately destroyed it.

Nineteen papyri exist today from the archives of St. Denis. In addition, at least three others were known to have existed in the seventeenth century.[114] These include a forged donation of Dagobert,[115] a forged bull of Stephen II, and the *Confessio Genechiseli*.[116] Although a number of the Sandionysian papyri are genuine, only two were used in the eleventh century because of their content: the diploma of Clovis II[117] and the bull of Nicholas I of 28 April 863.[118] However, even this latter document is suspect: Georges Tessier recognized in it the hand of the same scribe responsible for a number of diplomas of Charles the Bald which led him to suggest that the bull is either a ninth-century forgery or at least a copy that Nicholas I's chancery agreed to authenticate with a lead bull.[119] Without exception, the other documents survive only because, at a time when supplies of fresh papyrus were unobtainable, they became the raw material on which the diplomas and bulls needed for the successful pursuit of the monastery's conflict with the bishop of Paris were written. I would like to examine these documents for what they tell us about both the physical and technical possibilities of archivists at St. Denis in the eleventh century, and how the uses of these documents both determined and limited future understandings of the monastery's past and, by implication, that of the Frankish world.

Let us consider the materials available to eleventh-century forgers at St. Denis in their archives.[120] First, with two possible exceptions,[121] all of the papyri pertained directly to St. Denis. Judging from these documents, there is no reason to believe that St. Denis had served, for the first two thirds of the seventh century at least, as a depository of royal acts. The papyri included, first, a series of eight royal privileges, including two confirmations by Clothar II, one of Dagobert I, four of Clovis II, and one of one of his sons.[122] Second, the monastery had a series of four royal judgments in its favor by Clothar III.[123] Finally, the papyri included five private documents—two testaments, a private donation, an exchange, and a letter to Charlemagne.[124] Finally, St. Denis had a series of papal bulls, including at least one of Nicholas I and one of Formosus.[125]

How many other western papyri still existed at St. Denis by the end of the first millennium? We cannot be sure because, except for the three mentioned above, no others have survived or, indeed, seem to have survived the eleventh century. We can assume, from the uses made of preexisting documents in the forgeries, that some genuine papal bulls may have supplied the lead bulls for the forgeries. The originals were presumably then destroyed, as may have been the originals or presumed originals of the royal documents being reworked and the genuine privilege of Bishop Landry.

Losses of Merovingian diplomas did not begin with the eleventh century, although it may have ended with it. Forgery was also a venerable tradition in the monastery, a tradition that certainly continued for centuries. Hartmut Atsma has prepared a list of some seventy-four *acta deperdita*.[126] Twenty-two of these are known through the early ninth-century *Gesta Dagoberti*, which used or cited some twenty-four Merovingian diplomas (of which only two originals are extant: d. 14 and 19) and of the remaining twenty probably less than half were genuine.[127] The existence of other lost genuine, interpolated, and forged diplomas can be inferred from extant copies of genuine and forged diplomas. However, while the tradition of forging Merovingian diplomas continued, one need not posit the existence of lost Merovingian royal or episcopal papyri after the eleventh century to account for any of these. Later Merovingian forgeries for St. Denis seem to have used these forgeries rather than other genuine or earlier forgeries for their models.[128]

Not only did St. Denis still guard these papyri in its archives in the eleventh century, but at least some of its monks could still read them. This is by no means a minor consideration. The Merovingian cursive in which they were written was not an easy hand for later medieval readers. On the one genuine Merovingian papyrus,[129] the only dorsal inscriptions of the Middle Ages are those of the late eighth century and one contemporary to the creation of the cartulary. To judge from the dorsal inscriptions on parchment originals from the seventh century preserved at St. Denis, reading even them had become extremely difficult. Most contain contemporary notices, notations from the eighth- or ninth centuries, and then early modern notations. Notices from the twelfth through fourteenth centuries usually repeat earlier Carolingian indications. Thus on a precept of Theuderic III one reads in a ninth-century hand "conf de Saucido et Monticellis" and in a twelfth-century hand "Conf. de Saucido [et] Monticell."[130] A fourteenth-century hand indicates simply: "non legi p[ro] defectione [ ]inet" and its location, "de sc[ri]nio l[itte]rar[um] vetustissimar[um]." On another precept of Theuderic III of 688, the notice of the twelfth century, "donatio Theoderici regis de Latiniaco" simply copies exactly the eighth- or early ninth-century notice below it.[131] Other attempts at discerning the content indicate the great difficulty experienced by later generations. In the twelfth century, a judgment of Childebert III was interpreted as a donation.[132] On a *placitum* of Theuderic III of 679, a twelfth-century hand had written "Carta Almagero de porcione sua in Bestiliconivalle villa sati in pago Belvace[n]si," misreading "Almagero" for Amalgario, "Bestiliconivalle" for Bactilionevalle, and probably reading "Belvacensi" for

Belvacinse (not in the text but in the dorsal notice from the seventh century).[133] This inability to read seventh-century documents may account for the phenomenon, noted by Atsma, that later cartularies seem to have been made by copying previous ones, not by returning to originals.[134]

We are left then with the following image: In the early eleventh century, there still existed at St. Denis a collection of Merovingian papyri. Moreover, these papyri could still be read and appreciated by the monastery's archivists. However, the content of most of these documents, including genuine diplomas of the monastery's great patron Dagobert I, were of little importance to the monastery as it faced the needs of its time. More important was the papyrus on which they were written. Thus with the exception of ChLA 558, and the papal bulls K 13 10 and L 22 7, the extant Sandionysian papyri became the raw material for creating a new and more usable past for the monastery. They were turned over, the recto sides glued either to pieces of parchment or to the recto sides of other papyri in order to hide their content, and then they were reused to produce diplomas and privileges more appropriate to the needs of the eleventh century. We are certain of the uses of eleven of these since they still carry the forged texts. Four more bear traces of ink from papyri glued to their faces at one time, indicating that they too had been used to produce such forgeries. Since the monastic historian Jacques Doublet saw the pseudo-originals of Dagobert I and Stephen II in the seventeenth century, one can imagine that the traces on these four fragments may be evidence that they had been used as backing for these now lost pseudo-originals. Certainly during the later Middle Ages, none of these existed as an integral part of the charter collection of St. Denis, since none carries any dorsal notations.

Levillain and others have been dismissive of the efforts of the eleventh-century scribe to produce seemly seventh-century forgeries. He described the hand, which was the same in all of the forgeries, as "lourde et disgracieuse."[135] This may be, but one must still admire a certain level of technical ability. As can be seen from the facsimiles, the eleventh-century scribe did understand some of the characteristics of the hand he was copying. Moreover, working no doubt from genuine diplomas and bulls destroyed afterwards, he was not satisfied to imitate a single archaic hand. Instead, his royal diplomas imitate Merovingian chancellery cursive while his papal bulls imitate curial style. A major problem in his enterprise was caused by his writing instrument. While the ductus and the general forms of letters is followed, the pen he employed produced a much wider line than that of the originals. To the extent that it resembles Merovingian cursive, it is closer to what one might expect to find in a book hand than in charters. The result is disconcerting and, to a diplomatist accustomed to originals, obviously spurious. Moreover, as Levillain pointed out, at times the scribe slipped back to what is recognizably a tenth- or eleventh-century Caroline minuscule, for a few letters. Still, the effect is generally impressive: documents in an antique hand written on antique material. In the cases of the bulls of Zacharias, Stephen II, and Nicholas I, their authenticity was further enhanced by the attachment of bulls from genuine documents of these popes to the copies. And it was this visual impression more than the precision of the content that was paramount in this set of forgeries.

The "preservation" of these early Merovingian documents has been a boon to historians and diplomatists. As Leclercq suggested, without them diplomatics would be beheaded. However, it was not until the seventeenth century that this head was replaced. The only genuine Merovingian diploma of the first half of the seventh century to be known at St. Denis through the entire Middle Ages subsequent to the eleventh century was that of Clovis II (no. 19. ChLA 558). It alone bears any subsequent dorsal notations. It alone was copied into the later medieval cartularies of St. Denis: B.N. lat. 5415 and Arch. nat. LL 1156, 1157, and 1158.

The other genuine documents, including royal privileges, disappeared from sight and memory for over five hundred years. One of the documents used for forgery, namely ChLA 551, a donation by Dagobert of the villa Ezanville (Dept. Seine-et-Oise), had been known and used by the author of the ninth-century *Gesta Dagoberti*.[136] However, it disappeared from sight after the eleventh century. In contrast, the forged diplomas created in the eleventh century had a great success. DM 26 and 27 appear in all three subsequent cartularies along with other earlier and subsequent forgeries. As Atsma suggested, the three later cartularies may well have been copied one from the other, without reference to originals which, one can suspect, would have been almost impossible for the monks to read in any case. Thus, by the physical reappropriation of early papyrus documents to create an image of the monastery's pristine relationship with bishop and king, the eleventh-century forgers did more than offer a version of St. Denis's early history. By destroying originals of documents such as that of Bishop Landry after altering their contents, and by appropriating other originals for writing material, they made alternate pasts inaccessible. Much would be created at St. Denis in subsequent centuries that would serve as histories of the institution and of the monarchy to which it was intimately attached, but the destruction and appropriation of that century determined the primary materials that would be available to these subsequent generations. The rest of Sandionysian historiography would work within the radically reduced horizons of the eleventh century.

Conclusion

Arnold of St. Emmeram compared the process of sorting through the past to the process of clearing the arable, cutting down groves once sacred to the gods so that the land could be made useful for the present.[137] This same pruning was going on in archives across the continent. Both he and Paul of St. Père de Chartres emphasized that not everything was to be preserved, only that which was useful. However, many decisions and selections had already been made by their predecessors. Regional needs and traditions had determined in what form the records of the past would be transmitted: in the East, cartularies and *Traditionsbücher*; in the West, primarily originals. When, around the millennium, western churchmen became interested in organizing their past, they were faced with these collections that they then used as the raw material for the creation of a new past. In the East, more coherent records of the past often existed, but they had already been passed through a different kind of grid, that of geographically organized collections. This organization gave way to a chronological one as the same preoccupations with bridging the chasm of past and present became more important than the administration and defense of properties based on the written word. But in neither case were the creators of the eleventh century bound by what they found in their archives. They used this raw material with great freedom, destroying, revising, recopying, and especially reorganizing. The result was a winnowing and restructuring process that provided the parameters within which subsequent generations could hope to understand the past.

IV

UNROLLING INSTITUTIONAL MEMORIES

AROUND THE MIDDLE of the eleventh century, two monks, both living in ancient monasteries that had disappeared for a time in the course of the tenth century and that were struggling to reconstruct their identities in the face of powerful opposing forces, selected the same means by which to reinvent their lost pasts. The first, an anonymous monk moving back and forth between the monastery of Breme near Pavia, the Piedmontese cloister of Novalesa, and the city of Turin, scavenged odd scraps of parchment, either collected from the floor of his scriptorium or cut from the margins of books, and sewed them into a long roll on which he began to write a history of Novalesa from its mythical foundation until his own time. At exactly the same time, north of the Alps in Bavaria, another monk, Gottschalk of Benediktbeuern, was engaged in the same enterprise, compiling a "rotulus historicus" on which to write the history of his monastery. These two works, the only extant *rotulus* chronicles of the eleventh century, betray common concerns of monastic communities searching for a usable past among the scraps of parchment, odd charters, and miscellaneous written and oral fragments of their monastic inheritance.[1]

The *Chronicon Novaliciense*, although missing considerable portions of the first and fourth books, is over eleven meters in length and composed of thirty pieces of parchment varying between 90 and 110 mm in width.[2] The *rotulus* seems to have been a working copy of the chronicle used by the author and was never completed. Its chapter headings do not always correspond to the extant chapters, and following the fifth and last book the author included a series of documents, fragments from other texts and notes intended for later insertion into the chronicle.

The text, recently described by Chris Wickham as "a fascinating ragbag of a text,"[3] has frustrated historians and philologists for over a century by its apparently extraordinary level of misinformation, confusion, and conjecture. The author, it seems, ought to have been able to write history, but he somehow failed to do so. As Wickham wrote,

> The anonymous chronicler has a clear conception of writing *acta vel gesta* within which he explicitly interlaces discussion *de vassis* . . . and of monastic history. One could say that he recognized as possible a history of the Italian kings, and perhaps even of the kingdom. But the details of royal history, even where relevant to a monastic chronicle, are lost or garbled.[4]

Perhaps the author had such an option, but if so he chose not to follow it. The task he undertook was not to create a political history of Italian kings or even of the kingdom. Still less was it to create an "accurate" monastic chronicle. It was rather to create a past for his community, a past that corresponded to the mental, social, and political structures of the present. This was no easy task because the same political, social, and institutional discontinuities that had affected Provence had been felt even more forcefully in the Susa valley.

Novalesa had been founded in 726 by Abbo, an aristocrat whose family controlled the vital Alpine passes between Francia and Italy and who, through his cooperation with Charles Martel, had solidified his power in the lower Rhône.[5] In the eighth century, the area as far as Susa lay within the Frankish kingdom, and Novalesa's strategic position at the foot of the Mount Cenis pass made it a critical post for Frankish incursions into Italy. Under the Carolingians Novalesa became an important imperial monastery and stopping point on the route between Geneva and Turin.

By the mid-eleventh century, however, Novalesa was only beginning to recover after having been abandoned for more than a half century and had been reoccupied only a generation before that of the author. This hiatus, which had resulted from the political uncertainties of the tenth century and especially the presence of Saracens in the Alps, had transformed the geographical, political, economic, and cultural structures of the monastery's life. Before, Novalesa had been an important Frankish monastic community with close ties to Provence and to the Rhône valley. After, the community took refuge first in Turin and then resettled in Breme. After its restoration, Novalesa was a thoroughly Italian priory of the latter community, significantly weakened economically and prey to the pretensions of the rising aristocratic clans of the Piedmont.

The Benediktbeuern Rotulus historicus is considerably smaller than that of Novalesa's and is likewise missing its beginning and ending.[6] In its present state it consists of five sheets of parchment. The chronicle is written on one side; on the other is a contemporary list of "defenders and destroyers" of the monastery.[7] Its contents have been judged as harshly as those of the Novalesian chronicler by modern historians. Gottschalk has been described by Ludwig Holzfurtner as "one of the most unscrupulous forgers of the high Middle Ages."[8] And Gottschalk's most recent editor, Wilhelm Wattenbach, discussing in his introduction the transparent falsifications and outrageous chronology, commented laconically, "Who would believe this?"[9]

But again, like his Novalesian contemporary, an "accurate" monastic history was not Gottschalk's goal. He, too, lived in a community whose accessible history reached back less than a century, but whose dim past was more ancient and, from his perspective, largely unrecoverable. Benediktbeuern had been founded somewhat later than Novalesa, in the 760s, but under somewhat analogous circumstances.[10] Beuern had been the creation of members of a noble Bavarian family, Lantfrid, Waldram, and Eliland, who with their sister Kalswind had established three proprietary churches in Schlehdorf, Staffelsee, and Kochel. The founders obtained the permission of Duke Tassilo III, who also endowed the new institution. However, the founders apparently enjoyed close relations with the Carolingians. Shortly after the deposition of Tassilo and the confiscation of his property, Benediktbeuern obtained important donations from Charlemagne's sister Gisela of property that had belonged to the Agilolfings.[11] Under the Carolingians the monastery also obtained a relic, said to be the arm of Saint Benedict, that gave the monastery its name.

As an imperial monastery, Benediktbeuern continued to enjoy the protection of the Carolingians and their successors until the tenth century. In the early tenth century, the monastery began to see its widely scattered properties under increasing pressure. A *Descriptio praediorum* lists some 440 alienated manses.[12] Around 955 Benediktbeuern fell victim to Magyar raiders. The community's members were killed or scattered, its sacred ornaments and treasure sacked, and its library dispersed. Almost a decade later the community was reestablished as a dependency of Tegernsee and its buildings repaired and expanded; the monastery began to reconstitute its lands. In this it met opposition from the local aristocracy, in particular Counts Gaminolf and Unarc, who claimed that they were holding land demanded by the monastery for the king. Only in the first third of the eleventh century did Benediktbeuern once more become a monastery, when Abbot Ellinger of Tegernsee turned it over to Conrad II, who appointed Gotahelm abbot.

The newly refounded monastery did not long maintain its independence. The bishops of Freising claimed control over Benediktbeuern as an episcopal proprietary monastery. Under the direction of Abbot Gotahelm, Benediktbeuern attempted to defend itself against these claims. The abbot sought a privilege from Henry III while a monk, Gottschalk, sought to defend the institution by anchoring its rights in the past. Gottschalk's vigorous if ultimately unsuccessful defense of his institution's independence led him to reconstitute Benediktbeuern's past, reaching behind the destruction and confiscations of the tenth century to the earliest period of his institution's history.

For each institution then, the memory of its past was a key to its ability to meet the challenges of the present, and its loss of memory was its greatest danger. Forgetting was indeed the work of the devil, as the Novalesian chronicler explained in a story of a monk who, through negligence, allowed the devil to "steal his memory" so that he inadvertently celebrated mass with water but no wine.[13] More was at stake, however, than the memory of individual monks. The success of the refoundation of Novalesa required the successful recuperation of its lands, the reestablishment of the liturgical traditions of the community, and the defense of its ancient rights against upstart aristocrats and would-be Cluniac reformers. Benediktbeuern's chances to evade the control of the bishop of Freising and to recover the lands lost in the previous century likewise demanded a proper understanding of the foundation of the monastery as well as an accurate memory of those lands that it had controlled in the time before Magyars and restless Bavarian nobles had reduced it to a shadow of its former glory.

All of these required in turn the successful creation of a memory that would unite the institution's past prosperity and renown with the uncertain present. Gottschalk's work consists of three parts, each recording that which was *memoranda* for his monastery. Two are summary notices, one of land and one of people. The so-called *Breviarium Gotscalchi* contains a condensed history of the foundation, destruction, and refoundation of the monastery, followed by a *Descriptio praediorum* listing properties belonging to Benediktbeuern, and, finally, a list of properties alleged to have been alienated in the past.[14] The names of the donors are added interlinearly.[15] The second notice is a list of names of "defenders and destroyers" of the monastery found on the dorsal side of the *rotulus*.[16] The twenty names do not appear in any chronological order and include monastic advocates and important patrons of the monastery of the eleventh century, as well as the names of two of the monastery's most notable enemies. These are the above-mentioned Unarc, who in Gottschalk's *Rotulus historicus* is described, together with Count Gaminolf, as evil men "qui defensores debebant esse monasterii Sancti Benedicti,"[17] and Bishop Nitker of Freising, who is qualified in the list as "destructor libertatis Coenobii S. Benedicti."

Together these two lists, which are not entirely dependent on Gottschalk's history but represent rather an independent compilation, provide the two essential coordinates of monastic memory—land and names. They indicate what must be remembered: Those persons who had given property to the monastery *pro commemoratione sui*[18] (as well as what these persons had given) had the right to commemoration. But the alienators of monastic property and their unjust gains also had to be remembered so that some day justice might be done. The *rotulus* itself goes beyond these two laconic lists, attempting to connect people and land into a narrative framework that indicates not only what ought to be remembered but how it should be remembered.

Both the *Chronicon Novaliciense* and the Benediktbeuern *Rotulus historicus*, incomplete as they are, serve as this memory. In their structure, in their manipulation of oral, written, and monumental sources, and in their reinterpretation of these sources, they created mythic pasts whose contours provided the proper patterns for the present and future.

Structuring the Past

These chronicles are not as carefully constructed as others, such as that of Rodulfus Glaber, an older contemporary of the two authors. If the Benediktbeuern chronicle, like that of Novalesa, was a draft for a never-completed original, this might explain in part the lack of systematic structuring.[19] Still, they have structures that implicitly divide the past into discrete units that provide exemplars for the present.

The *Chronicon Novaliciense*'s five incomplete books were organized into a triad: The monastery's history consists of three ages, each marked by a legend, a destruction, and a conversion to the religious life. These ages do not correspond to classical or ecclesiastical divisions of history as in the case of Rodulfus' chronicle,[20] but rather to significant ages from the perspective of lesser vassals and monks of the Piedmont in the early eleventh century (the social circles from which the author himself came). The author describes his great-uncle as a warrior or "miles" and tells us that this uncle had been captured by the Saracens. The chronicler's grandfather, upon learning of the capture, goes to Bishop Ingo of Vercelli, his godfather, to ask help to ransom him. The bishop provides no assistance, but the captive is finally ransomed by his "neighbors and friends." In the age of the "moderni" one had to rely on this more humble, less formal but more accessible and ultimately more effective circle than on traditional lay and ecclesiastical lords.[21]

The first age in the chronicle's tripartite structure is the heroic age of the late migration period, at whose center stood Theodoric the Great (+526), the political hero of the Carolingians, the epic hero Dietrich of Bern of later German tradition, and the Ostrogothic king of Italy. The foundation of Novalesa, which was apparently preceded by a miraculous event at the site,[22] is placed during his reign: "Not the king [Theuderic] of the Franks who was the son of Queen Brunechild who expelled blessed Columbanus, but that king of the Goths who killed Symmachus and Boethius, two most excellent senators and former consuls."[23] Thus the foundation is firmly within the first great heroic age, in spite of the fact that the still-extant foundation charter known to the chronicler clearly presented the origins of the monastery in the time of the Frankish Theuderic IV. It was dated on "The third kalend of February in the fifth year of the reign of Lord Theuderic the King" and speaks of the founder's concern "for the stability of the kingdom of the Franks."[24] Similarly the founder's testament is explicitly dated on the "third day of the

nones of May in the twenty-first year of our most illustrious Charles ruling the kingdom of the Franks."[25] The author could suppose that
Theuderic was the great Gothic king for only two reasons: First, although at the time of its foundation in the early eighth century Novalesa
was in the Frankish kingdom, by the eleventh century it was part of the
kingdom of Pavia; looking back, the author would suppose that it always
had been. Second and more important, Theuderic could be the Ostro-
goth because he had to be: the distortion was essential if the history of
Novalesa was to fit the structure of the past as prefiguration of the present that the author had in mind.

Attila (+453) also belonged to the age of Theodoric (the chronological incongruity presented no more of a problem for the chronicler than
it did later in the German *Nibelungenlied*), and thus by placing the monastery's foundation in this period, Novalesa's origins were part of the
first heroic age. During this period, Novalesa became the home of a *conversus*, none other than Waltharius, the hero of the Latin epic composed
probably in the ninth century that tells of the son of the king of Aquitaine who, after having been raised as a hostage at the court of Attila,
makes his way home with his betrothed, the Burgundian princess Hil-
degunda, and in the process must fight his former cohostage, the Frank
Hagan.[26] The chronicle quotes from the poem at great length, but then
goes on to add information not found in the epic. Later in life Walter
becomes a monk at Novalesa and leads there a life of simplicity and humility, only once going out again to do battle against thieves who had
stolen the monastery's cart. In short, the chronicle contains a "Moniage
Gautier," extremely similar in specific details to other stories known
from later texts in which great warriors enter monastic life. Closest to
that of Walter are the *Moniage Guillaume, Ogiler,* and *Rainouard.*[27]
Some of the elements are so precisely the same that scholars have attempted to establish direct links from this text on the Italio-Provençal
border to the Latin and Old French *moniage* literature of the following
century. More important, Romance philologists and Germanicists have
argued about the origin of the "Moniage Gautier" tradition in Novalesa
and thus, by implication, about the origin and diffusion of the epic tradition in medieval France. Philipp Becker, Joseph Bédier, and more recently Félix Lecoy have argued for a clerical, Latin origin for these stories: Becker for a collection of clerical stories circulating widely in the
tenth century; Bédier for the strong influence of Paulus Diaconus on the
author of the chronicle; and Lecoy for the influence of Latin hagiography.[28] On the other hand, Pio Rajna and Jan de Vries have attempted to
defend the influence of oral epic tradition.[29] We shall return to the question of the chronicler's use of oral and written sources although, as
Lecoy rightly pointed out, the very categories of the debate—elite or

popular, clerical, or oral—are perhaps themselves oversimplifications and distortions.[30] For the present, I will simply note that this first age presents a paradigm for the future: the heroic age has its king (Theodoric) and its hero Walter, whose military prowess and courage, combined with the seriousness of his conversion, the excellence of his monastic humility, and his obedience, made him the perfect type of noble convert and patron.

The heroic age ended with the destruction of the monastery by the Lombards. In subsequent ages—that of the Carolingians and of the vassalic nobility—likewise appeared great men who, like Walter, epitomized their age, and who chose to enter the monastery of Novalesa.

The author's description of this second age in the chronicle's tripartite structure, the Carolingian age, centers, as do the others, on the events of the world at large only to the extent that they or their participants affect Novalesa. Here he tells at length of Charlemagne's invasion of the Lombard kingdom and of his capture of King Desiderius.[31] Whether his sources are lost heroic epics of Charlemagne, echoes from the last memories in northern Italy of Lombard traditions, or similar stories from Paulus Diaconus and other Latin authors, his interest is largely based on the desire to explain Charlemagne's largess toward Novalesa and its culmination in the second *moniage*—that of Charlemagne's own son Hugo.

The chronicle relates that, after Charlemagne's victory, he orders his young son Hugo to be brought before him and, commending him to Abbot Frodoinus of Novalesa, he asks that the boy be raised in the holy monastic profession.[32] For love of this son, the chronicle continues, Charlemagne is extremely generous to the monastery, increasing its lands, treasures, and store of sacred relics. Although this story has been dismissed as entirely without foundation, Charlemagne's illegitimate son Hugo did hold a plurality of abbacies, quite possibly including Novalesa (although the story of his oblation is without foundation).[33] The story serves to explain the Carolingians' generosity to Novalesa, a generosity that was genuine but based on Novalesa's strategic importance.[34] In addition to offering the example of Carolingian generosity to contemporaries, the episode suggests that in the Carolingian age, as in the previous heroic age, Novalesa was so highly respected that it was seen by the chief representatives of the period as an institution worthy of their religious conversion.

Of the three destructions of the monastery announced in the first book of the chronicle, the first, by the Lombards, is mythical; the second, designated only as "when they killed a certain very holy monk named Arnulphus," is not again mentioned; but the third, by the Saracens in 906, did indeed produce a crisis for the community. It is to this third age, ushered in by the Saracen pillage and the abandonment of Novalesa, that the third legend and the final *moniages* belongs. This was the chronicler's own age, and the entire narrative must be read as a reflection on and reaction to the circumstances of this present.

The legend of the third age is that of the founding of a noble house in the region, that of the counts of Aureate. After a confused account of kings Hugo of Arles and Berengar, the chronicler introduces a digression: "Accordingly as long as we unravel the acts or deeds of kings, it is fitting that we speak of vassals."[35] He then relates an "account of the ancients" that describes how two brothers, Roger and Arduin, "stripped of all their goods," come into the region from the "sterile mountains." Through force, duplicity, and cunning, Roger replaces Count Rodulf of Aureate and establishes his own family in the region. The story is quite similar to others relating the semimythical past of northern Italian families who traced their roots back to two brothers who arrived in the region in the early tenth century, took advantage of their situation, and in time received from the king de jure recognition of their de facto positions.[36] This particular family interested the chronicler because Roger's successors had had a long and varied relationship, usually hostile, with the monastery. His son Arduin the Bald seized the valley of the Susa from Novalesa shortly after it had been recaptured from the Saracens in the 940s.[37] Arduin V conspired in the mid-eleventh century with a disgruntled monk to establish the latter as abbot in return for annulling donations made by his father.[38] However, if some of the members of this family were hostile to the interests of the monastery, others had been generous. In particular, a Count Roger (possibly the brother of Arduin the Bald) was one of three "moderni" who, following in the tradition of Walter, entered the monastery of Breme. The chronicle describes Roger and Otbertus (of Asti) in terms reminiscent of Walter: "There were two great counts who at this time began to follow the way of Saint Benedict . . . both glorious according to their blood but even more glorious by divine laurels. . . . They exercised humility that is the queen of all virtues . . . feeding the hogs, collecting stale oil and left-over grain and giving it to them to eat."[39] This description is similar to that of Walter, also termed a "count"[40] who, according to the chronicle, had ended his days a humble gardener at the monastery.[41]

The choice of the monastery of Breme-Novalesa by these great counts, as well as by the Count Palatine Samson,[42] indicated that once more, in spite of the disasters that had befallen it, the community was so distinguished by its religious fervor that it attracted converts from the most important stratum of society. In the heroic age, this had been the heroes; in the age of Charlemagne, a Carolingian; now, in the age of vassals, it is counts. The tripartite division of the past and the repetition of essential events within each provided the conceptual framework, the generic memory, within which the chronicler constructed his past.

Gottschalk's text in the *Rotulus historicus* is roughly a *gesta abbatum*, but for reasons to be discussed he was unable to provide a satisfactory account of each abbot's reign. As in the *Breviarium Gotscalchi*, he divides the history of Benediktbeuern into three periods: its foundation, destruction, and refoundation (in which the third period mirrors the first).

The first part describes the age of the foundation and its first three abbots, whom the author identifies as the three brothers who founded the monastery on their family's lands. This section, like the foundation of Novalesa, begins with a miracle and then goes on to relate in detail the steps taken by the founders to establish the monastery, its putative consecration by Archbishop Boniface, and the consecration of Lantfrid as first abbot.

A second hand takes up the account after the consecration, describing donations made by Duke Tassilo and others and Lantfrid's establishment of monks and nuns in Beuern and in the family's proprietary churches and ends with his death. The reigns of each of Lantfrid's two brothers then follow, and the section ends with their epitaph, which Gottschalk claims to have copied from a wall of the church.

The second part (on the monastery's destruction) simply lists subsequent abbots and focuses on the destruction of the monastery by the Magyars and the beginning of its restoration following a nine-year hiatus. The final and longest section begins with the consecration of the church by Bishop Ulrich of Augsburg (924–973) and describes its history through the reign of Abbot Gotahelm.

Just as the author of the chronicle of Novalesa saw the present reflected in his invented past, Gottschalk understood the foundation of Benediktbeuern to have taken place in the same manner as its refoundation. As he describes it, the refoundation begins with the reconstruction and endowment of the monastery after the end of the Hungarian raids. The bishop of Augsburg is summoned to consecrate the new church. Finally, in 1033, through the intervention of Emperor Conrad II, it becomes once more an independent monastery under its abbot Gotahelm. The monastery's origins were similar. The founders endowed Beuern, with the permission of Duke Tassilo and the bishop of Augsburg, and then obtained, through the intervention of Boniface, privileges from Pippin and Carloman for the new foundation.

These differing tripartite visions of the past provided the frames within which to place the past, a past remembered through texts, through people, and through objects.

Tools for Remembering

Memories and legends tended to lend themselves to the physical contours of the landscape, to become incarnate in places. The Novalesian chronicler constantly attaches memories of the past to sites in the area of the monastery. A rocky formation suggestive of writhing serpents is the physical proof of the legend according to which Abbot Eldradus expelled poisonous snakes from the area.[43] The legend of Romulus, a leper king who was said to have summered in the area and to have buried a great treasure there, was preserved in the name of a nearby mountain: Mons Romuleus.[44] Besides, along the road, the author had himself seen the partially destroyed marble column that Walter had hit twice with his staff and that was called the "percussio vel ferita Vualtari."[45] The legend of Desiderius' defense of the Dora pass was preserved by the remains of the foundations of the walls, which could be seen "usque in presentem."[46] Charlemagne's grant of land to the musician who led his army through a secret pass in order to defeat Desiderius was said to have been as large as the territory in which one could hear his trumpet sound. The proof: this area "usque in presentem diem Transcornati vocantur."[47]

A second kind of physical memory was even more important to religious communities such as Novalesa and Benediktbeuern: that of their vast landholdings and economic rights. In the Piedmont, that remained profoundly attached to Roman legal tradition, and written proof played a vital role in the defense of property rights, but the validity of such documents was drawn not from the documents themselves but from the oral tradition that provided their context. Normally, this memory was preserved through institutional continuity and the collective memory of the region's population that served as a control on written documents. In 827, for example, a group of peasants from Oulx had appealed to Count Boso of Turin that Abbot Eldradus was unjustly holding them in servitude.[48] The abbot's advocate presented written evidence of a previous judgment that the "aviones vel patres vel parentes" of the plaintiffs had belonged to a certain Hunno, son of Dionisius, who had given all of his possessions to the monastery. The count then asked the plaintiffs if they were indeed "those men whose grandfathers or fathers or kinsmen had belonged to Dionisius, the father of Hunno."[49] Thus even written evidence had to be vindicated by oral testimony. The written evidence recorded rights transmitted in the past. Oral testimony confirmed generational links between that past and the present.

In Bavaria, donations had likewise long been recorded in writing, and monasteries and churches had maintained either individual charters or tradition notices since the eighth century (see chapter 3). However, possession was, even more than in the still Romanized world, dependent on witnesses and oral testimony for its guarantee. The disruptions of the tenth century risked destroying this important tie with the physical environment. When monks returned to Novalesa and Benediktbeuern, exactly such disruptions had taken place. When the hiatus extended beyond a century (the period Bernard Guenée indicates to be the outward limit of "living memory" in the Middle Ages),[50] this oral confirmation was impossible to obtain.

To recover geographical memory, the chroniclers turned to what remained of the region's oral traditions: The Novalesian chronicler was shown the tomb of Charles's wife "ab incole loci"; he learned the legends of the nearby Rocciamelone, Mons Rimuleus, from a certain "senex qui mihi tanta de eodem loco retulit";[51] and he learned of the location of the tomb of Waltharius from an old woman named Petronilla, who had lived in Susa for close to two hundred years.[52] Gottschalk knew of the portentous death of a monk, killed by a stag in the small wood next to the monastic church shortly before the Magyar raid, from the local laity.[53] Thus the memories attached to topography had to be rediscovered by the monks from the oral traditions of the local peasants, and fluid oral tradition had to restore learned written memory as well as liturgically perpetuated memory. Terms that indicate Gottschalk's and the Novalesian chronicler's reliance on oral tradition reoccur frequently: "asserit popularis vulgus; senex solitus erat narrare,"[54] "narrat sanctimonialem quandam,"[55] "a secularibus hominibus dicitur."[56] These oral traditions bridge the gap between past ages and the present: "usque in hodierum diem."[57]

Texts constituted a second category of "tools for remembering," and source-critical studies of the *Chronicon Novaliciense* have emphasized the documents available to the author as he compiled his text. These included the *Historia Langobardorum* of Paulus Diaconus, the *Liber pontificalis*, possibly some of the works of Liudprand of Cremona, the foundation charter and testament of Abbo mentioned above, the *Waltharius*, a monastic necrology, and various charters of the Carolingians and Ottonians as well as private patrons, a letter of Florus of Lyon to Hyldradus of Novalesa, hagiographical texts relating the life and miracles of Abbot Eldradus of Novalesa and other saints, and the Dialogues of Gregory the Great.

Two chance finds expanded our knowledge of what other texts the author might have had at his disposition. In the binding of a large Bible from Novalesa was found a fragment of a tenth-century list of books from its library which included a collection of homilies, the *Diadema monachorum* of Smaragdus, collections of miracles, and a passionary.[58] A miscellaneous manuscript from the later tenth century produced in

Novalesa included the Paulus Diaconus text but also Remigius of Auxerre's letter to Bernuin of Verdun on the origins of the Magyars (*De Gogh et Maghohg*), Bede's life of Gregory the Great, and a wide variety of hagiographical texts of western and eastern saints.[59]

Gottschalk had at hand necrological notices, charters and tradition notices, royal judgments, hagiographical texts, and inscriptions. The tradition notices in particular form the bulk of his sources.[60] They probably were already in a *Traditionsbuch* organized in roughly chronological order, and he seems to have excerpted extensively from them. However, the contents of these texts were not privileged in any sense. At Novalesa and Benediktbeuern, the monks clearly felt free to alter and adopt them to their own local needs. Thus, for example, a Novalesian version of the *Historia Langobardorum* contained an interpolated chapter in which was found the legend of Hugo's oblation.[61] This was a common practice. In another copy of the *Historia* made in Arles, a chapter had been inserted describing the Lombard invasion of Provence.[62] The author of the *Chronicon* made extensive and liberal use of such texts, assimilating events and accounts culled from Paulus Diaconus and other texts to the history of Novalesa. Stories told by Paulus about early Lombard kings could be reassigned to the time of Charlemagne; the *Waltharius* composed at St. Gall could be reintegrated into the Susa valley.

The chroniclers took the same liberty with charters and tradition notices. Gottschalk freely interpolated the earliest series of notices concerning the foundation of Benediktbeuern. He inserted a fictitious account of Boniface's involvement in the initial consecration of the monastery into what would otherwise be a typical account of the foundation of a Bavarian monastery. A miracle occurs that induces a noble individual to establish a proprietary church, endow it with land, and provide the necessary relics as well as the Bible. The family then attracts a community of monks, further endows the church with land from its inheritance, and arranges with the diocesan bishop (in this case Wikterp of Augsburg) for its consecration with the consent of the duke.[63] Boniface's purported role, like the equally fictitious *regali carta* Gottschalk claims the monastery received, were intended to protect the monastery from Freising's claims. Novalesa provides a similar example. Around 1030 the document that recorded its most important donations (the testament of its founder, the Patricius Abbo) was interpolated, recopied, and attached to a forged Carolingian charter in an attempt to establish an unambiguous imperial privilege guaranteeing its properties.[64] Elsewhere, where original charters were altogether lacking, such documents had to be produced from whole cloth, not in an effort to deceive (although the extent of property holdings might be remembered with more than total recall) but in an effort to provide documentary continuity in the place of lived memory that had been destroyed.

Such written texts could be attached to physical *memoria* of the region. The Novalesian author explains that after the foundation of Novalesa the Patricius Abbo had an arch constructed at Susa on the road across the Alps to Vienne. On this arch and on another in Vienne he had the text of his testament inscribed so that all who went from Italy to Gaul might have this text before their eyes.[65] The chronicler explained that Abbo had wanted this permanent record because he feared that "after the passage of many years this monastery might be destroyed by some people, which sadly happened three times."[66] The arch of Augustus in Susa does have an inscription legible today and perhaps legible to eleventh-century readers. However, it is a list of those who had dedicated the arch in the first century and has nothing to do with Abbo or Novalesa.[67] The chronicler's assertion is simply a claim based on the importance of a text as object—it bears no relation to the content of this text. Its meaning is entirely a function of the author's preoccupations.

Gottschalk makes similar use of an inscription. After describing the death of Eliland, he asserts that this abbot had ruled the monastery for nineteen years "as we found written on the wall by the efforts of his disciples." He then presents what he claims to be the epitaph of the first three abbots, which he allegedly transcribed from a wall of the church. Whether or not the epitaph is genuine, it contains no mention of the length of any of the three abbots' reigns.

Finally, both authors move without any hesitation from written to oral memory, hardly distinguishing between the two. At one point the Novalesian chronicler comments on his sources (oral testimony of written record):

> The facts that I have written in this book I learned not from the accounts of some person nor from my personal experience, but I have heard them from Bishop Peter [of Pavia? Vercelli?] who had read them when he was in Verona in a book in which he found many things about the monastery of Novalesa. We heard these things from him as we have told them.[68]

For the chronicler, the appeal to an unidentified book read by an otherwise unknown bishop is not "de relacione alicuis hominis," even though the author himself had not read the books (books that in fact probably never existed). Rather it is for him an appeal to written evidence supported in a circular way by oral testimony.

Books could be tools for remembering in other ways, quite apart from their content. Novalesa is remembered, even in Umberto Eco's *The Name of the Rose*, for its famous library of either six thousand (or 6,666) books, most of which were lost after the monks' flight to Turin in 906.[69]

However, the chronicler could still be reminded of the glories of the library when he handled the various books copied by Attepertus, the most accomplished scribe in the Carolingian scriptorium: "Whenever we find books written by him in his antique hand, we immediately recognize them."[70] Gottschalk may have been able to examine for himself the gospel books, homilies, and the precious copy of the rule of St. Benedict "copied from the same manuscript that the saint wrote with his own hand," allegedly given the monastery by Charlemagne.[71] Likewise, he could handle the precious liturgical vestments and books given by Abbot Ellinger of Tegernsee along with such books as the rule of Benedict, Bede's martyrology, an antiphonary, and a psalter.

Thus objects, places, books, or texts all served as touchstones for remembering—as concrete relics of the past, as model texts containing or reporting a past that could be attached to the monastery, or as both. The meanings of these *memoria* were never implicit. Rather they were derived from the overall intellectual structure of the monastery's past and the necessity to make this past conform to a pattern of its present. This past was thus created even as it was transmitted.

Forgetting

And yet each author was acutely aware of how fragmentary his knowledge actually was. Much of the geography—many of the important places, events, or persons of the monasteries—could not be recovered. Much had been forgotten, much that was vital.

What Gottschalk thought should be remembered is clear from his lengthy description of the reign of his own abbot, Gotahelm, whom he terms a "valde venerabilis vir." He describes how, after Abbot Ellinger of Tegernsee had surrendered governance of Benediktbeuern after one year, Gotahelm was consecrated abbot by order of Emperor Conrad II on 30 September 1032. He tells how Gotahelm immediately set about restoring the monastic observance, in particular the fasts, vigils, and liturgies of the saints. He lists those monks who entered the monastery during Gotahelm's abbacy, including a *conversus* Reginpert, who after his conversion distinguished himself in his fervor for fifteen years until his death. Gottschalk lists the names of the members of the congregation, distinguishing those Gotahelm had "nourished from childhood" from those who had entered religion as adults. He then describes the reconstruction and reparations Gotahelem undertook, the liturgical vestments and ornaments that he had inherited, purchased, or had made, and the books he had copied. He then turns to Gotahelm's land acquisitions, which were made by purchase, by payment in lieu of tithe, and by alms. "Not a year went by," Gottschalk reports proudly, "without him acquiring property for the altar of St. Benedict." He then mentions the most important benefactors of the monastery.

Twenty years after his installation, Gottschalk continues, Gotahelm faced the claims of Bishop Nicker of Freising who requested Henry IV to grant him the monastery "in servitium," and attempted by a stratagem to insert his control into Benediktbeuern. Gotahelm thwarted his plans, and after the bishop died in Ravenna, the abbot obtained confirmation of Benediktbeuern's liberty from the emperor.

The final, fragmentary description of Gotahelm's abbacy shows him fostering the efforts of his monks in all directions: "some writing, others preparing books, others acquiring land, others acquiring sisters and serving girls, others working with their hands to provide what was needed, others with the knowledge of fulfilling secular office. Others were diligent to collect relics of the saints in this place as much as they could."

In general, then, Gottschalk's ideal account of an abbacy included the details surrounding the abbot's accession, his supervision of its observance of the monastic rule, his augmentation of the community's size, his efforts to enrich its library and ecclesiastical treasury, its property, the names of its important benefactors, and the role of the abbot in the defense of the monastery's property.

For his own lifetime, Gottschalk could do this from his own memory since he lists himself among those Abbot Gotahelm had "nourished from childhood." Writing about similar aspects of his institution's history before his time was much more difficult. First, the materials he had at hand were sparse and lacunate. The general narrative framework of the text is provided by abbacies from which he was able to cull tradition notices and, for at least the more recent period, a necrology or martyrology.[72] However, none of these sources provided anno Domini dating, and thus while in general he presents his information in chronological order, he seems to have had no ability or interest in establishing any absolute chronology. The year of Abbot Gotahelm's election (1033) is the only year given in the *Rotulus historicus* and cannot be used to establish previous chronological guideposts. Nor is his attempt to establish a relative chronology for the reigns of the three brothers who founded the monastery and became its first three abbots any more successful.

Little of the information that, judging from his account of Gotahelm's reign, Gottschalk considered important could be culled from available necrological entries. The monastery's necrology may have dated only from the later tenth century. If an earlier one existed, it may have been destroyed by the Magyars. The dates of the deaths of the first three founding abbots may have been drawn exclusively from the mural inscription on the surviving wall of the church (assuming there really was such a wall), although the indication of the feasts with which they coincided suggest that by his time they had been reintroduced into the martyrology. Gottschalk knew that the first abbot, Lantfrid, had died on a tenth of July, "the vigil of the translation of St. Benedict";[73] that his brother and successor Waldram had died on a ninth of February "and was buried by Bishop Sintbert of Augsburg next to his brother the blessed Lantfrid, on the day of the deposition of St. Scholastica, the virgin of Christ";[74] and that the third brother, Eliland, was elected abbot the following day and had died "on the vigil of St. Mary ever Virgin, and on the day of her assumption was buried beside his brothers and father, next to the church of St. Benedict, on August 15."[75] The seventeenth-century necrology repeats this juxtaposition, although whether its author or the author of a previous necrology had drawn them from the *Rotulus historicus* or the later preface to the tradition book, or whether Gottschalk drew them from a necrology, is impossible to determine.[76]

In any case, he seems ignorant of the obits of the four abbots (Hrimgrin, Erpfmann, Yrolf, and Snelport) he places after Eliland and before the destruction of the monastery, but Gottschalk does provide the locations of their burials (Staffelsee, Regensburg, Schlehdorf, and Wessobrunn, respectively). These details may have been drawn from a catalogue of abbots rather than from a necrology.

Gottschalk was clearly drawing on a necrology for subsequent abbots Wolfidio,[77] Perhtrihcus,[78] Rihholf,[79] Reginbertus,[80] Ratoldus,[81] and Adalbero.[82] But even here the limitations of using a necrology to establish the history of the monastery are obvious. First, the obits are useful for liturgical commemoration but not for historical recording. Second, to judge from the necrology of St. Emmeram, Bavarian necrological notices prior to the eleventh century rarely gave the obits of any but abbots and the most important lay patrons. Gottschalk recorded only two other persons' dates of death. The first is a venerable monk Adalunc, who predicted his own death and the destruction of the monastery at the hands of the Magyars.[83] The miraculous circumstances of his death may have led to the development of a local cult included in the monastic calendar. The other exception is the "dominus Reginpertus" who entered the monastery as a *conversus* under Abbot Gotahelm and who died there fifteen years later on 11 February.[84] He may have included him because of the elevated social status of this *conversus* or because Gottschalk, who must have known him well, may have felt a particular affection for him. However, it was only possible because, by the eleventh century, necrologies were beginning to include obits of monks and patrons as well as of abbots. Gottschalk probably could not have known the obits of earlier *conversi* or patrons.

Information culled from tradition notices was more abundant and important, but here, too, his available resources limited his possibilities. First, the tradition notices seem to have dated primarily from the eighth and first half of the ninth centuries. This may be indicative of the rhythm of the compilation of tradition books in the monastery and may parallel developments in some other Bavarian institutions.[85] Second, the tradition notices seldom include the names of any of the community except for *conversi* and the abbot. Thus, Gottschalk, who was clearly interested in naming members of his community, can only mention abbots and *conversi* such as Count Engildeo[86] and the deacon Merigozus,[87] who made donations to the monastery upon entering monastic life. Of his other predecessors at Benediktbeuern, whom he firmly believed to number in the hundreds, he can say nothing.

Even his information on the abbots—whose names, at least, he had been able to record—was lamentably thin. Lacking access to such material, his account remained, by his own admission, incomplete. Speaking of the abbots who followed Eliland prior to the destruction of the monastery, he says sadly, "How or in what way they governed this monastery, we have been able to find but little."[88]

Ignorance of the past was not only unfortunate; it could be dangerous. This is clear from a number of stories in which the Novalesian author told of the dangers that forgetting could pose. In particular, the loss of the *memoria* of the dead posed a threat. The monastic community bore a primary obligation for the liturgical commemoration of the departed, and failure to perform this function haunted the author, quite literally:

> In this same monastery there were always many apparitions of saints who most frequently showed themselves to good monks and men of simplicity. I have heard about many of these. It is the witness of the lord, that there, in the silence of the night as many crowds of blessed men appeared as you would see men and women going out of the town when Christians make their rogation procession to the churches asking the help of the saints.[89]

To be ignorant of these holy people's presence could be dangerous. The chronicler tells of a soldier who unknowingly fell asleep on the unmarked tomb of a saint. He awoke shorn of his hair—a sign of the saint's displeasure at having been dishonored, even unknowingly.[90] On another occasion a "gentle and humble" monk, while at a dependency of the monastery, was visited by an apparition in the guise of a shepherd who identified himself as the leader of seven Greeks (presumably the Seven Sleepers of Ephesus) who were buried in that place. The vision wished that the monks might frequently visit the place of their burial, the memory of which had been lost.[91]

These and other apparitions are part of a more general eleventh-century phenomenon: the increasing frequency with which visions of the dead appear to warn, admonish, or instruct the living. Jean-Claude Schmitt has even written of the "invasion of ghosts" in the eleventh century.[92] The role of visions of the dead in medieval society is complex, but certainly in part their presence is evidence of an awareness, as on the part of the Novalesa chronicler, that the known past was fragmentary and inadequate. Much had been lost, and this loss was intimately tied to the problems of the present. One might recognize in this loss a sort of guilt, not in the modern, internalized sense of private sin but in the corporate sense of the inadequacy of the present age faced with the increasingly burdensome duty of preserving the *memoria* of a past that was on the whole much more glorious and worthy than the present. All the tools of memory available to the chronicler and his contemporaries—written texts, inscriptions, objects, places, rituals—proved finally inadequate because of their own shortcomings. At one point, while recording the glorious martyrdom of Novalesian monks who were killed by the Lombards, Gottschalk speaks of Iustus and Flavius. The epitaph of Iustus he recalled well if fantastically: "Here lies the monk Iustus, brother of Leo, companion of the true Saint Peter." Concerning the epitaph of the second, he writes sadly, "In truth, I do not remember it."[93]

The chroniclers are also responsible for another, more subtle loss of the past implicit in the manner in which they created their histories. Even when they have the names of founders, benefactors, and abbots, they have no understanding of the relationships among these persons or the political and social contexts within which they functioned. The relationships between monastic foundation, family power, and regional strategies, evident in the foundation of Novalesa[94] and so well investigated by Joachim Jahn for Benediktbeuern, while reconstructible from the information available to these authors, was entirely beyond their comprehension. Instead, both authors present the foundations as motivated, as we have seen, by miraculous events that led their founders to establish monasteries. The fabric of the past is thus depoliticized and decontextualized, projected out of the world of human events onto the miraculous world of sacred myth.

Finally, the two chroniclers were responsible for a third kind of forgetting as well, one about which they did not speak. Even as they created their pasts, they limited or denied access to future generations to alternative pasts for their respective institutions. In both cases, their accounts became the point of departure for subsequent institutional memory. At Novalesa, this meant largely placing the fragments of the past into a form that silenced other possible interpretations. At Benediktbeuern it meant something much more serious. As we have seen,

Gottschalk certainly had some charters, tradition notices, and royal judgments that reached back to the period of Benediktbeuern's foundation, and Jahn has recently shown how reliable most of the references to donations and donors from this early period, with certain important exceptions, actually are.[95] Gottschalk used these not only to write his *Rotulus historicus* but also for his *Descriptio praediorum*, which included the list of properties the monastery alleged had been alienated.[96] His was apparently the last use ever that was made of this rich archival tradition reaching back almost three hundred years. Roughly a century after Gottschalk, a new chronicle-*Traditionsbuch* was prepared at Benediktbeuern.[97] This text begins with an introduction that is an elaboration and continuation of the *rotulus* history to ca. 1139. However, it adds nothing substantive to the early period, for which it depends entirely on the work of Gottschalk. Nor does it include, in its tradition notices, any early notices other than two summaries of notices that Gottschalk certainly had seen and used. Perhaps the others had been destroyed through some accident; perhaps the new author felt no need to include them. More likely, however, once Gottschalk had done his work for Gotahelm, his *Rotulus historicus* and his *Breviarium* took the place of all of the monastery's older records. The latter may have been deemed unnecessary, perhaps even undesirable, given the interpolations and outright forgeries that they contained or to which they alluded. Thus they were probably destroyed, leaving as the only past the one Gottschalk had created in his *rotulus*.

V

POLITICAL MEMORY AND THE

RESTRUCTURING OF THE PAST

THE TENTH CENTURY saw the establishment of major new dynasties both east and west of the Rhine. In the East the last Carolingian kings disappeared, their places filled by the Saxon Ottonians, who after 951 reigned in northern Italy as well. In the West the Capetian family ruled France from 987 to the beginning of the fourteenth century and, through various branches, until 1789, while the Middle Kingdom of Lothar split definitively into fragments claimed by both sides or, as in Provence, left to local aristocracies.

These major political and dynastic changes, which we have rehearsed in the "canned histories" presented in chapter 1, obscured other tenth-century rulers who only in retrospect appear as minor actors on the European stage. Neither the polities that emerged from the tenth century nor the families that led them enjoyed any manifest destiny. Both the Carolingian family and regional aristocracies produced vigorous, capable, and innovative leaders, some of whom established what seemed, from the perspective of the early tenth century, polities of great promise. These leaders, such as Charles III (the Simple) in Neustria, Hugo of Arles in Italy and Provence, and Arnulf of Bavaria, drew on ancient traditions and contemporary possibilities in order to establish power and legitimacy in their respective regions. Ultimately, all three failed, and their opponents were left not only to enjoy the fruits of their efforts but also to control the manner in which the vanquished would be remembered or, more generally, forgotten. This chapter examines the fates of these three rulers in the memorial systems of the subsequent century. Many, indeed most, of these rulers, their intentions, the traditions from which they operated, and their considerable achievements were forgotten. What remained was depoliticized, deracinated from a specific historical context. Most of this chapter will concentrate on Hugo of Arles, who achieved the crown of Italy but could neither hold it nor realize his greater ambitions of reuniting the old Middle Kingdom of his ancestors. Two subsequent sections will examine Charles the Simple of western Francia and Arnulf ("the Bad") of Bavaria, two princes whose considerable achievements within the constraints of internal and external threats were quickly forgotten following their deaths.

Hugo of Arles

The refoundation of the monastery of St. Peter of Montmajour near Arles, according to an inscription allegedly found there in the Church of the Holy Cross, followed the victory of Charlemagne over the Saracens in Arles:

> Let all know that when the most serene prince Charles the Great, King of the Franks, was besieging the city of Arles which was being held by the infidels, and when he had captured it by force of arms most of the Saracens fled to the mountain of Montmajour, and there they held up and defended themselves. When the king had come there with his army to subdue them and had obtained a triumph over them, giving thanks to God for this and in a sign of this victory, he had this church dedicated in honor of the Holy Cross and he repaired the present monastery in honor of Saint Peter, prince of the Apostles, which had been destroyed and rendered inhabitable by these infidels, and he had monks come here to serve God and he endowed and gave many goods to this monastery where many of those from Francia who participated in the conquest were buried. Hence brothers pray for them.[1]

As far as is known, Charlemagne (Charles the Great) was never in Arles, so the tradition is clearly confusing him with his grandfather Charles Martel, who defeated the Saracens in the lower Rhône in 738. One cannot, moreover, suppose that Charles Martel or any other Carolingian had any role in the history of Montmajour. The Church of the Holy Cross was an eleventh-century foundation, having been consecrated in 1019. The monastery itself was formally established in 949. Just when the legend of a Carolingian foundation began is unknown, but by 1421, when the above legend was recorded (and probably forged to support the claims of Montmajour against the canons of the Cathedral of Arles), it had become an accepted part of the monastery's self-perception.

By the High Middle Ages claims to Carolingian origins had become widespread throughout Europe, and there is nothing particularly remarkable about Montmajour's claims in this regard. We have already seen the importance of Charlemagne both in Marseille and Novalesa as well as in Regensburg, Benediktbeuern, and St. Denis. Nor is the confusion of Charles Martel with Charles the Great unusual. However, this late medieval legend did not directly replace the tradition of its actual foundation in the tenth century. Already in 1205, when the papal legate Radulf visited the monastery, his brief account of the institution's history made no mention of the circumstances or the date of its foundation.[2] The origins of the monastery had apparently been forgotten in the first centuries following its foundation.

Many medieval monasteries forgot their past and replaced it with more venerable pedigrees. The banality of the Montmajour legend does not, however, detract from its historical interest or importance. On the contrary, it provides a favored case in which to examine the development of such legends, and its interest lies in the possibility to examine both high-medieval perceptions of the past and "scientific" perceptions of the past that can be reconstructed from archival sources.

The Last Lotharingian

If Montmajour was not restored by Charles the Great as a necropolis for the Franks slain in the "liberation" of Provence, it was founded by a claimant to the Carolingian tradition in the region; and it was intended to perpetuate the spiritual and temporal *memoria* of this individual and his party after the secular efforts to this end had met with failure. By the later eleventh century, not only was this Carolingian tradition discredited and a potential embarrassment to its most important secular patrons, but the very geographical, political, and social structures that formed the basis for aristocratic society were so transformed that the older traditions of the tenth century were well-nigh incomprehensible. As this old world slipped away, a new past had to be constructed, a past whose elements would serve the needs of a new form of identity.

A careful examination of the first decades of the monastery of Montmajour (founded 949) and in particular a prosopographical study of its early patrons suggest that it was founded to institutionalize and to perpetuate the memory of the Lotharingian family and political traditions of King Hugo of Italy (d. 947) in the lower Rhône valley. As such, it became the object of considerable dispute and controversy as the new family of counts establishing themselves in the region gradually appropriated it as their own necropolis as part of a strategy of consolidating their control over the region. The struggle to control Montmajour was a struggle for control over the institutional continuation of the past and thus held a key to future political legitimacy in Provence.

Hugo, Count of Vienne, Marquis of Provence, and king of Italy, embodies the last efforts of the party of Lothar II to control the Middle Kingdom of his grandfather. His family background combined both branches of the Lotharingian tradition. His father was Theobold, son of the Count-Abbot Hubert of Jura-Burgundy, who was the brother and ardent defender of his sister Tetburgis, whom Lothar had spent most of his reign trying to divorce. His mother was Bertha, daughter of Lothar II and his mistress Waldrada, whom the king had spent most of his reign

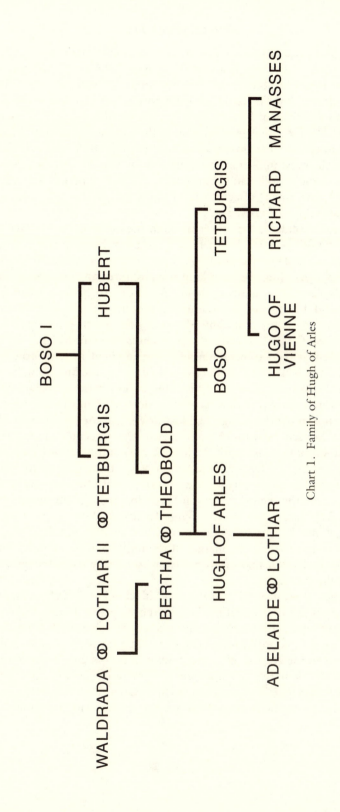

Chart 1. Family of Hugh of Arles

trying to marry.[3] His father had been closely allied with his brother-in-law Hugo, the illegitimate son of Lothar and Waldrada, and after the defeat of Hugo in 885 he had sought protection with his relative Boso, king of Provence.[4] Theobold's son Hugo was close to Boso's son Louis the Blind and from at least 903 was exercising the authority of count of Vienne.[5] His influence grew steadily at the expense of Count Teutbert, who had been Louis's closest agent, and from ca. 908 Hugo was established as the most important personage in the kingdom. After Louis had returned blinded following his disastrous second expedition to Italy in 905, Hugo became in effect the ruler of the kingdom. From at least 912 he was also duke of Provence.[6]

Hugo consolidated his power through the usual means of placing his kin in key positions. His brother Boso acquired the counties of Avignon and Vaison, and his nephew Manasses became archbishop of Arles. When, in 926, Hugo became king of Italy through the support of his mother's family, he increased these donations to his kin, establishing cousins and illegitimate children in major ecclesiastical and secular positions throughout the kingdom. Manasses received the episcopal sees of Verona, Trent, Mantua, and later the archbishopric of Milan.[7]

For the first years of his reign, Hugo maintained an active role in the Viennois and in Provence, effectively controlling the kingdom and preventing the succession of Louis the Blind's son Charles-Constantine. Although forced by circumstances to abandon his claims to the Viennois, this did not imply that Hugo had lost interest in the region west of the Alps. As Eduard Hlawitschka has shown, the agreement Hugo struck with the West Frankish king Rudolf (Raoul) and his vassal Herbert of Vermandois in 928, whereby the region of Vienne was given to Herbert for his son Odo, was actually a clever move. It effectively prevented the absorption of the region by Rudolf II of Upper Burgundy and probably left the way clear for Hugo to attempt to absorb Provence into his Italian kingdom.[8] During his reign prayers for him as "serenisimo Ugo regi nostro" were added in the margin of the ninth-century sacramentary of Arles, an indication that he was at least liturgically to be recognized as king in Provence.[9]

However, around 933, in the face of rebellion in Italy, which prevented him from completing his Provençal plans, Hugo reached an agreement with King Rudolf of Burgundy by which he ceded to the Burgundian ruler the public powers he had held in Provence while retaining vast lands in the region. Hugo saw this as a temporary, strategic retreat rather than a definitive abandonment of a political role in the area. At Rudolf's death in 937, Hugo rushed north, married Rudolf's widow Bertha five months after her husband's death, forced her daughter Adelaide to marry his son Lothar, and attempted thus to control the minority of Rudolf's minor son Conrad.[10] Otto I managed to take the young Conrad away from Hugo and serve as his tutor, thus thwarting Hugo's plans.

Hugo's final involvement in Provence came in 946 when, driven to abdicate his throne by an alliance around Berengar of Friuli and betrayed even by his close supporters and kinsmen, he returned to Arles and began to rebuild his network of alliances both in Provence and with the Aquitanians to the West. Only his death the following year removed the likelihood of a renewed struggle for control of the region.

Institutionalizing the Hugonid Tradition

The tangle of alliances built up over several generations and exploited by Hugo; his ruthless methods of reasserting his claims to Burgundy, Provence, and Italy; the elaborate network of relatives and allies he left behind him; his betrayal by his nephew Archbishop Manasses and his defeat at the hands of Berengar as well as the disintegration of his dreams throughout the region—all had major effects on the evolution of society and institutions in the Rhône valley.

The deaths of Hugo in 947 and of his son Lothar in 950 ended forever the aspirations of the party they led that sought to reunite the kingdom of Lothar II under a Carolingian descendant. The group that had risen with Hugo and had become established in the lower Rhône as a result of his gratitude was now faced with the necessity of taking defensive measures to safeguard itself from his former enemies and to save or at least neutralize what they could of his vast personal holdings in the region. The new count of Arles, Boso (probably the former husband of Hugo's niece Bertha), was clearly determined to absorb into his orbit the power base of his predecessor.[11] After the failure of Hugo's family to translate its aspirations into an institutional framework, Archbishop Manasses of Arles, his nephew, took steps with his followers to institutionalize something of Hugo's tradition in an ecclesiastical form through the establishment of the monastery of Montmajour in the Camargue.

The foundation and early history of this institution illustrate one role played by religious institutions in perpetuating the memory and structures of a faction after its political defeat (analogous to that played by the monastery of Lüneburg studied by Gerd Althoff in the continuation of Billung traditions).[12] Ultimately, by the early eleventh century, the original purpose of the foundation had been thwarted, but the effort and the opposition raised against it left a strong influence on the ecclesiastical configuration of the region.

Hugo's death had ended the political hopes of the Lothar-Waldrada party in the Rhône valley. The new Count Boso, installed in 942, had apparently gotten rid of any former connections with Hugo by divorcing his niece Bertha. And the success of his sons Rodbald II and William II (the Liberator) in driving the Saracens out of the Maritime Alps in 972—something Hugo had chosen not to do—firmly established the new family's position. The "Burgundian" alliance made up of relatives and *fideles* of Hugo who had descended the Rhône with him or who had joined forces with him in the south was on the point of dissolution. It had been seriously divided by the betrayal of Hugo's own nephew, Archbishop Manasses, although since Hugo had retreated to Arles after his defeat in Italy, this breach seems to have been repaired. Now, most would join the new count who would bring with him his own men from the north and west. One example was Arlulf, the father of the viscounts of Marseille, who was in the count's entourage in 949 and who had received an enormous grant of property in the region of Trets from King Conrad of Burgundy in 950.[13] Nevertheless, the tradition of Hugo was institutionalized and perpetuated for another generation, and the most significant properties in the hands of Hugo's party were kept out of the hands of the new family of counts through the foundation and their support of Montmajour. The web of patronage and the monastery's dealings with ecclesiastical and secular powers suggest that from 949 until 978 the monastery was the object of donations from outside the county of Arles, principally from the counties of Avignon, Aix, and Apt.

Hugo himself is not commemorated in any extant documents from Montmajour, although it is likely that this island, which had long been a place of burial in the Camargue, was his final resting place and owed to Hugo its first formal monastic foundation. According to the *Chronica Monasterii Casinensis*, in his old age Hugo returned to "Burgundy" and there established a monastery on his own property that was called "Saint Peter of Arles"; after greatly enriching it, he became a monk there.[14] This account has been disputed because the exchanges of property for the formal foundation of the monastery occurred in 949, two years after Hugo's death.[15] However, the description of the exchange strongly suggests that some sort of religious foundation already existed on Montmajour, particularly since it is referred to in that exchange as the "Island of St. Peter."[16] That a mortuary chapel would have existed at this ancient necropolis is certainly reasonable, and even though the extant church of St. Peter at Montmajour was probably completed between 1030 and 1050, the form of the church suggests a much more ancient origin.[17] The church, which is found on the southern side of the hill, has a double nave, the first of which is carved out of the living rock. The second nave is added parallel to the first. The columns that separate the first from the second and that support the south side of the second are probably of Roman origin or at least were reemployed from a previous construction. While the capitals date from the eleventh century and represent an important step in the development of Provençal sculpture, the very traditional form of the church itself suggests that it may have much earlier origins than the eleventh century.[18] If Hugo did establish or endow a community of religious at Montmajour, however, the monastery did not retain the memory in its liturgy or its monuments. The probable reasons are to be found in the history of Montmajour over the next sixty years.

The initial exchanges of land and donations were made between 949 and 954 between Manasses, Hugo's nephew and surviving representative in Provence, and a Theucinda,"sanctimonialia" who was the sister of Gontarus, provost of the church of Arles, who became in time abbot of Montmajour.[19] Theucinda was also the aunt of Riculf (who would later succeed his uncle Gontarus as bishop of Frejus and abbot of Montmajour) and was apparently the sister of Anno and the kinswoman of Atbertus and Landbertus.[20] The group including Theucinda, Anno, Gontarus, and Hugo is apparently represented as well in the *Liber memorialis* of Remiremont.[21] In 949 Manasses granted Theucinda the site of Montmajour as a *precaria*, in return for property at Barcianicus in the county of Arles, where she had a considerable inheritance.[22] Other donations followed in the counties of Avignon and Aix, with the exception of one from a Count Grifo, identified by Poly as a member of the family that would later be known as the Castellaine, an ally of the Sabran and the Burgundian party of Hugo of Arles, who held property in the area of Arles (although he himself seems to have been at Apt).[23] The new count of Arles, Boso, and his sons William and Boso witnessed some of these donations but were not themselves donors. In fact, in 977 they had apparently prevented a donation by one Lambert of fiscal property, and following the death of Manasses in 962–63, they seem to have attempted to seize the monastery's property. This attempt led to the confirmations by Pope Leo VIII in 963 and King Conrad of Burgundy in 964.[24]

The count's concerns about the monastery can be understood by an examination of the sources of the donations. Theucinda, Anno, and Riculf were in the circle of Manasses, who gave Riculf, a former canon of Arles, the diocese of Frejus. Count Grifo's nephew Rostagnus was apparently bishop of Uzès and hence a part of the "Burgundian faction" that had seized the county and bishopric when Hugo had gained control of Provence. Donations to Montmajour in the counties of Aix, Arles, and Avignon came from a variety of groups whose membership, while differing from charter to charter, tended to be constellations associated with the old supporters of Hugo, Gontarus, and Manasses.[25]

More telling were donations to Montmajour from outside Provence. In 960 Hugo's niece Bertha, whom Liutprand of Cremona identified as the heir of the vast treasure he had brought with him to Arles shortly before his death in the hopes of raising an army to expel Berengar,[26] donated to Montmajour all the property she had received from Hugo in Septimania in the county of Substancion and in Provence in the counties of Friul, Regenes, Gap, Vaison, Apt, Orange, Transe, and Digne.[27] As late as 1002 Montmajour received a donation from one Rotberga of property in the county of Vienne at St. Jean d'Octavéon near Romans (Drôme), which Hugo had granted in 936 to his nephew Hugo.[28]

Hugo's party thus attempted to keep his patrimony together and out of the hands of his enemies by establishing a sort of monastic trust fund to which it could be donated and thus neutralized. Papal and royal protection was secured, so that control and election of the abbot could take place without interference by the new count, who in return showed no generosity or direct involvement during the lifetime of the foundress and, until 977, owner of the property. Only after her death did the count allow Lambert, a former supporter of Manasses and Hugo and now a *fidelis* of William and Rodbald, to grant the monastery the vast marsh that surrounded it.[29] This donation was not simply a charitable grant but a bid to become the protector of the monastery. The bid was apparently rejected by the monks. On the death of the first abbot, Mauring, in 978, the leadership of the monastery passed to Poncio, his prior.

Forgetting the Hugonids

Possibly because the counts were unable to secure control of Montmajour, they were active in the refoundation of Psalmody, a monastery on the border between Provence and Septimania. This monastery, which had apparently been destroyed and largely abandoned in the late ninth century, began to receive new and important donations. The first of these was made by Counts Rodbald and his brother William on 24 November 979 and consisted of allodial property in the county of Aix.[30] The donation was witnessed by Aldebertus, Bonifilius, Amicus, and Poncius. These individuals, who were in the entourage of the new counts, were part of the kindred of Anno, a former supporter of Hugo of Arles, and had apparently shifted allegiance to the new counts. Since they had important holdings in the same location near Aix (the Church of St. Mary in the village of Vergerio), which they may have obtained from Hugo, this donation could have been a way to deny Montmajour property that it might otherwise have received. Some years later Anno's sons Amicus and Lambertus, along with one Bonafilia, made another donation to Psalmody from the same region.[31] This Lambertus is probably the same person who had obtained comitial permission to donate the marshes around Montmajour to that institution. In 993 the same counts gave Psalmody the Church of Saints Cosmas and Damien near Maguelon.[32] This donation clearly shows their desire to undercut Montmajour since this same church had been part of the large donation to Montmajour made by Bertha in 960. Apparently, the counts had confiscated the property from that monastery and were now attempting to give it to one more amenable to their influence.

In this same year (993), Count William II died and this donation of property usurped from Montmajour to Psalmody should be seen in conjunction with his establishment of the Church of Sarrians (Vaucluse) donated to Cluny as his place of burial.[33] Obviously, by 993 the counts were not yet in a position to adopt Montmajour as their necropolis. Instead, they favored Cluny and Psalmody.

The counts tried once more to gain control of the monastery upon the death of Abbot Poncio in 997. This time the monks attempted to continue the old tradition by electing Bishop Riculf of Frejus, the nephew of Theucinda, and thus maintain governance of the monastery within the survivors of the Hugo group, while Count Rodbald attempted to install a certain Paul, a monk of St. Gilles. The monks appealed to Pope Gregory V, claiming the right of free election of their abbot. The pope supported them and apparently defended Riculf, but he died within a year. Again the monks elected someone close to the original founders, Archinricus, one of the original monks of the community.[34]

Archinricus continued the independent tradition of the monastery for some ten years. Finally, in 1008, possibly under pressure of the counts, he left the monastery, retiring to the priory of Carluc in order to lead an eremitic life. Whatever the religious motives of Archinricus,[35] this departure can also be understood as the final defeat of the founding party and the victory of the counts. Their close involvement with the monastery is shown by its selection in 1018 as the burial place of Count William, and it served thereafter as the necropolis of the counts of Arles, just as it had once been probably the burial place of Hugo of Arles. With this victory, the counts of Provence seem to have lost interest in Psalmody. Subsequent donations to that monastery in the eleventh century came from the areas of Psalmody itself, from Nimes, or from the county of Toulouse.

As for Hugo, his memory, as far as can be determined, disappeared from the necrology of the community he and his party had done so much to establish. The same is true of the foundress Theucinda. Her name does not appear in the extant copies of the necrology or, apart from the charters, in other written sources from Montmajour. These omissions are unlikely to have been the result of random preservation of texts. Although the necrology used by Dom Chantelou to make his copy is fragmentary, breaking off on 22 May,[36] we know from the martyrology of Marseille that Theucinda died 7 May.[37] Moreover, she was certainly buried at the monastery. In this century a farmer working the land surrounding the island turned over a stone long used as a bridge over a small ditch and found that it was her tombstone. Except for Gontarius and Riculf, who were remembered as abbots of the community, the tradition of the last Lotharingian party was effaced from the community founded to be its heir.

The process by which the origins of Montmajour were forgotten and then reremembered in the Carolingian legend reported later is indicative not simply of the substitution of one comital family for another but also of the profound changes Provençal society was undergoing between 950 and 1050, changes represented and even fostered by the new comital family.

The geographical horizons of the two comital families were radically different. Hugo belonged to the wide world of late-Carolingian Europe, in which great aristocrats could and did hold widely dispersed properties and conducted their affairs on an international plane. Although he held property in the Viennois and in Provence, he also traveled widely both before and after his successes in Italy. However, north of the Alps, this movement was largely focused on the north-south axis of the Rhône, on the kingdoms of his grandfather and great-grandfather. It was in this same area that he had his coterie of kinsmen on whom he could call and who would look to him for help. He had useful, meaningful networks from as far north as Tongres to Arles. Likewise, thanks to the second marriage of his mother, he had powerful kin in the areas of Ivrea and Tuscany even before he entered Italy.

Virtually all of these contacts were with the north and east. Apart from his agreement with King Rodulf of France concerning the disposition of Vienne, he had little direct contact with or interest in western Francia. The focus of his political efforts and social ties were the Middle Kingdom. This orientation north along the Rhône and Rhine and southeast into Italy was by the tenth century a tradition over two centuries old. It began in the seventh century when aristocratic families closely allied to the Carolingians assisted the latter in gaining hegemony over the region in order to secure the Alpine passes into Italy. The earliest representative of the tradition was the Patricius Abbo, whose own estates and sphere of activities coincide with those of Hugo prior to the latter's coronation in Italy.[38] Abbo's kin and allies were found in Provence, western Lombardy, in the Viennois, and Burgundy, with probable connections to the region of Liège. Although a supporter of Charles Martel, Abbo and his supporters attempted to build regional hegemony within this area with Charles's support.

Boso, the founder of the new comital family, probably descended the Rhône with Hugo, with whom he was closely allied. When Hugo's brother left Provence in 931 for Italy, the other Boso seems to have taken his place and to have married Bertha, Hugo's niece and presumably the daughter of his brother. Other than the indication that his father was a certain Rodbald, Boso's family origins are unknown. Georges de Manteyer hypothesized that the family was Burgundian.[39] In spite of their close association with Hugo and his family, Poly suggests on the basis of their names and their devotion to Psalmody that they may have come from Septimania.[40] The evidence does not unambiguously support this hypothesis because Boso was a widely used name, as was Rodbald, which appeared frequently in ninth- and tenth-century Burgundy.

Much more significant than the origins of this family before arriving in the region are the measures that Boso and his successors took to solidify their position and identity in the immediate decades following the defeat and death of Hugo. The most evident break with the Burgundian party was Boso's and Bertha's divorce, which Poly has suggested was a means by which Boso disassociated himself from Hugo following the latter's loss of support among not only his Italian allies but even such people as his nephew, Archbishop Manasses.[41] Equally telling is the pattern of political alliances established by the count and his descendants into the 1030s. None of these, as far as can be determined, reinforced the family's ties to Vienne or the kingdom of Burgundy. To marry Boso's sons and grandchildren the family looked west, to Anjou, to Toulouse, to Catalonia, and to France, with the marriage of Constance, daughter of William II and Azalais of Anjou. The only alliance to the north was that of William III, count from 922–1019, who ca. 1009 married Gerberga, daughter of the count of Mâcon Otto-William. But even this alliance indicates the western focus of the counts of Provence since by this time Otto-William was a strong supporter of the Capetians.

Equally as important as the loss of continuity with the North is that with the East. The great event in the history of the comital family, which established them in Provence as nothing else did, was the defeat in 972 of the Saracens of Le Freinet by William II (the Liberator), with the assistance of Marquis Arduin of Turin. Nevertheless, following this victory one sees no evidence of further involvement in Italy or alliances with the lords of the region. Not only is this in marked contrast with the traditions of his predecessor but also with that of earlier governors of Provence going as far back as Abbo.

The horizons of the new family were smaller. They traveled less than Hugo, and unlike him they apparently had no possessions outside of Provence. When they did look beyond the frontiers of Provence, it was no longer to the ineffective king of Vienne or to the kingdom of Burgundy but rather to the west, to Catalonia, the Toulousain, to Anjou, and to the Ile de France. Within this new framework, their ancestry mattered little. Whether they were really "new men" of middling status raised by Hugo of Arles or whether they were actually part of the old aristocracy from Septimania, Burgundy, or Alemannia meant little in the new relationships into which the counts of Provence entered. Memories of former alliances and betrayals of Hugo and his Burgundians were not only embarrassing to the new counts but irrelevant.

Montmajour, their necropolis and the object of their charity, also took on this more limited perspective. For its new role, the memory of Hugo and even that of Theucinda meant nothing. What mattered was the counts' relationship to a new family, and it is this western-looking society that was remembered in their necrology and, indirectly, it was the mythic Carolingian Charlemagne, "king of the French," not the real Carolingian Hugo or even the pious woman who was remembered as the monastery's founder. To return to the legend of the Carolingian foundation, one sees the transference onto a mythic world, that of the Carolingian age, of the relationships and events to which the new comitial family owed its origins. The expulsion of the Saracens by Charlemagne and his subsequent support of the monastery as a burial place for his fallen warriors is the archetype for the role the new counts played. By defeating the Saracens and establishing Montmajour as their family burial place, they repeated the model established by the Carolingians. Of course, the modern historian would prefer to say that the counts provided the model for the Carolingian myth. That this memory did not correspond to the "facts" of the past is much less important in this context than that it corresponded to the circumstances of the present.[42]

Hugo of Arles had represented a particular configuration of the Carolingian tradition at the start of the tenth century, a configuration that, in its ultimate failure, rapidly lost its meaning for subsequent generations. Bavaria and Neustria had similar figures at the beginning of the tenth century. In Bavaria Duke Arnulf, in the dark days following the annihilation of the Bavarian leadership at the hands of the Magyars in 907, reached back to Agilolfing traditions to reestablish the Bavarian duchy. Charles III, the last effective Carolingian, likewise drew on the eighth-century models of his ancestors in an effort to assert his position, even while establishing the model for the West Frankish kingship for the next centuries. However, like Hugo, they, too, were failures, and the eleventh-century memory dealt harshly with them, excluding them from liturgical commemoration and denigrating or, more frequently, forgetting their achievements. Charles is known to subsequent history as "the Simple," and Arnulf is known by the epithet "the Bad" (although in the early eleventh century even these pejorative epithets had not taken hold). They were more ignored than vilified.

Charles III

In 893 magnates led by Archbishop Fulk of Reims and Count Herbert effected the consecration of Charles, the sole surviving son of the Carolingian Louis the Stammerer, as a rival king to the Robertinian Eudes (Odo), who had been elected during the crisis of 888. The magnates feared the way Eudes was concentrating power in his family, but nothing that Charles or his supporters could do could stop the process. Four years of violent confrontation followed, which were ended only when Eudes agreed to accept Charles as his successor. This recognition, however, cost Charles and his family dearly. In return for the kingship, Charles had to allow Eudes and his Robertinian heirs the estates, lands, and monasteries in Neustria, most notably St. Denis, which they had previously acquired.[43] This great monastery, where so many of Charles's ancestors had been buried, passed forever from his family. The loss was mutual. Charles was the last Carolingian to issue diplomas in favor of St. Denis, but the Robertinians were not immediately ready to accord the monastery the primacy that it had once known. In the tenth and eleventh centuries, as we have seen in chapter 4, St. Denis passed to the periphery of royal concern. As Thomas Waldman has observed, between the death of Charles and the ascension of Louis VI in 1108, St. Denis received only six royal privileges.[44]

After Eudes's death in 898 Charles succeeded him with the support of Eudes's brother Robert and the other Neustrian magnates. Almost immediately, Charles's chancery began a campaign to reestablish Carolingian political and ideological traditions.[45] Charles's diplomas, returning to formulas used by Louis the Pious following his reestablishment in 834, announced the "reintegration" of his rule. Deed followed word. Having renounced the centers of power in Neustria, Charles entered a long and ultimately successful effort to acquire Lotharingia, the traditional center of his family's power, where he worked to rebuild the kind of territorial basis of support now enjoyed by the Robertinians in Neustria. After his success in 911, he interpreted this feat in the traditional Carolingian manner as evidence of God's special favor shown them in the expansion of their realm. In the formulas used in his diplomas as well as in his reuse of Charlemagne's royal monogram, he attached himself specifically to Carolingian usages of the 770s.

Charles's propaganda and his Lotharingian politics thus aimed at a return to the early history of his family and to the traditional seat of its power. However, he was no nostalgic reactionary. In 911, after a Frankish force inflicted a crushing defeat on the Norman raiders established on the lower Seine, Charles accepted their leader, Rollo, as count in the

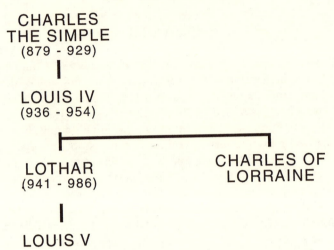

**CHARLES
THE SIMPLE**
(879 - 929)

LOUIS IV
(936 - 954)

LOTHAR
(941 - 986)

**CHARLES OF
LORRAINE**

LOUIS V

Chart 2. Principal Last Carolingians in the West

area around Rouen. This compromise, while it did not end the threat of Viking raids in the West, was the beginning of the end, since Charles apparently charged Rollo with the obligation to defend the mouth of the river against other Viking raiders and the treaty opened the way to fairly rapid Christianization of Rollo's Vikings.

Charles was as willing to compromise in the East as in the West. In 921, he met the East Frankish king Henry I on a barge in the Rhine so that they might deal on equal terms. The two kings, one a legitimate Carolingian and the other a Saxon upstart, recognized each other's legitimacy, thus ending any Carolingian pretensions to universal rule. In this acceptance of a limited kingship, just as in his adoption of the old Frankish royal title, "*rex Francorum*," in place of the absolute royal title in favor since 833,[46] Charles set the course of future West Frankish–French kingship well into the twelfth century. But if Charles's political instincts on these broad issues were sound, his ability to maintain his own position was not. His promotion of Hagano, a Lotharingian noble of lower status than the western magnates, to a position superior to them in the kingdom, led to rebellion.

The precipitating events to the rebellion appear to have been Charles's determined efforts to promote the *memoria* of his favorite to the same level as members of the royal family. In one diploma, the monks were obligated to offer prayers in perpetuity for the royal family and for Hagano.[47] Not content with this inclusion of Hagano in the Carolingian *memoria*, Charles went still further. In 922 he granted Hagano the royal

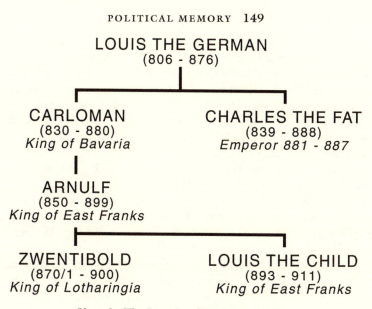

Chart 3. The Last Carolingians in the East

abbey of Chelles, the Neustrian nunnery most closely associated with the royal family and ruled by his aunt Rothildis, daughter of Charles the Bald and mother-in-law of Hugh the Great, son of Robert of Neustria.[48] By not only including Hagano in the Carolingian memorial tradition but by making him custodian of it, Charles seemed determined to transform him into a Carolingian.

Rothildis' Robertinian kin and their Neustrian allies found this last act intolerable and civil war broke out. Although Robert—who had been elected king by the magnates in 922 (in the same manner that Charles had been elected by rebel magnates twenty-nine years previously)—was killed, Charles was defeated and, tricked into capture by Herbert II of Vermandois, spent the last years of his life in helpless captivity.

Tenth-century historians were largely favorable to Charles, if universally hostile to his favorite Hagano. Richer, echoing what was probably the original sense of his epithet, describes him thus: "He strived for much good will, he was handsome in appearance, in character good and sincere" (ad multam benevolentiam intendebat. Corpore prestanti, ingenio bono simplicique).[49] The primary accusations made against the king were the advancement of Hagano and, by Flodoard, his alliance with the Vikings at the mouth of the Loire against Robert and the rebel Neustrian magnates.[50]

By the turn of the century, however, even these details had disappeared. With the exception of Dudo of St. Quentin's fanciful account of Rollo and Charles in which Charles appears a weak and at times ridiculous figure beside the Norman duke, Charles ceases to have an organic role in the crucial dynastic politics of the early tenth century.[51] The *Historia Francorum Senonensis*, written between 1015 and 1030, reduces its account of Charles to a minimum, eliminating the initial conflict between Charles and Eudes, the Lotharingian strategy, the Carolingian reform aspirations, his promotion of Hagano, and even his cooperation with the Normans.[52] The account jumps from the death of Eudes to Robert's rebellion, dwelling at length on Herbert's infidelity.[53] Aimoin of Fleury, writing around the turn of the century, describes only the rebellion of Robert, his death at the battle of Soissons, and Herbert's betrayal and capture of the king.[54]

In the hands of Rodulfus Glaber, Charles has ceased altogether to appear as an historical personage. In book 1 of his *Historia*, Charles becomes the point of departure for his narrative. However, the reign of Charles is situated neither chronologically nor politically. He is simply the last king to bear the name Charles, and the entire account of his reign is limited to Herbert's treason, elaborated and presented as typologically parallel to the betrayal of Jesus by Judas, the similarity of the two treasons being implied by Herbert's treacherous reception of the royal kiss.[55]

We can begin to understand this disappearance of Charles and the transference of the political turmoil of the early tenth century into myth by examining the manner in which Rodulfus treats Charles's competition, the ultimately successful Robertinians. About their origins he is equally vague. Discussing Hugh the Great, he says that he was the son of Robert of Paris. But he adds only that he does not speak of Robert's *genus* because "if one goes any distance back it becomes very obscure."[56] This obscurity, as Mireille Schmidt-Chazan has argued, is probably intentional on the part of the supporters of Hugh Capet, who deemphasized ancestry as a foundation for legitimacy, emphasizing instead the presumed absence of a Carolingian heir or the will of God.[57] Capetian ancestry, honorable as it was, could hardly stand comparison with that of the Carolingians. Nor could the rebellion of Robert against a Carolingian king, particularly one that ended in the former's death. Thus both Robert and Charles slip from a recognizable context: Robert is killed by "Saxons" (a reference perhaps to the Lotharingians in Charles's army). Charles is the type of the king betrayed by one closest to him because, according to Rodulfus, Charles had stood as godfather to Herbert's son.[58]

But in this image of betrayal there lurks a second, unmentioned betrayal that gave form and importance to this story: the even more striking and politically more significant betrayal of Charles of Lorraine by Bishop Adalbero/Ascelin of Laon.[59] After the death of Louis V without direct heirs, Archbishop Adalbero of Reims, who had been driven by Charles into Hugh's camp, quickly engineered the latter's election and coronation. However, Charles, Louis V's uncle, put forward his own claims, which gradually found adherents. In 988 the towns of Laon and then Reims came under Charles's control, and Hugh was unable to reduce them. But in 991 Bishop Adalbero of Laon, feigning to join the Carolingian pretender, entered the city and betrayed it to Hugh. Charles was imprisoned and died in captivity.[60]

The parallels between the fates of the two Charleses are striking. Both were passed over by the Neustrian magnates in favor of Robertinians, and both then managed to gain supporters, and finally, both were betrayed to their enemies by trusted confidants. The parallels are most clearly presented in the *Historia Francorum Senonensis*, whose author was particularly hostile to Hugh Capet. Both Robert and Hugh are said to "rebel" against the legitimate Carolingian. The revolts against Charles the Simple and Charles of Lorraine are presented in almost the same language: "In the second year after his death, Prince Robert rebelled against Charles the Simple."[61] And for Charles of Lorraine: "In the same year Hugo duke of the Franks rebelled against Charles."[62]

The traitors are similarly presented. Herbert is described as "infidelium nequissimus," while the bishop of Laon (called Ascelin rather than Adalbero), is termed an "old traitor, who was the false bishop of Laon and the adviser of Charles."[63]

Rodulfus Glaber, who elaborated at length on the treason of Herbert, entirely passes over that of Adalbero/Ascelin. He simply says that after the death of Lothar and Louis, "The government of the whole kingdom of France fell to Hugh, duke of Paris, son of Hugh the Great, whose brother was the very noble Henry, duke of Burgundy."[64] Hugh is elevated without any opposition, but shortly afterward some of his followers who previously had supported him become defiant. This lays the groundwork for the elevation of Hugh's son' Robert. Charles of Lorraine never appears.

Ademar does the opposite. He completely ignores the treason and capture of Charles the Simple and concentrates instead on that of Charles of Lorraine. In the first version of his chronicle, composed ca. 1026, his account of Charles the Simple (whom he calls Carolus Minor) is confused, perhaps intentionally.[65] In his account, Charles begins his reign after Louis's death. The Franks conspire against him and establish

Duke Eudes (whom Ademar misidentifies as the duke of Aquitaine) as king. Charles regains the kingdom, but the leaders of the Franks again conspire against him, this time driving him from the kingdom and establishing Duke Robert king. The Franks then become split, with the majority favoring Robert. However, with the help of Emperor Otto Charles raises an army of Bavarians and Franks that defeat the rebels and kill Robert. Charles recovers his kingdom but permits Hugo the son of duke Robert to rule. After his death, Charles is succeeded by Louis.[66]

In his revision, however, Ademar recounts a longer version of the same story, in which he attributes Charles's victory to St. Martial of Limoges. In the battle, he says that a Count Fulbert carried Charles's banner while Robert carried his own, his gray beard flowing outside his breastplate so that he can be recognized. Charles warns his own standard bearer, "Look out, Fulbert," from which, Ademar explains, arose the popularity of the phrase as a proverb. After Charles's victory Hugo comes to Charles and accepts his authority. Charles allows Hugo to retain the ducal position his father had enjoyed before him. Charles gives some of the spoils of victory to St. Martial of Limoges, including a precious Gospel book, two books of divine history, a *computus*, and banners of golden cloth. After his death, Louis rules in his place.[67]

If Ademar ignores the betrayal of Charles the Simple, he dwells at length on the treason of Ascelin (Bishop Adalbero) in the first and second versions of his *Chronicon*.[68] In the first, Ascelin is explicitly compared to Judas and said to have betrayed Charles during Holy Week in the manner of Judas: "For this reason Ascelin, bishop of Laon, betrayed Charles during the week in which falls Holy Thursday and Good Friday and the Saturday before Easter just as Judas betrayed Christ."[69] Only in Ademar's third version, written ca. 1028–29, is the comparison with Judas and the explicit mention of Bishop Ascelin removed.

Apparently, by the eleventh century, Charles the Simple, both for those supporting the new royal family and for its opponents, had lost an organic relationship to the political process of which he was a part. His diplomas, carefully modeled on those of his Carolingian predecessors, were easily mistaken in monastic archives for just that, and thus donations and privileges of Charles III were easily confused with those by Charles the Bald. Not only was Charles III confused with the earlier Charles, but his reign and betrayal had become sufficiently confused with that of the later Charles to be an interchangeable *exemplum* of treason. For Ademar, who at least originally opposed the Capetians, the story of the earlier elevation and betrayal was unnecessary. Instead, the reign of Charles became a frame within which to place an anecdote, drawn presumably from oral tradition but a tradition that had no particular relationship to Charles the Simple. For Rodulfus, who supported the Capetians, the story was retained, but at the expense of the second betrayal, which resulted in the final elimination of the Carolingians as royal pretenders.

In Provence, Hugo slipped from memory as an archaism and an embarrassment. In France, Charles the Simple lost his position as the founder of what might be termed the French monarchal formula and survived either as the archetype of the king betrayed by his vassal or, as with Ademar, as a patron of St. Martial, much in the manner that Arnold of Regensburg and Gottschalk of Benediktbeuern remembered kings who had been particularly generous to their monasteries and whose gifts of books, vessels, and rich vestments could be seen, handled, and used as nodal points around which to build memories. In Bavaria, another ruler, almost but not quite a king, who played an equally decisive role in the early tenth century was indeed remembered, but as a despoiler of the church: Arnulf the Bad.

Arnulf of Bavaria

In his 1974 study of the image of Arnulf in medieval historiography, Alois Schmid carefully and thoroughly outlined the development of the duke from "gloriosus dux" to "tyrannus."[70] Contemporary Bavarian sources recognized the continuity with the Carolingian and Agilolfing traditions that, as we have seen,[71] were the basis of his family's position. The anonymous author of the *Fragmentum de Arnulfo duce Bavariae*, a fragment of a propaganda text written at St. Emmeram of Regensburg during Arnulf's conflict with Henry I, emphasized his divinely granted *virtus*, his *fortitudo* and *victoria*, which resulted from his royal and imperial descent, and his victory over the Magyars by which he saved the Christian people.[72] It is the last that most impressed contemporaries. In particular, Arnulf's victory over a Magyar force on the Inn in 913 as the latter was returning from a raiding expedition into Swabia made a deep impression on Bavarians and Magyars alike and put Arnulf in a position to make a peace with the Magyars that essentially left Bavaria secure for the remainder of his life.[73]

Arnulf's victory over the Magyars was made possible by his use of monastic and church property to reward his followers. As Schmid has accurately pointed out, the confiscations of property in Bavaria were within a tradition that began at least with the early Carolingians.[74] Since the time of Charles Martel, or more accurately, his sons Carloman and

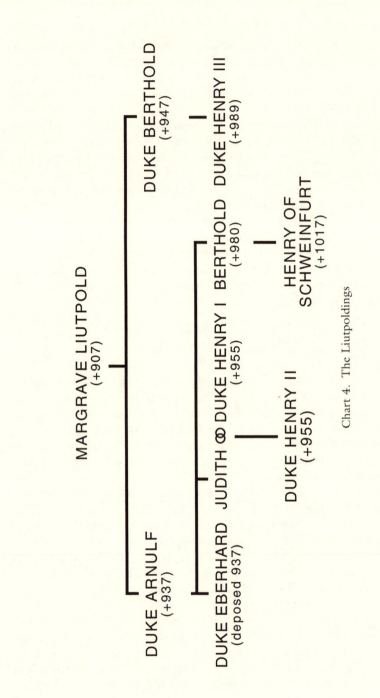

Chart 4. The Liutpoldings

Pippin III, such confiscations had not necessarily alienated property definitively but rather had granted it *in praecarium*, with the stipulation that the church continue to enjoy rights.[75] In using ecclesiastical property to support his defense of the duchy against Magyars and later against Conrad and Henry, Arnulf was acting in the recognized tradition that seems to have elicited no particular objections from contemporaries, even from those institutions whose property he granted *in beneficium*.[76] Moreover, if he was actively involved in the redistribution of church property, it was often from monasteries that had been devastated by the Magyars and whose lands were thus without effective lords.[77] Finally, this confiscation program was paralleled by one of restoration and the endowment of monasteries such as Kempten and the return of temporarily confiscated property.[78]

No wonder then that contemporary sources have nothing to say about Arnulf's secularizations, which were within the norms of tenth-century royal behavior and perfectly suited to a Bavarian duke whose claims were those of a sovereign within the Bavarian *regnum*. Even monasteries such as Benediktbeuern or Tegernsee, which retained records of property confiscated during the tenth century and maintained records of these precarial grants in the hope of recovering them at some future date, did not blame Arnulf for these confiscations until the twelfth century.[79] Arnulf is conspicuous in his absence from the list of "destructores libertatis Coenobii S. Benedicti."[80]

Unlike Hugo of Arles who died in disgraced exile or Charles III who died a captive, Arnulf survived Saxon and Magyar invasions of Bavaria and even managed to designate his son Eberhard as his successor before his death in 937. Only with the accession of Otto I did the Liutpoldings lose control over Bavaria. Although his conflicts with Conrad I and Henry I were often recorded as "rebellions," later tenth- and eleventh-century chroniclers (with the exception of Ottonian court historians such as Widukind of Corvey, Liudprand of Cremona, and Adalbert of Magdeburg) were generally positive in their estimations.[81] Thietmar of Merseburg, writing for Arnulf's descendant Henry II, characterized him as "precluus in mente pariter et corpore."[82] And yet, even before then, the memory of Arnulf began to fade from Bavarian memory.

Who was responsible for remembering Arnulf? During his lifetime, Regensburg seems to have played this central role, to judge both from the *Fragmentum de Arnulfo* and the Sacramentary of Regensburg, which contains prayers for "Arnolfum ducem nostrum."[83] He may have been buried in St. Emmeram or in Tegernsee.[84] After Arnulf's death Regensburg, or at least St. Emmeram, seems not to have long continued this commemoration. Arnold of Regensburg mentions him only for his having constructed the city walls that included the monastery.[85] While the anniversary of his death (14 July) was recorded in necrologies, including those of St. Gall and Fulda, the eleventh-century necrology of St. Emmeram ignores him completely. It appears in only one surviving example from Bavaria—Niederalteich.[86] During the crucial period of roughly a century and a half following his death and before the development of the "black legend" of Arnulf as tyrannical despoiler of churches, his memory seems to have faded in Bavaria.

This effacement is probably due to a series of factors. First, the replacement of Arnulf's son Eberhard by his brother Berthold and, on the death of the latter, by Otto's brother Henry ended the direct continuity of Arnulf's program and, following the violent confrontations between the Liutpoldings and the Ottonians, the virtual autonomy of the Bavarian *regnum*.[87] Second, Arnulf seems to have made few donations to major Bavarian institutions that would have left echoes in monastic *Traditionsbücher*. No donations meant no written memorialization of the duke—at St. Emmeram, for example, Arnulf appears nowhere in the extant *traditiones*.

Arnulf was much more directly involved with Salzburg, where he and his brother appear in a number of Salzburg traditions.[88] This may be explained in part by the kinship between Archbishop Odalbert (835–923) or his wife Rihni and Arnulf.[89] However, even there his memory seems to have become confused. In the Salzburg necrology, Arnulf is indeed remembered on the anniversary of his death, but as "Arnolfus rex" and not "Arnolfus dux."[90] But as Schmid has shown, this must not be attributed to his putative royal aspirations (also recorded in Salzburg) but rather to a confusion with Arnulf of Carinthia.[91]

This confusion of the two Arnulfs to the advantage of the emperor may explain the disappearance of Duke Arnulf in the historical consciousness of Arnold of St. Emmeram as well. For that author, as we shall see in the following chapter, the Emperor Arnulf was the most important royal patron of his monastery, and Arnold attributed to him a devotion to the monastery that is difficult to document. As royal patron, the Emperor Arnulf became the kernel around which the legends of royal favor coalesced, to the disadvantage of others. Even the only account of Conrad I's hostile relationships with Regensburg, which took place during the life of Duke Arnulf, are connected with the donations allegedly made by the earlier like-named king. In Regensburg as in Salzburg, the memories of the two Arnulfs seem to have merged, a process that continued in the following century. As Schmid has remarked, between the twelfth and fourteenth centuries, Emperor Arnulf, Count Arnulf of Wels-Lambach, and Duke Arnulf coalesced in Bavarian historiography.[92]

What had happened to Hugh, to Arnulf, and perhaps to some extent to Charles III, is in some sense the logical outcome both of their programs of self-representation and of the means by which *memoria* was preserved. Arnulf and Charles had sought, through conscious imitation of Carolingian precedent, to associate their reigns with the ideals and ideologies of previous, like-named Carolingians. If Charles III's diplomas resembled closely those of Charlemagne and Charles the Bald, if Arnulf's autonomous rule in the *regnum* of Bavaria paralleled that of Arnulf of Carinthia before his election to the monarchy, then the assimilation of the individuals could follow. Their names, which indeed announced a program, aided this confusion, particularly in necrological entries.

Hugo of Arles also sought to revive a Carolingian tradition that was too far beyond the ken of succeeding generations to make a lasting impact. Instead, his Provençal foundation was attributed to his distant ancestor Charlemagne. Charles III and Arnulf might be said to have succeeded too well in their attempts to incarnate Carolingian royal traditions. Their names and their diplomas, stripped by the memorial systems of monastic archives and necrologies, merged with those of their predecessors. As individual rulers, the memorial process of the eleventh century left them blank slates on which future generations could write.

VI

REMEMBERING PANNONIAN DRAGONS

IN THE PRECEDING CHAPTERS we have examined how individuals and groups from across Europe reformed elements of the liturgical, oral, onomastic, archival, and literary fragments of their pasts in accord with the needs of their present. This penultimate chapter will bring this disparate series of examinations together by focusing on the memorial activities of a single individual. Through his reflections of his personal experiences, his family traditions, the history of his monastery and its patron saint, his city, and finally his region, we shall see how one man went about creating a useful past.

Around 1030 Arnold, a monk of the Bavarian monastery of St. Emmeram of Regensburg (ca. 1000–1050), traveled to Pannonia on a mission for his abbot.[1] Years later he remembered a most impressive event during that journey. On the second Friday after Pentecost, at the third hour, Arnold met a dragon.[2] The monster was suspended in the air and stretched for a distance of almost one mile. It had a plumed head the height of a mountain and a body covered with scales that protected it like armor or shields of iron. Its sides and back were blackened as by soot; its belly was a lighter color, similar to that of sulfur. This monster remained in sight for three hours before suddenly flying over Arnold and his companions at great speed.

This very personal and extraordinary memory is recorded in an apparently rambling dialogue whose professed subject is the miracles of St. Emmeram, in which Arnold quite accurately calls himself the "collectitius," or the one who gathers together, while his interlocutor is "Ammonicius," the one who constantly urges him back to the task at hand. Examining in some detail just how Arnold collects and recollects—how he reflects on, remembers, and describes remembering—this event raises once more some of the primary characteristics of remembering and forgetting of the decades immediately preceding and following the year one thousand.

Medieval hagiography and historiography are filled with visions, dreams, miracles, and other extraordinary experiences that rival Arnold's. Indeed, the desire to transmit these extraordinary occurrences to posterity motivated many hagiographers and historians to set them down.[3] But these same texts are also filled with more mundane accounts that often draw on archival records such as charters, diplomas, records of court proceedings, and the like to demonstrate the proper relationship between their institutions and the rest of the world.[4] Historians have tended to take these latter sources very seriously, assuming that archival documents exploited by medieval authors could put us in touch with a "real" world of social and political interaction, while the former category is seen as an important but quite different world, that of the imaginary. Thus reliance on archival evidence is seen as proof of the author's critical sense, while reliance on visions, dreams, and dragons shows evidence of credulity. What one sometimes forgets is that visionaries were often also people of great practical ability and interest and that in their construction of reality dragons and charters formed part of a whole. The difference between hagiography and archival evidence is a modern, not a medieval, one. The author of the cartulary of St. Père of Chartres, writing in the later eleventh century, even uses the term *agiographa* to describe, among other kinds of texts, the charters of his monastery.[5] Both saints' lives and charters are writings recording the glory of the saints. In the words of Michael Clanchy, monastic scribes were primarily concerned "with making liturgical books for worship and with keeping in charters and chronicles a record, for future generations of monks, of the working of God's providence as revealed in gifts and portents."[6] Moreover, when reflecting on the range of experiences, both personal and mediated through oral or written tradition that composed one's memory, the ways in which one re-collected these fragments were essentially the same.

One sees this in the memories and the remembering of Arnold, who was not only a pious monk given to visions of dragons and saints but also a member of an important Bavarian noble family and the provost of his monastery, and thus responsible for the acquisition, recording, and management of the property of St. Emmeram during a complex period in that institution's history. During his lifetime, conflict between St. Emmeram and the bishop of Regensburg came to a head over the autonomy of the monastic community. In defense of their autonomy, the monks sought the intervention of the emperor, claiming a special relationship with the monarchy that reached into the distant past. In his writings, Arnold was determined to show the proper relationship between St. Emmeram and the various powers with which the saint and his community had to contend: with aristocratic families such as Arnold's own, with the bishops of Regensburg, and with the monarchy. These relationships were to be found in the past, which provided models for the present and future; but in order for this past to provide this model, it had to be properly ordered and useful.

To this end, Arnold the *collectitius* gathered together disparate fragments of personal, institutional, and regional memories. These range from personal experiences of his dragon, to texts, to oral traditions, to charters, to tombs. In this chapter we will examine how he recalled his grandparents, his kings, and his dragon. The first two instances appear initially to be classic, if precocious, cases of the use of archival and necrological notices to present an account of dealings between Arnold's grandfather and his monastery a generation before his birth. The last seems at first glance to be a total fantasy. However, the commemorative and forgetting processes are the same in all. Arnold remembers his dragon, his grandfathers, and his kings in the same way. We will begin with the dragon.

Arnold, like other eleventh-century men and women, lived with many memories, both personal and collective. It would be a serious mistake to think that this collection of memories is simply the sum total of what he had experienced, heard, and read. Rather memory is an active and creative faculty, constantly selecting, interpreting, and transforming experience. Whether Arnold actually saw a dragon is less important than that he remembered seeing one—that is to say, his perception and memory operated differently from that of modern historians, according to a different system that was dependent less on the input of experience than on the commemorative and referential systems of which he was a part.

What does one do when one sees a dragon? First, Arnold recognized it as a dragon, although he had never before seen one and it did not resemble pictures he had seen previously. Then he observed it, giving a detailed description that he compared with that of the Leviathan in Job (Job 41) and also, interestingly enough, with depictions he had seen of dragons, either in illuminated manuscripts or in frescoes.[7] The former he judged to be accurate, the latter not at all. The book of Job, he explained, rightly observes that these monsters are covered with scales. Pictorial representations of dragons, however, indicated wings and legs or feet. Arnold's beast had neither, for its scales and ribs were sufficient for movement.

Arnold's interlocutor asks if he did not remember, at the time that he saw the dragon, the dragon and the beast described by John in the Apocalypse. Arnold replies that these things had come to mind ("in memoriam venerunt haec"), especially the verse, "Woe to you because the dragon comes to you with great wrath, knowing that he may have but little time."[8] However, he had soon dismissed this recollection because he knew that the beast and the dragon symbolized the Antichrist and the devil, and since the day of universal judgment had hardly arrived, he gradually lost his fear for his life and the lives of his colleagues. Then he began to turn over ("volvere") or to treat ("tractare") mentally, whether in reading or in scrutinizing scriptures he had ever found anything such as he was seeing that day. And among the things that had run through ("percurrere") his mind were the words and writings ("dicta et scripta") of Isidore of Seville in his *Etymologiae* on the nature of dragons.[9] This description, which he cites at length, is entirely without supernatural meaning or religious significance. It is also no memory. Unlike the biblical text that he cites with characteristic creative restructuring, the Isidorian text is a verbatim citation from Isidore, presumably copied from the manuscript of Isidore we know to have been in St. Emmeram's at the end of the tenth century.[10]

Arnold thus describes a process in which a new experience is first perceived, evaluated, and then made meaningful within a preexisting context that was a literate and pictorial tradition. What he perceived passed through a filter of prior knowledge—although in the case of the Pannonian dragon it did take some time, some due consideration and mental gymnastics, before his mind could run through all the possibilities. Within this tradition he made certain critical choices: judging the description of the Leviathan in Job as an accurate image of a dragon while rejecting those of pictures he had seen; perhaps initially accepting the apocalyptic meaning of the dragon but then later rejecting that idea along with the possibility that he had ever long entertained it in order to accept the natural one of Isidore.

Here one sees an eleventh-century person's memory at work, not just accessing and reproducing stored memories in some mechanical manner but actively recollecting, in the literal sense of "re-collecting" and thus selecting and emending, his past experience. His account provides an unusually clear opportunity to see how he went about making and judging his collection, and in particular how deeply interdependent were what he experienced and what he recollected as well as what he later recalled having experienced and recollected.

First, he identified the dragon with the description from Job, in which the Lord speaks to Job: "Canst thou draw out Leviathan with a hook?"(Job 41:1). Arnold uses the vocabulary from Job to describe his dragon, particularly its "scales horribly compact as though covered with shields or iron,"[11] which echoes Job 41:6 ("its body compact and glorying in its scales like fused shields").[12] But what is perhaps most interesting in the use of this passage is that in Job the Leviathan is not identified as a dragon. Arnold may have made this connection because the beast he saw appeared to resemble the description of the Leviathan more than those of dragons because of its scales and for its lack of limbs. It may also be that images of the Leviathan with which he was familiar, unlike those of monsters specifically identified in scripture as dragons, conformed to what he had seen. In this connection one can compare the Leviathan in the Utrecht Psalter, which appears as a great serpent without legs or wings, with Arnold's description. Here his experience is assimilated to an already known image, which both determines how he is to process the one (that is, to describe his beast with the language of Job) and to label the other (the Leviathan becomes a dragon). Within this assimilative process, Arnold makes no reference to any popular traditions concerning dragons. All of his explicit connections are to biblical sources. However, the ready identification of a great snakelike beast with a dragon may have been influenced by traditions of the *Wurm* of Germanic folklore. If so, Arnold avoids any allusions that would take his memories out of a Christian biblical context.

The second comparison that he makes, this one to be rejected, is even more interesting. He compares his beast to pictures he had seen of dragons (that is, of beasts specifically labeled dragons, as opposed to the Leviathan) and finds them incorrect because they depict wings and legs and feet. Exactly what Arnold had in mind we cannot know; no extant St. Emmeram manuscripts contain images of dragons. However, the dragon from the Bamberg Apocalypse (and in particular those illustrating chapter 12, verse 12, which he cites, only to reject the apocalyptic interpretation) is probably close to the sorts of dragons Arnold would have seen illustrated: here we see indeed a monster with wings, legs, and feet, exactly as he says the inaccurate pictures he had seen suggested (see plate 14). The iconographic tradition, which was by this time fairly fixed, gave dragons limbs—clearly in Arnold's judgment an error.

But if Arnold detected an error in the pictorial representation of dragons, we can recognize an error in his quotation of scripture. Arnold quotes the Apocalypse as follows: "Woe to you because the dragon comes to you with great wrath, knowing that he may have but little time."[13] This quotation is inexact in several particulars. The actual text reads, "Woe to the earth, and to the sea, because the devil is come down upon you, having great wrath, knowing that he hath but a short time."[14]

It is not unusual to take liberties with the text, even for quotations from scripture. As Quintilian noted, quoting *ad litteram* suggests a poor assimilation of what is memorized, while paraphrases that fit more closely to the discourse are signs of true skills of memory.[15] But exactly how Arnold recollected this scriptural passage indicates much about how he reworked his experience that day in Pannonia. This reworking is very similar to the patterns observed by experimental psychologists such as F. C. Bartlett, who, as we have seen, gave subjects short stories to memorize and then asked them to repeat the stories at fixed intervals over subsequent days, months, and even years.[16] The stories changed as the remembering subject simplified them, resolved ambiguities or contradictions, and brought them into conformity with other experiences.

In the same way, Arnold first simplified the text, substituting "you" for "the inhabitants of the earth and of the sea" (a legitimate sense of the

nam. ſcienſ quod modicum tempuſ habe̒.

Plate 14. Dragons in the Bamberg Apocalypse (fol. 30v).

text since "you" appears in the next line and is clearly the referent of "the inhabitants of the earth and of the sea"). His second change is not quite so straightforward. Arnold replaced the devil of the text with the dragon, thus making the equation between the devil descending to the earth with great wrath and the dragon that is seen falling to the earth in the next verse. Since the context of Arnold's discussion is dragons and not devils, one understands the error, but this substitution, unlike the first, is supported less by grammar than by exegesis that clearly identifies the dragon and the devil. The third and most subtle change in Arnold's quotation is to change *habet* to *habeat* (from "knowing that he hath but a short time" to "knowing that he may have but little time")—that is, from the indicative to the subjunctive mood. This may seem a trivial change, but actually, shifting from certainty to possibility makes more sense in the context within which Arnold was writing and remembering.

To understand Arnold's memories of the dragon, scripture, and of his initial understanding of the dragon, we must not examine simply his description but also his circumstances in 1030 and then later when he was writing. The context of the vision and its initial meaning is probably provided by the interlocutor's query (the interlocutor being an external projection of Arnold's own mind arguing with itself). In asking if he did not first think of the dragon of the Apocalypse, he is probably reflecting what was his original concern. In 1030, as Richard Landes and Johannes Fried have recently argued, the end of the world was indeed very much in peoples' minds, especially but not exclusively reformed monks.[17] Rodulfus Glaber reported that, in the second year from the millennium, "A wonderful portent appeared in the sky. It had the shape of (or perhaps it simply was) a huge dragon, and it traveled from north to south, shimmering with a great light. This portent terrified almost all the men in Gaul who saw it."[18] This report was taken up by Hugh of Flavigny, and the *Annales Floriacenses* also report the appearance of a great, headless dragon in 956.[19] Thus Arnold probably did first understand the dragon not simply as the monster of Isidore, but as a sign of the end. Later, after the millennium of the crucifixion, when the end did not come, the meaning and thus the memory had to be recast. The apocalyptic meaning of the dragon is thus explicitly discarded as though it had never mattered, and the suggestion that the dragon's descent is proof that "he hath but a short time" is likewise downgraded from certainty to possibility. It remains nevertheless as a sort of pentimento, expressed in the question of the Ammonicius. The new meaning likewise came from the specific circumstances within which the events were remembered, not from the memories themselves.

The story of the dragon occurs in the context of a discussion of the crystalline spheres, a natural history discussion, not a discussion of the end of the world or of signs and portents. Arnold contends that the crystalline spheres are not solid but that bodies can pass through them. As proof, he offers his experience of the dragon. Thus why the events of the past are recalled give form to how they are recalled. In the context of postmillennarian disenchantment and in a discussion of natural history, Arnold needed to recall a real, physical dragon, one capable of passing through the heavenly spheres rather than one associated with the end of the world.

The Ordered and the Useful

This liberty of recollection, of judging experience remembered according to social and cultural categories of the present, appears not only in Arnold's personal recollections but also in his construction of familial, institutional, and regional pasts. His raw materials are the places, texts, objects, and persons by which he is in touch with these pasts. But as with his own memories, he judges, selects, and reshapes them, determining what the past was and meant by what it ought to have been.

Most of Arnold's two books are focused not on natural science but on the history of his institution. He was writing at a time when the future of St. Emmeram was seriously in question because of the radical break with its past occasioned by the separation of the monastic and episcopal offices, the dispute between bishop and monks over the property of the monastery, and the dissipation of monastic property.[20] More fundamental was the question of the place of the monastery and its patron within the empire and its relationship with emperor and Bavarian nobles. Arnold was convinced of the central place he thought the monastery had played in the past. Now that position was threatened. In fulfillment of a vow he had made to St. Emmeram in return for the miraculous cure of an eye ailment, he undertook to record the miracles of the saint, to praise his deeds, and "to transmit by letters the words and deeds of the elect to the memory of posterity."[21] Thus the *De miraculis* is not focused simply on the miracles of the saint but on those of his monastery, from its foundation to Arnold's day.

In describing these miracles, in ruminating on the physical remains of the past, and in selecting and interpreting the written evidence of this past, Arnold was consciously participating in a great mystery, that of the Trinity, reflected, as he reminded his reader, in human intellect, memory, and will. Here he echoes St. Augustine's concept of memory as the primary human faculty of knowledge and image of the divine.[22] Several years before his dragon sighting, Arnold's independent attitude toward the past resulted in his temporary banishment to Saxony. Around 1022 as a young monk, he had proposed to revise the venerable life of St. Emmeram composed more than two centuries earlier by Bishop Arbeo of Freising. Arnold's reasoning was that the original text, written, he believed, correctly by Arbeo, had become corrupt by the negligence of his predecessors.[23] Although his abbot fully agreed, many of the brothers did not. They were scandalized that someone would dare to add to or to diminish the past. Arnold's response was bold: "Not only is it proper for the new to change the old, but even, if the old is disordered [at variance with the divinely willed order], it should be entirely thrown away, or if it conforms to the proper order of things but is of less use, it should be buried with reverence."[24] These are strong words for a monk of any period, and Arnold's abbot sent him north to Magdeburg in order to prevent further animosity within the community. However, Arnold carried with him into exile a copy of the *passio* and while in Magdeburg convinced the provost Meginfred to rework it in accordance with Arnold's sense of what was ordered and useful. A few years later he returned in triumph with the new version.

But what, precisely, did the disorder or uselessness Arnold found in Arbeo's venerable text consist of? On first thought, one might imagine that it was its Latinity. As norms of Latin style changed, medieval authors frequently sought to bring older texts up to the standards of their own age. Literary taste mattered in medieval monasteries, and it mattered more than the patina of venerable antiquity. In the preface to his life of Saint Lambert, Bishop Stephen of Liège (from 901 to 920) explained that he had revised the earlier, eighth-century vita because, when the old text was read aloud on the saint's feast, its simple, unadorned Latin was met with derisive laughter by the listeners.[25] Bishop Stephen, therefore, undertook the task of reworking the text in a manner conforming to the literary tastes of the educated clergy of his day. The result is a text in an ornate, obscure style, replete with Greek words, complex rhythms, and other adornments of tenth-century fashion. About a century later Vitalis of Fleury reworked the life of Saint Paul of Orléans because "the old one was so tediously lengthy and because the Latin of its author was so wretched that reading it became an onerous burden."[26]

Arbeo's text shows similar aesthetic problems. As Bernhard Bischoff pointed out, Arbeo's Latin was quite likely strongly influenced by the vulgar Romance dialect spoken in the southern Tirol valley of the Etsch/Adige River.[27] Cases and conjugations bear little resemblance to classical norms; deponent and passive verbs appear in active forms; modifiers often assume cases of that which they modify; and the generous use of prepositions and the ignorance of the cases they govern announce the vernacular. His vocabulary is likewise far from the norms of Classical or even Carolingian Latinity. He favored obscure and rare terms culled from glossaries. Like poor German prose, his sentences are strongly substantive and participial but often lack a principal verb. Still, he tried for a sublime style by attempting complex periodic sentences, but often these periods are not followed through. Such writing would undoubtedly have profoundly troubled an educated person of the Carolingian or post-Carolingian period. All of these would have led Arnold and his contemporaries to pronounce Arbeo's text *inordinata*. However, if we compare the various versions of the *vita*, we see that more has taken place than Arnold suggested, and in fact the realities of the text's history before Arnold were quite other than he pretended. It is not at all clear that Arnold even had before him Arbeo's text but one revised and corrected at Regensburg in the ninth century. Rather, his objections were probably not primarily that the *passio* was *inordinata* but rather that it was of less utility. Again, utility was judged, as in his vision, in terms of his presentist understanding of his monastic community.[28]

Already in the ninth century copiers had begun to correct the most glaring barbarisms in Arbeo's text. Only one extant early manuscript retains the Latin of the eighth-century bishop of Freising (BN MS lat. 2990A). This manuscript, which was apparently copied at Saint-Amand in northwest France, may have reached Neustria through Archbishop Arn of Salzburg, who was also abbot of Saint-Amand until 821. Sometime in the ninth century, an anonymous editor, working almost certainly in Regensburg, went still further toward correcting the greater barbarisms in Arbeo's text as well as making some subtle changes in the text.[29]

One can see the kinds of changes made by these anonymous editors and revisers by comparing the original version's account of Emmeram's arrival in Regensburg with corrected manuscripts and the revised ninth-century version. Brackets indicate the first corrections of the text made in the early ninth century. The second text indicates the second, more systematic revision:

Arbeo's text:

Dum intentione huius sollicitudinis perfecisset iter, ut eorum postponeret partes, caepit Germaniam austri ingredere [ingredi], ad fluenta Danubii amnem [amnis] in partibus Baiuvariorum. Cuius dum sequeret [sequeretur] fluentis [fluentia] ad Radasponam pervenit urbem, qui [quae] ex sectis lapidibus constructa, in metropolim huius gentis in arce [arcem *om.* in] decreverat [creverat].

Second Revision:

Dumque hac intentione iter perageret, ut praedictarum provinciarum partes postponeret, coepit austri Germaniam ingredi, donec veniret ad amnis Danubii fluentia in partibus Bawariorum. Cuius dum fluentia sequeretur, ad Radasponam urbem pervenit, que sectis constructa lapidibus, in metropolim arcem huius gentis excreverat.

(While he was completing his journey according to his intention, in order to leave behind the regions of the above-mentioned provinces [of the Alemanni], he began to enter southern Germany to the flood of the Danube River in the region of the Bavarians. He followed its course until he came to the town of Regensburg that, built of cut stones, had grown into the fortified capital of this people.)

The corrections of the first ninth-century scribe or scribes were quite minor and stayed very close to the vocabulary and word order of Arbeo's text. They consist principally of the substitution of deponent forms for Arbeo's active forms (*ingredi* for *ingredere*; *sequeretur* for *sequeret*); the elimination of prepositions (*arcem* for *in arce*); and the correction of gender and cases (*quae* for *qui*, *amnis* for *amnem*) and minor vocabulary corrections (*creverat* for *decreverat*).

The second revision went considerably further than the earlier one, not only correcting grammar and syntax but reforming the phrases in order to clarify and simplify the text. In this particular passage, the changes are typical but minor: the reworking of the initial clauses, correction of verb forms (*coepit* for *caepit*, *excreverat* for *decreverat* or *creverat*.)

Elsewhere, however, the editor made small but important changes in not only the form but also the sense of the text. The most important is the explicit linkage of the killing of Emmeram to the fall of the Agilolfing family, to bring the life into conformity with Carolingian Bavarian policy. Arbeo had written that Lambert, the duke's son who had had Emmeram tortured and killed, had ended his life in the exile of his damnation and that the blood of Emmeram had been avenged in his children and his children's children, since "this race was exterminated, such that not one of them remains."[30] The ninth-century editor had taken the judgment against Lambert still further, explaining that, as a result of his crime, within a few years there remained not one of his vast offspring who deserved to receive from God the paternal kingdom.[31]

But if Arnold had before him the ninth-century revision of the *vita*, or even the earlier corrections, what was it about the text that seemed to him *inordinata*? Was it the grammar and syntax? These, as we have seen, had been corrected. We can get a hint of what Arnold felt was out of order by examining how Meginfred (who had presumably no other source for his version than the revised *vita* brought by Arnold to Magdeburg and Arnold's own account) described Emmeram's arrival in Regensburg. Meginfred's text is considerably shorter than the earlier versions and much less closely connected to Arbeo's original. Words and phrases found only in the second revision and repeated in Meginfred's text suggest that he worked from the most corrected version. The style is more in keeping with eleventh-century convention, employing periodic sentences and rhetorical elaboration. However, more than the form is changed.

In describing the arrival of Emmeram in Regensburg, Meginfred elaborated on the earlier account in a subtle manner to establish precisely the image of the city that Arnold, in ruminating on its past, was most concerned to present.

In this manner the faithful one, unafraid of this limit, came down to the Bavarian borders that stretch the boundaries of Germany south against the Alps, east to the Hungarians, and north to the Nordgau forest. There since he followed the command of the Danube's current he came to the city of Regensburg, which of old had been both in name and in dignity of its princes the head (or capital) of all Germany, and which is still the chief metropolis of the ancient leading family of this same people.[32]

In the original version, Regensburg is described as a city constructed of stone, which had grown into the "metropolim huius gentis" (that is, of the Bavarians). In Meginfred's text it is much more. Now Regensburg is remembered as "the capital of all Germany." Moreover, it is today the "eiusdem gentis metropolis antiquae prosapiae caput." Which *gens* does Arnold intend? Is it the Bavarians, or all the Germans? The proximity of *Germaniae* argues for the latter interpretation, which fits Arnold's claims that Regensburg enjoyed a special relationship with the kings of the East Franks. This interpretation also reflects his disdain for the old ducal family.

This was not the only sort of correction Arnold presumably induced Meginfred to make in the text. In the description of the punishment inflicted on Lambert and the Agilolfings, Meginfred (no doubt following information supplied him by Arnold) contradicts the earlier version. While the earlier versions describe the extinction of Lambert's *proginies*, Meginfred announces that all did not die out "within a few years," but rather that "within a few years, cut down by the sickle of premature death, their lives surrendered in agony, almost all were scattered for the innocent blood of the martyr."[33] Others, he stated, survive, "even until today," their miserable condition testifying to the continuing vengeance of Saint Emmeram. This suggestion of the survival of the Agilolfings into the eleventh century, contradicting the received tradition, clearly comes from Arnold since in his book of miracles he tells of a patron of the monastery of St. Emmeram *e stirpe Lantperti* who was struck with blindness when he attempted to enter the church.[34]

In both instances, the text commissioned by Arnold in the name of style subtly changes the content as well. Regensburg's dignity and importance ceases to be regional and becomes rather one for all of Germany. The Agilolfings, eliminated by divine vengeance in the revised account from which Meginfred worked, survive, but as a cursed race, a living symbol of divine wrath. Once more, one sees Meginfred at Arnold's behest, revising the evidence of the past, reworking and reinterpreting it in light of his present.

Arnold was not only interested in the past of his monastery and his city as presented in hagiography. As provost, Arnold was keeper of the most vital portion of his community's memory—its archives. We have seen that Regensburg, like other Bavarian institutions, had a rich collection of cartularies and *Traditionsbücher* reaching back to the ninth century. These recorded the fundamental relationships between the lay society and the community solidified by exchanges of land. We have also seen that in 975 Bishop Wolfgang separated the monastery from the cathedral and established Ramwold (975–1001), whom he had invited from Trier and made provost, as first independent abbot. A new and carefully prepared *Traditionsbuch* was begun in his abbacy, periodically recording transactions involving property that was the exclusive possession of the monastery. The calm of the monastery was broken by Bishop Gebhard I (995–1023), who strove to reestablish control of St. Emmeram, beginning a long period of friction between monks on the one hand and bishops, canons, and their lay supporters on the other. During this time, traditions are noted in a much more frequent but haphazard manner by a variety of scribes. Only in the middle of the twelfth century did regular record keeping again appear.

Thus at the time that Arnold was responsible for the monastic property, periodic, summary entries in *Traditionsbücher* had given way to sporadic, ad hoc notices destined to protect the monastery's claims against episcopal pretensions that questioned the material, physical, and jurisdictional continuity of the institution. The separation of cathedral and monastery and subsequent disputes had disrupted both the historical identity of the monastic community and the system by which this community remembered and thus defended its property. Such disruptions were particularly important to a writer who, as provost, was responsible for the collection of dues from *censuales* and the supervision of monastic property. Part of his efforts to recover this continuity are reflected in the Urbar or monastic estate inventory prepared under the direction of Abbot Burchard and Arnold in 1031[35] and Arnold's uses of the monastic archives with which he was intimately familiar.

Reading the *De miraculis* gives us an insight into the organization of St. Emmeram's archives and the manner in which they were used to restructure the community's memory. The collection was divided into royal and ducal privileges on the one hand and private acts on the other. He talks first about royal and ducal donations: "With what honor and reverence, with what affection the princes venerated blessed Emmeram is shown among other things by the lands by the valuable gifts given him by them."[36] These include a donation by Charlemagne of property adjacent to the monastery, donations by Louis the Pious, and the donation of Mondsee by Louis the German.[37] He also recalls unspecified donations from dukes of Bavaria before the Carolingian absorption: "The property that the dukes who ruled the duchy of Bavaria under the kings of the Franks before this prince [Charlemagne] gave to blessed Emmeram are well shown by their parchments and testaments found in our possession."[38]

The original of the Charlemagne diploma was preserved at St. Emmeram, but no originals or copies of genuine diplomas of Louis the Pious for St. Emmeram exist. The only extant copy of a diploma of Louis's is a forgery based on a later diploma of his son Louis the German found in a collection of charters and traditions from the second half of the eleventh century.[39] Eight genuine diplomas of Louis the German for St. Emmeram are extant but that which purports to be a donation of Mondsee is a forgery of the eleventh century.[40] However, Arnold seems to have relied for his information not on this forgery (which may have been made after his lifetime) but on a tradition notice that Anamot had recorded in his *Traditionsbuch*.[41] Rather than assuming that Arnold either used or had a part in the creation of these forgeries, one might imagine that his text gave the impetus to create the documents he seems to cite. Arnold's work was the reproduction of a narrow, skeletal history of his institution that his successors would flesh out, producing when necessary documents whose existence was at most only hinted at by Arnold.

His fondest memories were, however, of Arnulf of Carinthia, the illegitimate son of Carloman, whose donations, like those of the other kings and emperors, were preserved in Arnulf's time in originals and only copied (along with more recent forgeries) in the later eleventh century. Arnold considered him the ruler most devoted to St. Emmeram and recounts his career, first as duke, then king, and then emperor.[42] All the stages of his career appear in the St. Emmeram archives, which preserved three of his diplomas, two as king and one as emperor.[43] In addition, he appears in the *Traditionsbuch* of Anamot, first as son of Carloman,[44] then as duke of Bavaria,[45] and finally as king of the Franks.[46] As emperor he is remembered at Regensburg in his diploma of 898.[47]

However, while Arnulf's diplomas and the tradition notices mentioning him could assist the provost in establishing the stages of his career, they do not actually establish his particular devotion to Regensburg and its patron. The only diploma that does this explicitly is a forgery devised by Otloh, possibly on the model established by Arnold.[48] The diploma speaks of Arnulf's "love and honor of our patron and the most precious martyr of God Emmeram,"[49] echoing Arnold's claim that Arnulf "chose blessed Emmeram the patron of his life and for his kingdom."[50] The genuine diplomas are merely exchanges[51] and restorations of confiscated property.[52] Thus Arnold and later Otloh, while using the archives of their institution, see them as general guides but not the limiting and defining sources of their vision of the past. They do not draw on them for its essence.

The most important donations of Arnulf that, in Arnold's mind, proved the king's particular devotion to St. Emmeram were not lands but rather the gifts of movables to the church that Arnold describes in detail. The most important of these were the *codex aureus*, a magnificent Gospel book prepared for the coronation of Charles the Bald, and the portable ciborium of Arnulf of Carinthia.[53] Alois Schmid has suggested that these were not gifts of Arnulf at all, but rather remained in Regensburg after the death of his son Louis the Child.[54] Arnold explained within a miracle account how in the year 918 Conrad I claimed them and tried to take possession of these treasures.[55] Arnold suggests that Conrad had come to pray at the tombs of Emmeram (Arnulf, and Louis thus, in a sense, to see in the *civitas regia* a source of legitimacy). On the advice of his chaplain, who tells him "that by royal right and in as much as it was in the power of his antecessors, he should claim aforesaid book of great value,"[56] Conrad does so, but the bishop of Regensburg places the precious book on the altar and announces that whoever takes it would be in the debt of St. Emmeram on the day of judgment. The king soon develops dysentery, which he interprets as punishment for the alienation. Seeking forgiveness he returns the book but fails to recover and goes back to Francia where he dies soon after. Schmid suggested that Conrad's claim actually resulted from the circumstance that there had never been a formal donation to the monastery. In any case, the existence of the portable ciborium, books, precious objects, and cloths, and not records of royal favor, was the foundation for Arnold's image of Arnulf's dedication to the monastery. Here the traditions were physical, not written.

Arnold discussed private *traditiones* in even greater detail. He saw three central kinds of private donations: *censuales*, servants, and land. These other types of donations, private ones, are clearly described later in his text. "Those who come with humility and trembling are received and are not admitted in vain."[57] He described the types of donations made by "noble men of noble family and a time well known to us whose names we pass over in silence."[58] These included those who, "placing their heads and their hands reverently on the altar, professed themselves to be the perpetual *censuales* of the martyr."[59] The second category of donors are those who "hand over male and female servants so that they might find thanks in the sight of so great a patron."[60] Examples of these are numerous throughout the *Traditionsbücher*. Finally, "others hand over allodial property so that it will no longer belong to them."[61]

All of these types of alienations are abundantly documented in the archives. But what was equally visible to Arnold were the alienations invisible in the texts. He explained that one person deposits on the altar over three years of weakness, another over two years of illness, still others because of possession by evil spirits. His image of donations, of what is left on the altar, is thus only partially reflected in the *Traditionsbuch*. The other equally important type of "donation"—the illnesses, cares, and worries from which donors are freed—were no doubt just as real but rarely appear in the notices.

Arnold presented two examples from his family of how such donations might come about. Following these examples allows us to see both how actual transactions took place and how Arnold used oral and archival traditions to reconstruct and transform such transactions. The first describes a dispute with Adalrammus, who claimed a portion of land that his *nepos* had given "sub testibus in hereditatem" to the saint. "Sub testibus" seems to be the key, as it is in the *Traditionsbücher*. The wording of the donation is not as important in the record as the witnesses, whose presence, not the document itself, makes the donation valid. Adalrammus repossessed the property and was struck with illness. Lingering, and unable either to die or recover, Adalrammus sends his wife (Arnold's niece, or kinswoman) and his son to return the property. They arrive on the vigil of the saint's feast. The next morning Arnold makes the arrangements. She goes to the altar of St. Emmeram and first pays the census of her son to the saint. Then, "drawn by the hands according to the Bavarian custom, she returned the *predia* in the presence of witnesses as it had previously been given."[62] The ceremony itself took place on the feast of the saint. She paid the census for her son (apparently they were already *censuales* of Saint Emmeram, unless she was now dedicating him to the saint for the first time), as in the first type of donation Arnold described. Then, before witnesses, she went through the formal gesture by which the redonation was made before the saint's altar.

Because Arnold does not supply the names of his relatives, we cannot be sure that this donation was entered in the extant *Traditionsbücher*. The notice of the second donation that Arnold described in detail does exist. This is a donation by Arnold's maternal grandfather. Arnold indicates that the events took place during the episcopacy of Michael (ca. 980), about which he had heard from "very prudent elders who have memory of this time." His maternal grandfather, Margrave Berthold, was engaged in a long conflict with St. Emmeram. At one point the conflict was to be ended by the swearing of an oath by twelve nobles, including Arnold's own paternal grandfather, on the staff of St. Emmeram, a relic preserved in the monastery. The twelve swear a false oath and all are struck down. His grandfather Arnold is immediately paralyzed in his right arm and drowns shortly after. The others meet similar fates. Terrified, Berthold donates a piece of property at Isling to the saint, specifying that it is to be used to provide twelve special meals and drinks for the monks and charity for twelve paupers.[63]

The transaction is recorded in two notices, one of five such double records in the St. Emmeram *Traditionsbuch*.[64] Both were possibly expansions from an original, very brief notice, expansions that relied more on the memory and rhetorical standards of the two scribes than on the content of the original except for the donation itself, the names of the principals, and the list of witnesses. Thus in version *a* Berthold is described as "Orientali Frantia comes"; in *b* as "marchio comes." In *b* the circumstances that gave rise to the donation are not mentioned, while version *a* indicates that the donation took place as Berthold lay gravely ill and dying. Both versions record that Berthold's wife Helicsuinda transmitted to his vassal Arpo property at Isling as well as four serfs, all of which Arpo, "with the hand of Helicsuinda and of her son Heinric," then transmitted to St. Emmeram. In *b* no particular purpose is given for the donation. In *a* the donation is made "for the assistance of the monks here serving God and so that paupers and pilgrims may be consoled and rested with food and clothing."[65]

Thus it would appear that the notices, particularly *a*, expanded on what may have been a very brief record of the transaction, relying on an oral tradition about the circumstances and the identity of the donor. In a similar way, Arnold's account continued to expand on the transaction, particularly that in version *a*. However, although he claims to be relying on oral tradition, Arnold is actually expanding the transaction in terms of a religious and theological elaboration more connected with his understanding of St. Emmeram, the importance of the twelve oath helpers, and the twelve monks and poor than with the history of his family. Thus he takes considerable liberties with both the written notice and the oral tradition, recasting both in terms of a symbolic and exemplary account that glorifies St. Emmeram. First, his grandmother Helicsuinda disappears entirely. The offense and the recompense involves only men. Second, just as Emmeram had punished the irreligiosity of the twelve through twelve miracles, the donation repeats the apostolic number in its largess. Regardless of his access to tradition notices and the testimony of "seniores," the meaning of the past is found not in them but in the typological schema imposed by his religious understanding. The hostility of Arnold's ancestors is also less a memory of the past than a reflection of the present, strained relationship between St. Emmeram and local powers. As we have seen, in his own lifetime Adalrammus, his kinswoman's husband, had attempted to recover property donated to the monastery and had paid for the effort with his agonizing death. By contrast, Berthold had apparently been, despite Arnold's characterization of him, a favored patron of the monastery.

This close relationship is clear from Berthold's inclusion in the monastery's necrology, in which he has an honored place.[66] This necrology was compiled in 1045, specifically for the monastic community of St. Emmeram.[67] It contains the names of deceased members of the monastery since its separation from the cathedral chapter in 975 as well as the names of members of monasteries with which St. Emmeram had agreements of confraternity—bishops of Regensburg, and lay and ecclesiastical dignitaries. The selection of these names from earlier, now lost necrologies, was not indiscriminate. Instead, as Eckhard Freise has shown, the selection and position of these names, and in particular those of Regensburg bishops and lay patrons, was done with great attention to their relationship with the monastery.[68] Berthold's appearance in the necrology is thus a clear indication of the continuing respect his memory was accorded.

The respect was apparently mutual. That Arnold's family placed him in the monastery as a novice speaks for positive rather than conflictual relationships between his kin and the institution. Once more, the created past is the product of a present. Arnold may thus have transferred the hostile relationships between local aristocrats and St. Emmeram of his own time onto those between his ancestors and his institution.

In the examples Arnold drew from his institutions' diplomas and *Traditionsbücher* to mold his account of the past. We can thus see a continuing re-forming and reinterpreting of this material. *Collecticius* though he may have been, he does more than simply collect. His *persona* is only part of the story. The other part is a very utilitarian attitude toward the past, one that must not be forgotten. Tradition notices, like other sources, are but the raw material from which he created a past, one less in conformity with his sources than with his present. Arnold's remembering was an active process not simply of storage and retrieval but of selection and interpretation. Whether looking at the Pannonian horizon or at the archives of his institution, Arnold saw more than we would have seen, and he remembered that which he saw differently from us. In the Pannonian sky he saw a dragon, perhaps announcing the end of the world, which he later remembered as a natural phenomenon, the "Greatest of all Serpents," according to Isidore. In the dry archival notices of his archive he saw the power of his patron acting to crush the pride of a hostile and threatening world. We see no movement from oral to written tradition or from individual to collective memory, but rather an interplay of oral and written, individual and collective, constantly being re-formed to the needs of the present. To understand Arnold's memory of his grandfather, or to understand his memory of his dragon, we must understand the double process of memory systems—*Traditionsnotizen*, necrological entries, personal recollections, on the one hand; and the logical, theological, and circumstantial contexts within which these transmissions were re-formed and reinterpreted. Only then can we understand not simply what Arnold and his contemporaries preserved but also what they forgot, what was "entirely thrown away," and what was "buried with reverence."

VII

CONCLUSIONS

Vergangen nicht, Verwandelt ist was war
(Rilke, *Gedichtkreis für Madeleine Broglie*)

THIS STUDY BEGAN with the premise that what we think we know about the early Middle Ages is largely determined by what people of the early eleventh century wished themselves and their contemporaries to know about the past. Thus I have attempted to recover some of the circumstances in which these people went about re-remembering their past in relationship to their own present. This process, which involved creating new systems and structures, both social and textual, within which the past was preserved, necessarily changed the very nature of what would be preserved through elimination, elaboration, and reinterpretation.

For the most part, this process took place for very local and specific reasons and often followed regional forms—although from region to region across Europe striking similarities can be detected. Moreover, if the process was local and ad hoc, the effects were broad and long-lasting. The filter of the eleventh century determined in a fundamental way the access that all future generations would have to alternative pasts.

Men and women dealt with the dilemma constituted by the obligation to remember and the frailty of human memory by developing new techniques for sorting and preserving the past. Aristocratic families, splintered by the disintegration of the Carolingian world, entrusted the preservation of their dead to memory specialists, both women within the kindred and monks without. The latter especially preserved the *memoria* of their patrons, but in ways that emphasized those who were directly connected to the concerns of the religious communities themselves. Institutions sorted, pruned, and reorganized their archives with an eye toward making the record of these donations and privileges tell a story, not simply in order to facilitate access to individual documents for narrow legal or administrative needs. Chroniclers in turn exploited these quasi-narrative collections as well as liturgical materials and physical relics of the past in order to fit the past into what they recognized as an appropriate, typological reflection of the divine order in human activities. Throughout all these processes, the raw material of the past was transformed in ways similar to those described by Frederic Bartlett: to the extent that the past could be made to conform to the present, it was retained. Persons, events, and traditions that eluded contemporary systems of understanding and perceiving were quickly lost or transformed. These transformations, whether of kings and princes, or of dragons and grandfathers, owed more to superimposed interpretative schemas than to the raw materials by which eleventh-century people encountered them.

If this study contributes anything to the debate over the "mutation" of the year one thousand, it is that perhaps the most profound transformation of this period was in the nature of the written record, a transformation that relates to changes in self and group perception. Changes in social and political traditions there certainly were, but these had begun in the late ninth century across Europe and had been under way for more than a century. What changed in the generation around the millennium was a belief that things were indeed different, that the received past no longer coincided with the present.

Nevertheless, throughout the cases we have examined, this process of creative memory has owed less to overarching political or ideological programs or to subconscious processes such as the transition from an oral to a literate society than to particular, and to us seemingly trivial, circumstances of the moment. These losses, creations, and transformations were thus broadly political, in the sense that they resulted from decisions made in terms of contemporary needs within the contest for status, power, and privilege of the eleventh century. There is little evidence that the guardians of memory around the first millennium even perceived the wider implications of the fundamental work they had set in motion. In this parochialism, they differed greatly from their immediate successors in subsequent generations, and it is this parochialism that has largely led to their neglect by modern historians.

St. Emmeram of Regensburg in the eleventh century is known in German historiography not for Arnold, whose hagiographical, liturgical, and administrative efforts are largely forgotten, but primarily as the monastery of his younger brother-monk Otloh (ca. 1010–post-1070), one of the most creative and extraordinary authors of the eleventh century. His autobiography (often seen as the first since St. Augustine), his hagiographic production, his book of visions, and his work as diplomatic and hagiographic forger (culminating in his account of the theft of the relics of St. Denis from Paris to his monastery) are extraordinary texts that, were they better known in French and English historical circles, would force considerable redefinition of the age preceding the so-called twelfth-century renaissance.[1]

But as extraordinary as he undoubtedly was, Otloh's career and writings have eclipsed unnecessarily those of the slightly older provost Arnold. Although his extant writings are much less extensive than those of Otloh, they announce already much that the younger monk would develop: an autobiographical focus in his writing, his vivid reports of visions, his concern with the renown of his institution, and the freedom which he, like Otloh, displayed in dealing with its past. Reading Arnold's *Vita S. Emmerammi*, it is hard not to see this text as the foundation for Otloh's works, both in what it says and in what it fails to say about Regensburg and its past.

And yet Arnold is no Otloh. He belongs to a generation only beginning to meditate on the meaning of the monastery's past as he was able to perceive it through the objects, places, and texts that survived to his day, and on its place in the long sweep of Bavarian-Germanic history from the eighth to the eleventh centuries. But this interest has a double effect. At the same time that he was concerned to preserve and interpret the fragments of the past, he was also prepared to make a selection, preserving some, eliminating others. In his own metaphor, he is the pioneer, participating in the expansion of the arable, cutting down the forest of useless or disordered past. In this carefully cultivated clearing, Arnold's successors such as Otloh would build the edifice of a monastic memory conforming to the needs of a new age.

In the same way that St. Emmeram is known for Otloh and not Arnold, St. Denis is known for the twelfth-century historiographical tradition that would give rise to Suger's *Vita Ludovici Grossi Regis* and the *Grandes Chroniques*, not for the anonymous calligrapher who furnished the abbey with new Merovingian papyri. And yet this monk and his confederates, faced with the necessity of protecting their institution against episcopal authority and ruminating on the richness of their archive, determined what raw materials these later historians would have with which to erect the new edifice of French history.

This new edifice had many facades. The ones most familiar to many are the series of attempts to assign a global meaning to the past (collectively designated as the Gregorian Reform) or the historical propaganda efforts on behalf of the rising Capetian dynasty. None of our archivists, liturgists, chroniclers, hagiographers, or forgers was directly involved in either of these movements. What they did rather was to establish the parameters within which such global readings of the past could be established.

We have seen some of the ways that Arnold and his generation did this. They determined who would be responsible for remembering—increasingly, both in the West and in the East, Benedictine monks. They determined how the past was to be recalled: in function of names and land, both of which were entrusted to religious professionals. They systematically abstracted these names from the social and political contexts within which they had been embedded and placed them in new ones. These contexts were heavily influenced by liturgy, by local geography, and by a schematization that saw pasts as discrete moments represented by archetypical figures of good or evil.

This process was entirely presentist and ruthlessly efficient. The past could be useful either as a model for the present or as justification for the future. The obligation of perpetual memorialization took second place to the utilitarian model. As new cartularies were created, old charters were destroyed; as new necrologies were produced, older ones were not copied in their entirety. As chroniclers reflected on the kings and princes of their day, that material considered to be *inordinata* was either transformed or omitted. Hugo, the Carolingian, was replaced by Charlemagne; Charles III the Simple, when he was not assimilated to his predecessors Charlemagne and Charles the Bald, was abandoned as an exemplar of a victim of betrayal to the later Charles of Lorraine; Arnulf, the savior of Bavaria, became either Arnulf the Bad, who, like Charles Martel before him, served the ends of monastic reformers or was elided with Arnulf of Carinthia, thus losing his individuality to a distant but homonymous ruler.

Arnold and his contemporaries attempted to bury much of the past with reverence, and they were largely successful. They so thoroughly shattered the image of the past that the next generations of reformers, forgers, polemicists, and dynasts could pick up the remaining fragments and use them to create a new image, one that was bolder, more universal, and more elaborate than that of the generation of the millennium, but entirely dependent on it for the selection of their materials.

And yet not all the past would stay buried. Like the ghosts in Thietmar of Merseburg and the *Chronicon Novaliciense*, bits of the buried past refused to stay buried. Texts, names, traditions, inscriptions, and objects continued to haunt the landscape of the eleventh and twelfth centuries, wraiths of earlier ages that fit uneasily into the constructed pasts of our memory specialists. The very attempts to reassimilate them, to place them in a proper schema, betray the vague and occasionally threatening if unexpressed fear that in remembering the past, Augustine's "vast courts" and "boundless chambers" of memory held less than perhaps they should.

Who, then, are the phantoms of remembrance? Are they Hugh of Arles and Petronilla, Ambricho of Regensburg and Charles of Lorraine, Flavius of Novalesa and the nameless specters seen in the churchyards at Walsleben and Magdeburg, whose lives and deaths, once preserved in the oral traditions of their families and the prayers of their religious communities, gradually disappeared or merged with those of similar names or similar deeds? Or are the phantoms Gottschalk of Bene-

diktbeuern, Arnold of Regensburg, and the anonymous chroniclers, archivists, and forgers of Novalesa and St. Denis whose pioneering work in
the early years of this millennium set the parameters for all subsequent
interpretations of the past, interpretations that rarely credit them or
even recognize their existence? Or perhaps the phantoms of remembrance are actually Jacques Le Goff, Mary Carruthers, Chris Wickham,
Otto Gerhard Oexle, Patrick Geary, and other modern historians intent
on creating our own versions of the past and hoping that our creation
will be so successful in selecting, suppressing, and manipulating our data
that the evidence of our subjective intervention, like that of our eleventh-century predecessors, will vanish before the eyes of our audience,
present and future.

NOTES

ACKNOWLEDGMENTS

1. Friedrich-Wilhelm Westerhoff, *Gruppensuche. Ein Verfahren zur Identifizierung von Personengruppen in mittelalterlichen Namen-Quellen. Beschreibung des Verfahrens und der Programme.* Rechenzentrum Universität Münster. Schriftenreihe 61 (December, 1988).

INTRODUCTION

1. Andrew Lewis, *Royal Succession*, 22–26.

2. Rodulfus Glaber, *Historiarum libri quinque* (ed. and trans. France) 164–67. See Platelle, "Le problème du scandale," *Revue belge de philologie et d'histoire* 53 (1975): 1071–96; Andrew Lewis, *Royal Succession*, 22–26; Pfister, *Etudes sur le règne de Robert le Pieux*, 60–69.

3. Neithard Bulst, "Rodulfus Glabers *Vita domni Willelmi abbatis*," 450–87, esp. 482; reprinted and translated by John France in Rodulfus Glaber, *Historiarum libri quinque* (ed. France), 254–99, esp. 290–91.

4. On the weakness of Rodulfus as a reliable witness for positivistic history and on the political context of condemnations of the queen, see Bautier, "L'hérésie d'Orléans," in *Actes du 95e congrès national des sociétés savantes*, 63–88, esp. 66–67.

5. Pfister, *Etudes sur le règne de Robert le Pieux*, 60–69, and most recently Andrew Lewis, *Royal Succession*, 22.

6. See John France's questioning in Rodulfus Glaber, *Historiarum libri quinque*, xxvii. France is skeptical because the context for the criticism in the sermon is the consecration of the church of St. Benigne while that in the *Historia* is the entourage of Constance. However, as we shall see, the two are closely related.

7. See Bulst, *Untersuchungen zu den Klosterreformen Wilhelms von Dijon (962–1013)*, 78–80; and Carolyn Marino-Malone, "Les fouilles de Saint-Bénigne de Dijon (1976–1978)," *Bulletin monumental* 138 (1980): 253–91.

8. On the family of William of Volpiano see Bulst, *Untersuchungen*, esp. 39 and 97.

9. Rodulfus Glaber is finally receiving the attention that his work merits. See Ortigues and Iogna-Prat, "Raoul Glaber et l'historiographie clunisienne," *Studi Medievali*, 3d ser., 26 (1985): 537–72; and Iogna-Prat, "Continence et virginité dans la conception clunisienne de l'ordre du monde autour de l'an mil," *Académie des inscriptions et belles-lettres, comptes rendus* (1985): 127–46.

10. On Fulk's family, see Werner, "Untersuchungen zur Frühzeit des französischen Fürstentums (9.-10. Jahrhundert)," *Die Welt als Geschichte* 18 (1958): 256–89; 19 (1959): 146–93; and 20 (1960): 87–119 (but esp. vol. 18, 264–79); Guillot, *Le Comte d'Anjou et son entourage au XIe siècle*; and most recently the studies by Bachrach, "The Angevin Strategy of Castle Building in

the Reign of Fulk Nerra, 987–1040," *American Historical Review* 88 (1983): 533–60; "The Idea of the Angevin Empire," *Albion* 10 (1978): 293–99; "A Study in Feudal Politics," *Viator* 7 (1976): 111–22; and "Toward a Reappraisal of William the Great, Duke of Aquitaine, 995–1030," *Journal of Medieval History* 5 (1979): 11–21. On the importance of Constance's ties to Anjou, see Andrew Lewis, *Royal Succession*, 23–24.

11. Poly, in *La Provence*, 33, suggests that Boso was from Septimania. However, the hypothesis of G. de Manteyer, in *La Provence du première au douzième siècle* 1:208–21, that he was from the Viennois or Burgundy, is perhaps equally defensible (as we shall see in chapter 5).

12. See Geary, "Ethnic Identity as a Situational Construct," 15–26, reprinted in *Folk Life in the Middle Ages*, ed. Edward Peters, *Medieval Perspectives* 3 (1988) [1991]: 1–17.

13. Bulst, *Untersuchungen*, 22–23. On such northern aristocratic families in Italy see Hlawitschka, *Franken, Alemannen, Bayern und Burgunder*, who nevertheless does not include William's grandfather Vibo or his father Robert, presumably because, although Bulst assumes that Robert held the title of count, he is never so described in contemporary sources.

14. On Cluny in the tenth century, see most recently Rosenwein, *Rhinoceros Bound: Cluny in the Tenth Century*, and Poeck, "Laienbegräbnisse in Cluny," *Frühmittelalterliche Studien* 15 (1981): 68–179.

15. This theme has been treated most recently by Duby, *Les trois ordres ou l'imaginaire du féodalisme*.

16. In particular see Hlawitschka, *Franken, Alemannen, Bayern und Burgunder* and, on the continuing connections between the Piedmont and the North, Sergi, *Potere e territorio*, esp. Part I, "Alle origini dei poteri regionali di strada nel medioevo," 19–69.

17. For an exemplary model of how categories of perception influence the possibilities of writing history in the eleventh century see Vollrath, "Konfliktwahrnehmung und Konfliktdarstellung in erzählenden Quellen des 11. Jahrhunderts," in *Die Salier und das Reich*, ed. Weinfurter, 3:279–96.

18. "Non solum novis vetera licet mutare, sed etiam, si sint inordinata, penitus abjicere, sin vero ordinaria sed minus utilia, eum veneratione sepelire" (PL 141:992). MGH SS IV, 547, which reproduces only a portion of Arnold's text, correctly reads "inordinata" (the PL erroneously reads "ordinata").

19. Pocock, "The Origins of the Study of the Past," *Comparative Studies in Society and History* 4 (1962): 217. This insight is developed for the northern French aristocracy of the early thirteenth century by Spiegel in her *Romancing the Past*, esp. 111–13.

20. The importance of the past on ecclesiastical reform is the theme of Ladner's classic, *The Idea of Reform*. The Gregorian reform of the eleventh century can in a sense be interpreted as the greatest example of an invented (or perhaps even forged) past in Western history. On one aspect of the elaborate series of forgeries—not only of individual documents but of the past itself—on which the Investiture controversy was based, see Goetz, "Fälschung und Verfälschung der Vergangenheit," in *Fälschungen im Mittelalter* 1:165–88.

21. On the distinction, expressed at the end of the eleventh century by Gervase of Canterbury, see Clanchy, *From Memory to Written Record*, 147.

22. The bibliography on medieval historiography is enormous. In addition to the specialized studies of individual historians, one should cite in particular Guenée, *Histoire et culture historique*, and Davis and Wallace-Hadrill, eds., *The Writing of History in the Middle Ages*.

23. See especially Yates, *The Art of Memory*, 2–26, and most recently Carruthers, *The Book of Memory*, and Coleman, *Ancient and Medieval Memories*.

24. The outstanding example of this approach to memory is Clanchy's *From Memory to Written Record*, although for reasons presented below the evolutionary model Clanchy presents for the eleventh to the fourteenth centuries is not particularly useful to understanding the working of memory in the tenth and eleventh centuries.

25. Halbwachs, *Mémoires collectives* (in English: *The Collective Memory*, trans. F. L. Ditter, Jr., and V. Y. Ditter, with an introduction by Mary Douglas). More satisfactory than Halbwachs' formulation of the theory of collective memory are his actual studies of memory and its relationship to society, especially *Les cadres sociaux de la Mémoire* and his extraordinary *La topographie légendaire des évangiles en terre sainte*.

26. On the background to Halbwachs' role in the sociology of memory, which (along with Aby Warburg's theory of cultural memory elaborated at the same time) was a rejection of attempts to elaborate a biological theory of "racial memory," see Assmann, "Kollektives Gedächtnis und kulturelle Identität," in *Kultur und Gedächtnis*, ed. Assmann and Hölscher, 9–19.

27. For an excellent summary of Halbwachs' thesis and an insightful critique, see Baker, "Memory and Practice," *Representations* 11 (1985): 134–64, esp. 156–58.

28. Thelen, "Memory and American History," *Journal of American History* 75, no. 4 (1989): 1117–29.

29. Ibid., 1118.

30. See especially Nora's article, "Mémoire collective," in *La Nouvelle Histoire*, ed. Le Goff, Chartier, and Revel, 398–401, as well as the important series he is editing, *Les lieux de mémoire* (vol. 1, *La République*; vol. 2, *La Nation*; vol. 3, *Les France*).

31. Letaldus of Micy, "Revocabantque nostrae memoriae inter multa hoc quod dicturi sumus miraculum." *Miracula S. Maximini*, in *Acta Sanctorum Ordinis Sancti Benedicti* 1:610. Cited and discussed by Thomas Head in *Hagiography and the Cult of Saints: The Diocese of Orleans, 800–1200* (Cambridge, 1990), 74.

32. Baker, "Memory and Practice," 156.

33. An example is the apparent suppression of negative wartime memories in the village of Minot studied by Zonabend in *The Enduring Memory*, 196–97. One of the finest studies of the radical limitation and fragmentation of oral memory under the influence of social structures is Dakhlia, *L'oublie de la cité*.

34. Nora "Mémoire collective," 399.

35. Fentress and Wickham, *Social Memory*.

36. Ibid., 26.

37. This is especially elaborated in Goody's work, including *The Domestication of the Savage Mind*, *The Logic of Writing and the Organization of Society*, *Literacy in Traditional Societies*, *The Interface Between the Written and the Oral*; and Goody and Watt, "The Consequences of Literacy," *Comparative Studies in Society and History* 5 (1963): 304–45. Goody was in turn influenced by the work of Eric A. Havelock on orality in Ancient Greece. See particularly Havelock's *The Literate Revolution in Greece and Its Cultural Consequences*.

38. Clanchy, *From Memory to Written Record*.

39. Ibid., 12.

40. Ibid., 18.

41. Ibid., 21.

42. Stock, *The Implications of Literacy*.

43. Ibid., 16.

44. Ibid., 526.

45. Although even this is by no means certain. See the penetrating critiques of of the Goody and Havelock traditions in Street, *Literacy in Theory and Practice*.

46. See Eric John's summary of the problem in Campbell, ed., *The Anglo-Saxons*, 238–39.

47. See especially Rosamond McKitterick, *The Carolingians and the Written Word*, for the eighth- and ninth-century evidence. McKitterick may overestimate the extent to which laymen and women, particularly in Germanic-speaking regions, were fully integrated into a literate culture. However, her evidence does support the contention that writing, even if largely controlled by a clerical elite, permeated every level of society. Moreover, the Carolingian uses of the written word, which continued in spite of the decline of local schools, municipal curias, and other late antique traditions, was certainly significantly less than had been the norm in the sixth and seventh centuries.

48. See most recently the essays edited by McKitterick in *The Uses of Literacy in Early Mediaeval Europe*.

49. See Fentress and Wickham, *Social Memory*, 96–98, drawing on the work of Finnegan, *Literacy and Orality*, and Tonkin, *Narrating Our Pasts*.

50. One might say the same about the later periods they study as well. The "textual community" may appear to favor the text over the oral tradition, but the interpretation remains external to the text—in essence, an oral tradition, even if it expresses itself in a rhetorical mode that implies that it is privileging the text.

51. Carruthers, *The Book of Memory*, 11.

52. Le Goff, *Histoire et mémoire*, esp. 130–48.

53. "Quoniam ualde labilis est humana memoria." See the discussions of this medieval commonplace in Le Goff, *Histoire et mémoire*, 140, where he rightly sees it as evidence of the equilibrium between written and oral in medieval society, and in Fentress and Wickham, *Social Memory*, 8–10.

54. For a brief summary of remembrance in Plato see Coleman, *Ancient and Medieval Memories*, 5–14, and Taylor, *Plato: The Man and His Work*, 136–63 and 186–89. The significance of orality for Plato and the problems of mimesis

and social memory in Plato are studied in Havelock's classic *Preface to Plato*. For the classic neo-Platonic position see Plotinus, *Enneads* 4.6, and Coleman, *Ancient and Medieval Memories*, 63–79.

55. The essential formulations are *Ad C. Herennium libri IV* and Quintilian's *Institutio oratoria* 11.11. See Yates, *The Art of Memory*, 2–26, and Carruthers, *The Book of Memory*.

56. "Magna ista vis est memoriae, magna nimis, Deus meus, penetrale amplum et infinitum. Quis ad fundum eius pervenit?" Augustine *Confessiones* (ed. Luc Verheijen) 10.8.15.

57. On memory in Augustine, see Yates, *The Art of Memory*, 46–49; Coleman, *Ancient and Medieval Memories*, 80–111; and Söhngen, "Der Aufbau der augustinischen Gedächtnislehre: Augustine *Confessiones* X.c.6–27," in *Die Einheit in der Theologie*, ed. Söhngen, 63–100; and Pelikan, *The Mystery of Continuity*, esp. 19–27.

58. Augustine *Confessiones* 10.11.18; Augustine *De Trinitate* (ed. Mountain) 14.10.440; Pelikan, *The Mystery of Continuity*, 20.

59. Augustine *Confessiones* 1.6; Pelikan, *The Mystery of Continuity*, 22.

60. Carruthers, *The Book of Memory*, 146, doubts that Augustine practiced an art of memory in spite of his descriptions of the spatial characteristics of memory, arguing that such descriptions are "archetypal." While one need not believe that Augustine was a "philosopher of memory" in the technical sense of *ars memoriae*, it is difficult to imagine a rhetorician of his stature using such descriptions coincidentally. He, even more than Carruthers' thirteenth- and fourteenth-century mendicant preachers, was trained in the tradition of classical rhetoric, even if he was not a practitioner of the narrow sort of memory tricks proposed by the *Rhetorica ad Herennium*.

61. Augustine *Confessiones* 10.8.

62. *Confessiones* 10.9.

63. *Confessiones* 10.11.

64. *Confessiones* 10.15. For a summary of these types of consciousness, see Söhngen, "Der Aufbau der augustinischen Gedächtnislehre," 89.

65. "sive per imagines, sicut omnium corporum, sive per praesentiam, sicut artium, sive per nescio quas notiones vel notationes, sicut affectionum animi." *Confessiones* 10.17.

66. Augustine *De Trinitate* 14.12.442–43.

67. *De Trinitate* 15.21.517–18.

68. Ladner, *The Idea of Reform*, 202.

69. "Habet igitur anima in sua natura, ut diximus, imaginem sanctae Trinitatis in eo quod intelligentiam, voluntatem, et memoriam habet. . . . Intelligo me intelligere, velle et meminisse; et volo me intelligere et meminisse et velle; et memini me intelligere et velle et meminisse." PL 101:641–42. In the eleventh century, this tradition is reformulated by Anselm, *Monologium* 48.

70. "Quandoquidem homo habet Trinitatem in semetipso, necesse est ut creatura subdita sit Creatori, cuius nihil praeponendum est amori. . . . Quamobrem intime corde tenusve mecum perpendens quantum periculi gignat et ferat negligentia eius quae in me est trinitatis, id est intellectus, memoriae, ac voluntatis." PL 141:1063.

71. Ladner, *The Idea of Reform*, passim.

72. See Carruthers, *The Book of Memory*, 46–79, on the Aristotelian tradition of *memoria* in the later Middle Ages.

73. See the article on "Memoria" in C. du F. du Cange, *Glossarium mediae et infimae latinitatis* 5:335–36. On the role of physical objects as *memoria* see Clanchy, *From Memory to Written Record*. On liturgical *memoria* see above all *Memoria*, ed. K. Schmid and Wollasch. On the "very special dead" see P. Brown, *The Cult of the Saints*, 69–85; and Geary, *Living with the Dead*.

74. See the articles by Otto Gerhard Oexle, "Memoria und Memorial-überlieferung im früheren Mittelalter," *Frühmittelalterliche Studien* 10 (1976): 70–95; "Liturgische Memoria und historische Erinnerung. Zur Frage nach dem Gruppenbewußtsein und dem Wissen der eigenen Geschichte in den mittelalterlichen Gilden," in *Tradition als historische Kraft*, ed. Kamp and Wollasch, 323–40; "Die Gegenwart der Toten," in *Death in the Middle Ages*, ed. Braet and Verbeke, 19–77; and "Die Gegenwart der Lebenden und der Toten: Gedanken über *Memoria*," in *Gedächtnis, das Gemeinschaft Stiftet*, ed. K. Schmid, 74–107.

75. Oexle, "Die Gegenwart der Toten."

76. For a general introduction to the psychology of memory, see the first chapter of Von Wright, *Forgetting and Interference*, and Baddeley, *The Psychology of Memory* and *Human Memory*. For a more detailed discussion of the relationship between these theories and the history of memory, see Fentress and Wickham, *Social Memory*, chaps. 1 and 2, 1–86. Much of the most important recent research on memory has been in the area of neurobiology. For a clear exposition see Dudai, *The Neurobiology of Memory*.

77. Ebbinghaus, *Über das Gedächtnis* (in English: *Memory: A Contribution to Experimental Psychology*, trans. Ruger and Bussenius).

78. For studies in this tradition see *Aspects of Memory*, ed. Gruneberg and Morris.

79. Bartlett, *Remembering*.

80. Among Bartlett's successors and their works are Bransford, *Human Cognition*; *Perceiving, Acting, and Knowing*, ed. Bransford and Shaw; and Schonen, *La Mémoire, connaissance active du passé*.

81. Tulving, "Episodic and Semantic Memory," in *Organization of Memory*, ed. Tulving and Donaldson, 381–403, and more recently *Elements of Episodic Memory*.

82. McClelland, "On the Time Relations of Mental Processes," *Psychological Review* 86 (1979): 287–330. I am grateful to my colleague Robin West for her advice on the psychology of memory.

CHAPTER ONE
REMEMBERING AND FORGETTING IN THE ELEVENTH CENTURY

1. Bloch, *Feudal Society*, trans. Manyon, 1:39–41.

2. Duby, *La société aux XIe et XIIe siècles dans la région mâconnaise* (Paris, 1953); Southern, *The Making of the Middle Ages*.

3. Poly and Bournazel, *La mutation féodale Xe–XIIe siècles* (2d ed.).

4. Bois, *La mutation de l'an mil* (in English: *The Transformation of the Year One Thousand*, trans. Birrell).

5. The most exaggerated example being that of Bois, *La mutation de l'an mil*. See the devastatingly effective critiques of Guy Bois's work in "L'an mil: Rythmes et acteurs d'une croissance," *Médiévales* 21 (1991): 5–114, in which a series of scholars point out the evidentary, methodological, and conceptual weaknesses of his study. Guerreau, "Lournand au Xe siècle," *Le Moyen Age* 96 (1990): 519–37, provides an equally negative appraisal.

6. Barthélemy, "La mutation féodale a-t-elle eu lieu?" *Annales ESC* 47 (1992): 767–77. Barthélemy defends in detail the case for his thesis that the apparent transformations of the eleventh century are largely the effect of changes in documentation in the Vendôme in *La société dans le comté de Vendôme de l'an mil au XIVe siècle*, 19–83.

7. For more moderate statements of the thesis of the survival of ancient slavery see Bonnassie, *From Slavery to Feudalism*. Responses include Verhulst, "The Decline of Slavery," *Past and Present* 133 (1991): 195–203; Barthélemy, "Qu'est-ce que le servage, en France, au XIe siècle," *Revue Historique* 287 (1992): 233–84; and Goetz, "Serfdom and the Beginnings of a 'Seigneurial System,'" *Early Medieval Europe* 2 (1993): 29–51.

8. Barthélemy, "La mutation féodale," 652–80 and 772–74; Geary, "Moral Obligations and Peer Pressure," in *Hommage à Georges Duby*, ed. Lobrichon and Amado.

9. See particularly Fried, "Neue Historische Literatur," *Historische Zeitschrift* 245 (1987): 625–59, esp. 644–57.

10. Especially McKitterick, *The Carolingians and the Written Word*, and McKitterick, ed., *The Uses of Literacy*.

11. The formation of a disjointed, isolated memory is not unique to medieval society. See Frisch, "The Memory of History," *Radical History Review* 25 (1981): 9–23, in which the author argues that often today "the past is severed from the present almost entirely, sealed in a kind of protective wrapping, either of forgetfulness or artificial distance." While Frisch's description of the phenomenon of memory is accurate, his remedy, which includes "actively remembering the past" rather than producing "images of the past for our more passive consumption" (p. 21), fails to recognize the very active and selective process by which the sealed-off past he bemoans is created.

12. See Wickham, "Lawyers' Time," in *Studies in Medieval History*, ed. Mayr-Harting and Moore, 53–71, esp. 61; and Bisson, "Unheroed Pasts," *Speculum* 65 (1990): 281–308. However, neither author sufficiently considers the significance of hagiographical writing, which presents a very localized form of historical commemoration (see especially Head, *Hagiography and the Cult of Saints*).

13. On the historiographical tradition of Fleury see especially Werner, "Die literarischen Vorbilder des Aimon von Fleury und die Entstehung seiner *Gesta Francorum*," in *Medium Aevum Vivum*, ed. Jauss and Schaller, 69–103; and Bautier, "La Place de l'abbaye de Fleury-sur-Loire," in *Études ligériennes d'histoire et d'archéologie médiévales*, ed. Louis, 25–33. On the later development of this tradition see Spiegel, *The Chronicle Tradition of Saint-Denis*.

14. Carruthers, *The Book of Memory*, 123, 144–46. The *Ad Herennium* is first mentioned in the Middle Ages by Lupus of Ferrières in a letter to Einhard, indicating that a faulty copy was in Einhard's library. Four ninth-century manuscripts exist, all apparently descending from the same defective exemplar lacking the first eight paragraphs. The first complete manuscripts date from the late tenth and early eleventh centuries, presumably from a Northern Italian exemplar. The earliest evidence of its use is by Anselm de Besate in his *Rhetorimachia*. See the introduction to Guy Achard's edition, *Rhétorique à Herennius*.

15. Coleman, *Ancient and Medieval Memories*, 146–54, does write briefly concerning Ratramnus of Corbie and Cluniac customaries but finds little of significance to her subject in the later tenth and earlier eleventh centuries.

16. Guido of Arezzo, *Epistola Guidonis Michaeli monacho de ignoto cantu* (PL 141:423–32). In his *Micrologus* he boasted that he could teach his method in only one month (Jos. Smits van Waesberghe, ed., *Corpus scriptorum de musica* 4:85).

17. On the continuing controversy over the relationship between the introduction of musical notation, memorization, and inprovisation, see most recently Treitler, "Medieval Improvisation," *World of Music* 33 (1991): 66–91.

18. Schmid and Wollasch, eds., *Memoria*.

19. Nietzsche, *Vom Nutzen und Nachtheil der Historie für das Leben*, vol. 2 of *Nietzsches Werke, Klassiker Ausgabe*, 134: "plastische Kraft eines Menschen, eines Volkes, eine Cultur . . . aus sich heraus eigenartig zu wachsen, Vergangnes und Fremdes umzubilden und einzuverleiben, Wunden auszuheilen."

20. Fichtenau, *Living in the Tenth Century*, trans. Geary.

21. In general on Provence in antiquity and the Middle Ages, see Bourrilly et al., *Les Bouches-du-Rhône: Encyclopédie Départmentale*, vol. 2: *Antiquité et Moyen Age*.

22. On early medieval Provence see Buchner, *Die Provence in merowingischer Zeit: Verfassung—Wirtschaft—Kultur*.

23. On the Alpine region in the late seventh and early eighth centuries, see Geary, *Aristocracy in Provence*.

24. In general, see Poupardin, *Le royaume de Provence* and *Le royaume de Bourgogne*.

25. *Annales Fuldenses* 845. In the *Annales Bertiniani* Folcrad is termed *comes*, and he is said to act simply with "ceteri Provinciales."

26. McKitterick, *The Frankish Kingdoms*, 262–66.

27. Poly, *La Provence*, 3–55.

28. On the counts of Arles, see Poly, *La Provence*, 32–34. On the Arduini, see Sergi, "Una grande circoscrizione," *Studi medievali*, 3d ser., 12 (1971): 637–712, and Sergi, *Potere e territorio*, 47–69.

29. On Neustria see most recently the important collection of essays edited by Hartmut Atsma, *La Neustrie*.

30. For an excellent general introduction to early Bavaria, see Reuter, *Germany in the Early Middle Ages, 800–1056*, 54–58, 128–47, and passim. On the end of the Roman presence in Noricum see Lotter, *Severinus von Noricum*, and more generally Wolfram, *Die Geburt Mitteleuropas*, chap. 1, "Die Umgestaltung der römischen Staatlichkeit (378–536/68)," 19–81.

31. On the Bavarian ethnogenesis see the essays in *Die Bayern und ihre Nachbarn*, vol. 1, ed. Wolfram and Schwarcz; vol. 2, ed. Friesinger and Daim.

32. On the particularly important continuity at Lorch, see Eckhart, "Die Kontinuität in der Lorcher Kirchenbauten mit besonderer Berücksichtigung der Kirche des 5. Jahrhunderts," in *Die Völker an der mitteleren und unteren Donau im fünften und sechsten Jahrhundert*, ed. Wolfram and Daim, 23–27.

33. Hageneder, "Die Kirchliche Organisation im Zentralalpenraum vom 6. bis 10. Jahrhundert," in *Frühmittelalterliche Ethnogenese im Alpenraum*, ed. Beumann and Schröder, 201–35.

34. Wolfram, *Die Geburt Mitteleuropas*, 96–98, 118–25.

35. Mayr, "Neuerliche Anmerkungen zur Todeszeit des heiligen Emmeram und zur Kirchenpolitik Herzog Theodos," in *Typen der Ethnogenese*, vol. 1, ed. Wolfram and Pohl, 199–215.

36. *Anglo-Saxon Chronicle: Two of the Saxon Chronicles Parallel*, ed. Plummer (revising Dorothy Whitelock), vol. 1, 80.

37. See Brunner, "Der fränkische Fürstentitel im neunten und zehnten Jahrhundert," in *Intitulatio II*, ed. Wolfram, 179–340.

38. Freed, "Medieval German Social History," *Central European History* (1992): 1–26, esp. 19–26.

39. Augustine *Confessiones* (ed. Luc Verheijen) 10.8.

CHAPTER TWO
MEN, WOMEN, AND FAMILY MEMORY

1. *Cartulaire de l'abbaye de Cysoing*, ed. Ignace de Coussemaker, 1–5.

2. Riché, "Les bibliothèques de trois aristocrates laïcs carolingiens," *Le Moyen Age* 69 (1963): 87–104; McKitterick, *The Carolingians and the Written Word*, esp. 245–48.

3. Werner, "Bedeutende Adelsfamilien im Reich Karls des Großen," in *Karl der Große*, vol. 1, *Persönlichkeit und Geschichte*, ed. Beumann, 133–37. On northern families such as the Unrochs in Italy see Hlawitschka, *Franken, Alemannen, Bayern und Burgunder*.

4. Dhuoda, *Manuel pour mon fils*, ed. Riché.

5. Riché, "Les bibliothèques," 88–89.

6. See Wollasch, "Eine adlige Familie des frühen Mittelalters," *Archiv für Kulturgeschichte* 392 (1957): 150–88; Geary, "Échanges et relations," *Droit et Cultures* 12 (1986): 3–17; and, most recently Bouchard, "Family Structure and Family Consciousness," *Francia* 14 (1986): 639–58.

7. *Cartulaire de l'abbaye de Cysoing*, 1.

8. See Lauranson-Rosaz, *L'Auvergne et ses marges (Velay, Gévaudan)*, 58–78.

9. The image of the transformation of the aristocracy from horizontal to vertical organization and identity has recently been challenged, most forcefully by Bouchard in "Family Structure and Family Consciousness" as well as in "The Origins of the French Nobility," *American Historical Review* 86 (1981): 501–32. One must certainly note a tendency, as early as the seventh century at least, for fathers to attempt to pass property and office to their sons. (See Geary,

Aristocracy in Provence, esp. 131–38.) However, largely because of royal intervention and interfamilial rivalry, such attempts were frequently not successful over many generations. The broader diffusion of property and office within wider kindreds can perhaps be seen as an alternative strategy, but one that, prior to the tenth century, did characterize much of Europe's aristocratic families.

10. On these three models of aristocratic memory, see Bournazel, "Mémoire et parenté," *La France de l'an Mil*, ed. Delort, 114–24.

11. MGH SS XIII, 733–374.

12. On the self-perception of the Welfs, see K. Schmid's classic article, "Welfisches Selbstverständnis," in K. Schmid, *Gebetsgedenken und adliges Selbstverständnis im Mittelalter*, 424–53.

13. See Dunbabin, "Aristocratic Families." On aristocratic family memory see Ruiz Domenec, *La memoria de los feudales*.

14. "Ibi tum facta pro defunctis memoria . . ." (*Thietmari Chronicon*). Thietmar of Merseburg, *Chronicon* (ed. Holtzmann) 6.73 (MGH SSRG IX, 362).

15. On dying around the year one thousand see Fichtenau, *Living in the Tenth Century*, 42–43.

16. Thietmar of Merseburg, *Chronicon* 6.71 (MGH SSRG IX, 360).

17. "Fuit itaque militum luctus, famulorum clamor, feminarum frequens exclamatio." Richer, *Histoire de France (888–995)* (ed. Latouche), IV, 94 (2:300).

18. "Sed archipresul, cum iam finis adesset, nescio quid videns ad levam, signo sanctae crucis potenter dextera se munit et aversus corpore et vultu contraxit faciem quasi ploraturus et mox remisit laetus." Thietmar of Merseburg, *Chronicon* 6.71.

19. "Nam cum levatum e lecto humi deposuissemus, primum brachiis quasi contra aliquem reluctatus, demum ad sinistram acutissime flectens obtutus, adeo abhorrebat a facie inimici, ut oculorum versione capitisque aversione ac impulsu, ut gestum exprimam, capitali, pene loco sibi astantes propelleret; et ut patesceret, quantum fides Christi valet ubi meritum habet, quantumve deest ubi mortua est, nisu quo potuit dextram manum extendit, signum salutis facere volens; sed exprimere minime valens, subita concussione contremuit, ac pallore obductus irriguit; sicque exalavit." Arnoldus S. Emmerammensis, *De miraculis S. Emmerammi Libri Duo*, I (PL 141:991).

20. "Quis non tunc plangeret, cum talia videret?" Thietmar of Merseburg, *Chronicon* 6.73 (MGH SSRG IX, 362). "Funebre melos, lacrimis impedientibus vix proferebatur." Richer, *Histoire de France* (ed. Latouche) III, 110 (2:142).

21. Biblioteca Capitolare d'Ivrea MS. 86. See the facsimilie edition *Sacramentario del vescovo Warmondo di Ivrea* (Ivrea, 1990). The miniatures were previously published in Magnani, *Le miniature del sacramentario d'Ivrea*; see Schmitt, *La Raison des gestes dans l'Occident médiéval*, 223.

22. Plate 1: Biblioteca Capitolare d'Ivrea MS. 31 (LXXXVI), fol. 191r.

23. Plate 2: Ibid., fol. 193r.

24. Plate 3: Ibid., fol. 195v.

25. Plate 4: Ibid., fol. 198v.

26. Plate 5: Ibid., fol. 199v.

27. Plate 6: Ibid., fol. 200v.
28. Plate 7: Ibid., fol. 201v.
29. Plate 8: Ibid., fol. 203v.
30. Plate 9: Ibid., fol. 205r.
31. Plate 10: Ibid., fol. 206v.
32. Corbet, *Les saints ottoniens.*
33. Odilo of Cluny, *Die Lebensbeschreibung der Kaiserin Adelheid von Abt Odilo von Cluny*, ed. Paulhart. MGH SS IV, 633–49.
34. Corbet, *Les saints ottoniens*, 82.
35. Leyser, *Rule and Conflict*, 49.
36. MGH SS IV, 301.
37. *Vita Mahthildis Reginae antiquior*, MGH SS X, 573–82.
38. Corbet, *Les saints ottoniens*, 194–96.
39. MGH SS IV, c. 8, 288.
40. Thietmar of Merseburg, *Chronicon* 2.44 (MGH SSRG IX, 92).
41. *Chronicon* 6.85.
42. *Chronicon* 7.14.
43. *Chronicon* 6.76 (MGH SSRG IX, 364). See Leyser, *Rule and Conflict*, 61.
44. Thietmar of Merseburg, *Chronicon* 3.10 (MGH SSRG IX, 108).
45. For a general survey of female monasteries, particularly in Saxony from the ninth to the twelfth centuries, see Parisse, " Die Frauenstifte," in *Die Salier und das Reich*, vol. 2, *Die Reichskirche in der Salierzeit*, ed. Weinfurter, 465–501. Parisse points out (483–84) that such cloisters, while most common in Saxony, were also founded in other regions of the empire, especially in Lotharingia, but were rare to nonexistent between Lake Constance and the Rhein and Main and between the Danube and the southern border of Saxony.
46. Leyser, *Rule and Conflict*, 72. Parisse counts, in addition to the obligation of *memoria*, that of the education of young women ("Die Frauenstifte," 480).
47. Leyser, *Rule and Conflict*, 72; Althoff, *Adels- und Königsfamilien*, 170.
48. Corbet, *Les saints ottoniens*, 199. See also Schneider, "Zum Bild von der Frau in der Chronistik des früheren Mittelalters," *Forschungen und Fortschritte* 35 (1961): 112–14.
49. On Constance and her role in the royal succession, see Andrew Lewis, "Successions ottoniennes et robertiennes," in *Le roi de France*, ed. Parisse and Barral i Altet, 51–53.
50. Odorannus of Sens, *Chronique* in *Opera omnia*, ed. and trans. Bautier and Gilles, 84–113. On Odorannus, protégé of Thierry, future Bishop of Orléans and in the entourage of Constance, see Bautier, "L'hérésie d'Orléans," 82–83.
51. Helgaud of Fleury, *Vie de Robert le Pieux*, ed. and trans. Bautier and Labory, 106–109.
52. Poly, "L'oeuf du griffon," *Droit et cultures* 22 (1991): 101–102.
53. Helgaud of Fleury, *Vie die Robert le Pieux*, c. 10, 72. See Poly, "L'oeuf du griffon," 111–12.

54. Herlihy, "Land, Family, and Women," *Traditio* 18 (1962): 89–120, reprinted in *Women in Medieval Society*, ed. Stuard, 13–45 (these statistics come from table 3, 28).

55. Gold, *The Lady and the Virgin*, 130.

56. Hajdu, "The Position of Noblewomen," *Journal of Family History* 5 (1980): 122–44, esp. 130.

57. On tenth-century queens see, in general, Stafford, *Queens, Concubines and Dowagers*; and on Gerberga in particular, ibid., esp. 117–23, and McKitterick, *The Frankish Kingdoms*, 313–18.

58. Richer, *Histoire de France* (ed Latouche) III, 92 (2:116). Also III, 86: "Lotharius rex necnon et Emma regina insidias ubique parabant" (2:114). On Emma's lot after the death of Lothar, see Stafford, *Queens, Concubines and Dowagers*, 167 and 175–76.

59. For a preliminary list of women's monastic institutions in France between the ninth and twelfth centuries see the two articles by Jean Verdon, "Recherches sur les monastères féminins dans la France du nord," *Revue Mabillon* 59 (1976): 49–96, and "Recherches sur les monastères féminins dans la France du sud," *Annales du midi* 88 (1976): 117–38. Most recently on religious women in France see Johnson, *Equal in Monastic Profession*. To a lesser extent, the existence of women's cloisters in Bavaria and Swabia may also temper the image of women's institutions in the empire, although these southern institutions did not play the role of their northern counterparts. See Parisse, "Die Frauenstifte," 483.

60. "Le lien matrimonial se dénouait donc fort aisément à la cour de France, dans une province moins attardée que ne l'était la Germanie de saint Henri." Duby, *Le Chevalier, la femme et le prêtre*, 90.

61. PL 189:903–908.

62. PL 189:912.

63. Bouchard, *Sword, Miter and the Cloister*, 142–48.

64. "bona mulier est domna Regina nomine, quae multa praedicto loco [Micy] pro salute sua, et pro remidio animarum videlicet sui mariti et filiorum suorum iam defunctorum, Deo et sanctis ibidem venerans obtulit. PL 131:439–40. See Head, *Hagiography and the Cult of Saints*, 229.

65. Althoff, *Adels- und Königsfamilien*, 170.

66. *Vita Sanctae Odiliae virginis* MGH SSRM VI, 45, c. 15. See Zoepf, *Das Heiligen-Leben*, 227, who seems however to have misunderstood the sense of the text.

67. *Cronaca di Novalesa*, ed. Alessio.

68. *Cronaca di Novalesa* 2.8.112.

69. See Lambert and Grilletto, "Le sepolture e il cimitero della chiesa abbaziale della Novalesa," *Archeologia Medievale* 16 (1989): 336–38, on tomb T 28, an important ninth-century burial that includes the remains of two men and one woman. On the excavations of Novalesa in general see Wataghin-Cantino, "Prima campagna," *Archeologia Medievale* 6 (1979): 289–317; "Seconda campagna," in *Atti del V Congresso Nazionale di Archeologia Cristiana*, 89–101; and "Le ricerche archeologiche in corso all'Abbazia della Novalesa," in *La Novalesa* 1:329–57.

70. Thietmar of Merseburg, *Chronicon* 1.12–13. On ghosts in Thietmar see Schmitt, *Les Revenants*, 52–55.

71. See Biblioteca Capitolare d'Ivrea MS. 31, fol. 61v, where they stand in the first rank of those designated as the "plebs."

72. Detailed statistical studies of the name pool for regions of the empire have yet to be undertaken. For one region of Bavaria (Salzburg) one can consult the preliminary study of Dittrich, "Personennamen im *Codex Odalberti*," *Mitteilungen der Gesellschaft für Salzburger Landeskunde* 61 (1921): 55–60, which identifies over six hundred different names in the 102 entries of the first Salzburg Traditionsbuch. I am grateful to John Freed for pointing out this article to me as well as for his observation that, by the twelfth century, the royal names Frederick, Henry, Otto, and Conrad predominated in Salzburg.

73. "tam scavinis, tam romanis quam salicis, vel iudicibus." *Cartulaire de l'abbaye de Saint Victor de Marseille* (hereafter, *CSV*), ed. Guérard, no. 26, pp. 32–34.

74. *CSV*, no. 447, pp. 452–53.

75. A rough estimate of the frequency of names in Provence has been calculated by an analysis of the charters principally from Arles: Archives communales, *Authentique de S. Trophime*; Apt: *Cartulaire de l'église d'Apt*, ed. Didier, Dubled, and Barruol; St. Victor of Marseille: *CSV*; Lérins: *Cartulaire de l'abbaye de Lérins* (hereafter, *Cart. Lérins*), ed. Moris and Blanc; Montmajour: Marseilles, Arch. départ. Bouches du Rhône 2 H 2; Avignon: *Les chartes du pays d'Avignon (439–1040)*, ed. de Manteyer; and Psalmody: Nimes, Arch. départ. du Gard, H 106, as well as charters from Cluny (relating to Provence): *Recueil des chartes de l'abbaye de Cluny*, ed. Bernard and Bruel.

Variant forms of the names were then automatically standardized using a system developed at the University of Freiburg by Dieter Geuenich and then the frequency of each name was calculated at fifty-year intervals. The mean, variance, and standard deviation were then calculated for frequency of names, and the most frequent were determined based on standard scores. These statistics should be understood only as presenting a very general qualitative image of the onomastic changes in Provence and not as a precise quantitative analysis of Provençal onomastics.

76. Beech, "Les noms de personne," *Revue Internationale d'Onomastique* 26 (1974): 81–100.

77. Barrière, "L'anthroponymie en Limousin," *Genèse médiévale*, 23–34.

78. See Bourin, "Les formes anthroponymiques," *Genèse médiévale*, 179–217; Patrice Beck, "Évolution des formes anthroponymiques en Bourgogne," *Genèse médiévale*, 61–85.

79. See Bourin's concluding remarks in "Bilan de l'enquête," *Genèse médiévale*, 233–46, esp. 244.

80. Historians are only beginning to look in a systematic, statistical way at the transformations of onomastic traditions as keys to social and cultural identity. In addition to the important series of studies of medieval naming patterns that has emerged from a series of conferences organized by the University of Tours at the château d'Azay-le-Ferron—*Genèse médiévale de l'anthroponymie moderne* (Tours, s.d. [1988])—see Littger, *Studien zum Auftreten der Heili-*

gennamen im Rheinland; Lynch, *Godparents and Kinship*; Fine, "L'heritage du nom de Baptême," *Annales ESC* 42 (1987): 853–77, and "Transmission des prénoms et parenté en Pays-en-Sault," in *Le Prénom*, ed. Dupâquier, Bideau, and Ducreux, 109–25. For comparative methodological insights into naming and social structure see Cody, "There Was No 'Absalom' on the Ball Plantations," *American Historical Review* 92 (1987): 563–96.

81. Bourin, "Bilan de l'enquête" *Genèse médiévale*, 245.

82. See note 71, above.

83. Poly, *La Provence*, 33.

84. "Rodbald" disappears with Rombald II (965–1008) and Boso never reappeared. Poly, "Catalogue des actes des comtes de Provence," appendix to "Listes épiscopales de Provence Xe–XIe siècles" (Ph.D. diss., University of Paris, 1972).

85. *Actes concernant les vicomtes de Marseille et leurs descendants*, ed. Gérin-Richard and Isnard; Poly, "Lignées et domaines en Provence Xe-XIe siècles" (appendix to his unpublished thèse de droit, 1972), ser. 1.

86. See most recently the essays in the collection *Memoria*, ed. K. Schmid and Wollasch.

87. Geary, "Échanges et relations," 13–17. Barbara Rosenwein disputes the suggestion that land was exchanged for prayers and argues instead that "the social meaning of gift giving alone is enough" (*To Be the Neighbor of Saint Peter*, 38–43 and 138–39; the quote is from p. 138). The question requires further investigation, both at Cluny and at other eleventh-century monasteries where different liturgical and social bonds may have developed.

88. Geary, "Échanges et relations," 6–7.

89. For example, see *Cartulaire de l'abbaye de Saint Bernard de Romans*, ed. Chevalier, 27 n. CVIII, in which Arlulfus makes a donation "pro remedio animae genitoris mei Teodbert et genitricis mee Aimenradane et germanis mei Sigibodo."

90. *Cart. Lérins*, no. 132, pp. 119–20.

91. Poly, *La Provence*, 158–59.

92. Ibid., 140.

93. "Fulko, filius Guillelmi predicti, multociens ibi iniurias intulit." See Poly, *La Provence*, 140 n. 51.

94. Ibid.

95. The necrology of Lérins is no longer extant but enumerations of names in the "genealogy" read as though they may well have come from necrological notices. For unambiguous examples of the use of necrologies in creating histories, see chapter 6.

96. *Cart. Lérins*, pp. 2–3, n. 3.

97. Including the donation made by Bishop Aldebert (*Cart. Lérins*, no. 131), the donation by William the Lombard (no. 137), and the final *guriptio* by his son Fulk (no. 343).

98. "Hic jacet domnus et amabilis Willelmus, comes Engolismae, qui ipso anno, quo venit de Hierusalem, obiit in pace VIII idus aprilis, vigilia osanna, MXXVIII anno ab Incarnatione, et tota sua progenies jacet in loco sancti Eparchii." Ademar of Chabannes, *Chronicon* (ed. Jules Chavanon) 3.66. See Lemâitre, *Mourir à Saint-Martial*, 151–52.

99. Rosenwein convincingly shows the importance of continued renewals of gifts and exchanges made between Cluny and lay kindreds in reaffirming these relations in *To Be the Neighbor of Saint Peter*.

CHAPTER THREE
ARCHIVAL MEMORY AND THE DESTRUCTION OF THE PAST

1. See McKitterick, *The Carolingians and the Written Word*, chap. 3, "A Literate Community: The Evidence of the Charters," 77–131.

2. On these collections in general one must still consult the scholarship of the late nineteenth and early twentieth centuries, in particular Oesterley, *Wegweiser durch die Literatur der Urkunden sammlungen*; Redlich, "Ueber bairische Traditionsbücher und Traditionen," *MIÖG* 5 (1884): 1–82; Grüner, "Schwäbische Urkunden und Traditionsbücher," *MIÖG* 33 (1912): 1–78; and Bresslau, *Handbuch der Urkundenlehre* 1:94–99. More recent systematic examinations of groups of such collections include Wanderwitz, "Traditionsbücher bayerische Klöster und Stifte," *Archiv für Diplomatik* 24 (1978): 359–380, and Guyotjeannin, *Les Cartulaires*.

3. Editions of a given institution's charters are often referred to as *Urkundenbücher*, which are normally modern compilations of tradition notices, cartulary copies, and originals organized chronologically. In France the term *cartulaire* usually refers to what I call a cartulary, although published collections of archival material of disparate origins are occasionally termed *cartulaires*.

4. Notable exceptions are the recent publications of the *Traditiones Wizenburgenses: Die Urkunden des Klosters Weißenburg 661–864*, ed. Glöckner and Doll, and that of Mondsee in the edition begun by Gebhard Rath and completed by Erich Reiter, *Das älteste Traditionsbuch des Klosters Mondsee*, both of which publish the charters in the order of the manuscript.

5. Exceptions are Walker, "The Organization of Material in Medieval Cartularies," in *The Study of Medieval Records*, ed. Bullough and Storey, 132–50, and Genet, "Cartulaires, registres, et histoire," in *Le métier d'historien au moyen âge*, ed. Guenée, 95–138. In addition, some scholars have studied the history of particular cartularies in considerable detail. Especially significant are the studies of Léon Levillain on the earliest cartularies of Corbie, *Examen critique des chartes . . . de Corbie* and his studies of the earliest cartulary of St. Denis discussed later in this chapter.

6. "Chaque cartulaire est un témoin de l'état des archives d'une église au temps où il a été composé." Lesne, *Histoire de la propriété ecclésiastique en France*, vol. 4, *Les livres "Scriptoria" et Bibliothèques* (Appendix: "Les archives ecclésiastiques et monastiques"), 809.

7. For example, see the use of private charters in legal proceedings in Provence in Geary, "Die Provence zur Zeit Karl Martells," in *Karl Martell und seiner Zeit*, ed. Jarnut et al. For a German example see *Die Traditionen des Hochstifts Freising* (ed. Bitterauf) 1:207 no. 223, from 806: "Et vincebat eum cum carta atque veraces testibus." The *carta* was a donation of 769–77. No. 37, pp. 64–65.

8. Dopsch, *Die Wirtschaftsentwicklung der Karolingerzeit vornehmlich in Deutschland* 1:110; *Traditiones Wizenburgenses* (ed. Glöckner-Doll), 40.

9. Metz, "Zur Geschichte und Kritik der frühmittelalterlichen Güter-verzeichnisse Deutschlands," *Archiv für Diplomatik* 4 (1958): 183–206, and *Das Karolingische Reichsgut*, 45–53.

10. See note 25, below.

11. Metz, *Das Karolingische Reichsgut*, 18–19.

12. *Brevium Exempla*, MGH Capit. I, 250–56.

13. Metz, *Das Karolingische Reichsgut*, 46–48; *Codex Diplomaticus Fuldensis* (ed. Dronke), Trad. c. 44. See Werner-Hasselbach, *Die älteren Güterverzeichnisse der Reichsabtei Fulda*.

14. Goffart, *The Le Mans Forgeries*, 10–13.

15. "*Notitia Arnonis* und *Breves Notitiae*," ed. Lošek, in *Mitteilungen der Gesellschaft für Salzburger Landeskunde* 130 (1990): 5–193.

16. Fichtenau, *Das Urkundenwesen*, 77–78.

17. Goffart, *The Le Mans Forgeries*, Appendix B. "The Textual Transmission of the Cartulary of St. Calais," 321–26; Levillain, *Examen critique des chartes . . . de Corbie*, 13. This Corbie collection, today Berlin MS 79, is a composite. Only fols. 93r to 128r contain charters all of which, with the exception of the first, are papal bulls or royal diplomas. Neither it nor the second oldest Corbie cartulary, BN MS lat. 17764, contains private charters or translation notices.

18. Johanek, "Zur rechtlichen Funktion von Traditionsnotiz, Traditions-buch und früher Siegelurkunde," in *Recht und Schrift im Mittelalter*, ed. Classen, 131–62.

19. Molitor, "Das Traditionsbuch," *Archiv für Diplomatik* 36 (1990): 61–92.

20. See in general Werner, "Les principautés périphériques dans le monde franc du VIIIe siècle," in *I problemi dell'Occidente nel secolo VIII* 2:483–532; Archibald R. Lewis, "The Dukes in the *Regnum Francorum*," *Speculum* 51 (1976): 381–410, esp. 404.

21. See Wolfram, "*Libellus Virgilii*," in *Mönchtum, Episcopat und Adel zur Gründungszeit des Klosters Reichenau*, ed. Borst, 177–214; Wolfram, "Die *Notitia Arnonis*," in *Recht und Schrift im Mittelalter*, ed. Classen, 115–30; and Wolfram, *Die Geburt Mitteleuropas*.

22. See most recently Jahn, "Virgil, Arbeo und Cozroh," *Mitteilungen des Gesellschaft für salzburger Landeskunde* 130 (1990): 201–91, esp. 213–17.

23. They are not "Besitzertragsverzeichnisse, sondern Besitztitelverzeich-nisse" (Wolfram, *Die Geburt Mitteleuropas*, 171).

24. "per iam per dicti Tassiloni traditionem hoc firmiter et stabile minime permanere poterat" (DKar I 169); Wolfram, "*Libellus Virgilii*," 182.

25. The earliest Fulda cartulary, prepared under the direction of Hrabanus Maurus, must have contained almost two thousand charters. Only fragments of this collection, written ca. 828, survive: eighty-six leaves in the Marburg Staats-archiv, Kop. no. 1; and a double leaf now in Sarnen from ca. 833. See *Ur-kundenbuch des Klosters Fulda* (ed. Stengel) 1:xvii–xxi. The Fulda charters to 802 are edited by Stengel, ibid., vols. 1 and 2. For the others, one must still rely on the *Codex Diplomaticus Fuldensis* (ed. Dronke, 1850). The contents of the *libelli* are as follows: 1. Alsace; 2. Wormsgau; 3. Rheingau and Nahegau; 4. the East Frankish Gaue of Volkfeld, Gollachgau, Taubergau, Jagstgau, Rangau, and

Badenachgau; 5. Saalegau; 6. Aschfeld and Werngau; 7. Grabfeld; 8. Hessengau and Lahngau; 9. Thuringia; 10. Bavaria and Swabia; 11. Saxony; 12. Frisia; 13. Niddagau; 14. Wetterau; and 15. Maingau.

26. On the manuscripts and organization, see the introduction to Stengel's edition of *Urkundenbuch des Klosters Fulda* 1:xviii–xxi.

27. *Urkundenbuch des Klosters Fulda* (ed. Stengel) 1:xlviii–xlvix.

28. Nos. 286 and 287. See introduction, *Urkundenbuch des Klosters Fulda* (ed. Stengel) 1:lii–liii.

29. Munich, Hauptstaatsarchiv Regensburg, St. Emmeram KL 5 1/2, fols. 9–14.

30. Ibid., fols. 9–14. See *Die Traditionen des Hochstifts Regensburg* (ed. Widemann).

31. Vienna Staatsarchiv. Cod. 179. See Hauthaler, "Der Mondseer Codex traditionum," *MIÖG* 7 (1886): 223–39; Fichtenau, *Urkundenlehre*, 15.

32. On the date of the Mondsee cartulary see the introduction to *Das älteste Traditionsbuch des Klosters Mondsee* (ed. Rath and Reiter), 36–38. The manuscript is dated on paleographic grounds to the second half of the ninth or the beginning of the tenth centuries. The editors believe that the practical nature of the collection suggests a date close to the date of the last document it contains.

33. The regions are: Matahgau (with the Quinzingau and Donaugau), Atargau, Rottachgau, Sundargau, Trungau, and Salzpurggau.

34. Munich, Bayerische Hauptstaatsarchiv, Hochstift Passau Lit. 1., *Die Traditionen des Hochstifts Passau* (ed. Heuwieser).

35. *Die Traditionen des Hochstifts Passau* (ed. Heuwieser), fols. 1–10, Rottachgau; fols. 23–42, Mattachgau. Fols. 1 and 2, although contemporary with the earliest section and containing material from Rottachgau, were attached later.

36. Such as document no. 1, which appears to be a fragment of a document of sale whose language and personal names suggest late Roman forms (although whether this document is evidence of the survival of such diplomatic traditions into the early eighth century, or if it is itself a copy of a late Roman document possibly written on a wooden tablet, is impossible to know). See Fichtenau, *Das Urkundenwesen*, 12–15.

37. Nos. 2, 3, 63, 70, and 75.

38. See Wolfram, "*Libellus Virgilii,*" 177; "Die *Notitia Arnonis,*" 155; and *Die Geburt Mitteleuropas*, 88.

39. No. 33 (DD. Kar I, 170).

40. "*Notitia Arnonis* und *Breves Notitiae*" (ed. Lošek), 16.

41. "The charters which comprise this collection were first arranged in about 815." McKitterick, *The Uses of Literacy*, 80, citing Albert Bruckner, "Die Anfänge des St. Gallen Stiftsarchivs," *Festschrift Gustav Binz* (Basel, 1935): 119–31.

42. *Die Traditionen des Hochstifts Freising* (ed. Bitterauf) 1:xix–xxii. See Jahn's perceptive treatment of Cozroh's cartulary as a memorial text in "Virgil, Arbeo und Cozroh," 240–76.

43. See Jahn, "Virgil, Arbeo und Cozroh," 245–46.

44. *Die Traditionen des Hochstifts Freising* (ed. Bitterauf) 1:1–2.

45. "Ut in perpetuum permaneret eorum memoria qui hanc domum suis rebus ditaverunt et hereditaverunt, seu quicquid pro remedio animarum suarum ad ipsam domum tradiderunt et condonaverunt." *Die Traditionen des Hochstifts Freising* (ed. Bitterauf).

46. Jahn, "Virgil, Arbeo und Cozroh," 241, goes so far as to argue that Freising needed no *liber vitae* because it had Cozroh's cartulary: "Somit liegen aus Freising und von der Reichenau spiegelbildliche Überlieferungen vor: Während man im Inselkloster einem Liber Vitae, aber offenbar kein Kopialbuch der Traditionsurkunden anlegte, schuf man in Freising einen Traditionskodex, verzichtete aber auf ein Verbrüderungsbuch."

47. MGH SS XXIV, 314–31.

48. "Les gesta sont aussi, et parfois d'abord, une histoire du patrimoine foncier." Sot, *Gesta Episcoporum*, 20–21.

49. See *Traditiones Wizenburgensis* (ed. Glöckner-Doll), 40–41, on the date of the codex.

50. Judgment, no. 196a; *praestaria*, no. 196.

51. *Traditiones Wizenburgensis* (ed. Glöckner-Doll), 42–43. Not all the evidence is equally convincing. The editors cite references to royal diplomas in the lost volume. However, since Carolingian cartularies rarely contain royal diplomas, which seem to have been preserved separately and copied (often with the intention to interpolate or defraud) in the tenth and eleventh centuries, the existence of such a document would suggest a post–ninth century date for the lost "Salbuch."

52. Wilsdorf, "Le *monasterium Scottorum* de Honau," *Francia* 3 (1975): 1–87, esp. 11.

53. Davies, "The Composition of the Redon Cartulary," *Francia* 17 (1990): 69–90.

54. Ibid., 81.

55. Bresslau, *Handbuch der Urkundenlehre* 1:179. Capitula Pistensia, 12: "Et episcopi privilegia Romanae sedis et regum praecepta ecclesiis suis confirmata vigili solertia custodiant, ut exinde auctorabili firmitate tueantur." MGH Capit. II, 336.

56. Goffart, "The Privilege of Nicholas I for St. Calais," *Revue Bénédictine* 71 (1961): 287–337, and *The Le Mans Forgeries*, Appendix B, 321–26.

57. Bretholz, "Studien zu den Traditionsbüchern von S. Emmeram in Regensburg," *MIÖG* 12 (1891): 1–45.

58. Munich, Hauptstaatsarchiv, Regensburg St. Emmeram, Lit. 5 1/2. Fols. 9–14 consist of a ternio from the oldest Regensburg *Traditionsbuch*, bound into a younger one. According to Bischoff, *Die Südostdeutschen Schreibschulen und Bibliotheken in der Karolingerzeit* 1:210, it is apparently entirely from one hand that is close to that of Dignus in Clm 14437, 14727, and possibly 14468. Clm 14437 was finished in 824. Bischoff also says Bishop Baturich was in the circle of Hrabanus Maurus of Fulda, in whose company he had been consecrated and with whom he corresponded. Hrabanus Maurus had dedicated a poem to him *ex persona Isanberti*. An unknown person (probably also Hrabanus Maurus) dedicated to him a treatise on the benedictions of God. Bischoff, "Literarisches und

künstlerisches Leben in St. Emmeram (Regensburg)," in *Mittelalterliche Studien* 2:77–115.

59. St. Emmeram KL Lit. 5 1/3, fols. 70–165, Anamot's *Codex traditionum*, written between 891 and 894, contains in addition fols. 1–69, Kopial- und Salbuch saec. XI–XIII. Lit. 5 1/4 b. contains two double leaves from a second exemplar of Anamot's *Codex* and six leaves from a *Traditionscodex* from the period of Bishop Tuto (years 900–901).

60. "Presulis hic pulchram venerandi cernite formam." The verse and the picture were scraped away in the fifteenth century. However, the dedicatory verse was copied onto fol. 71v. A twelfth-century image of abbot Berthold I (1143–1149) on fol. 146v is probably modeled on the now lost image of Ambricho.

61. "Uestram igitur mentem, quoniam in omni librorum studio ceteroque divini cultus mancipatu semper inherere cognoveram." *Die Traditionen des Hochstifts Regensburg* (ed. Widemann) 8.

62. Bretholz, "Studien zu den Traditionsbüchern von S. Emmeram in Regensburg," 12.

63. St. Emmeram KL Lit. 5 1/2. The manuscript begins with fols. 15–22 since fols. 1–8 were leaves from the tenth to twelfth centuries reused in the sixteenth and fols. 9–14 are fragments of the oldest *Traditionsbuch*. The fourth, fifth, and sixth *Lage* contain only traditions from the period of the first independent abbot, Ramwold (975–1001). The first quaternio, fols. 15–22, containing nos. 32–49 (Pez 11–28), formed a unified text. The next *Lage* is a ternio, fols. 23–28, and contains nos. 50–79 (Pez 26–36), written in a poorer hand, but it is contemporaneous with the previous portion.

64. Ibid., fols. 15–22v.

65. To no. 188, fol. 56.

66. Ker, "Hemming's Cartulary," *Studies in Medieval History*, ed. Hunt, Pantin, and Southern, 49–75. The following description is taken from Ker's detailed analysis. See also Mason, *Saint Wulfstan of Worcester*.

67. BL Cotton Tiberius A. XIII, ff. 1–57 and 103–109.

68. Ibid., ff. 57–101 and 111–13.

69. According to Ker, those from Worcestershire, Wincombeshire, and Oxfordshire have occupied their present relative positions on quires 1–5 from the first. Documents from Gloucestershire and Warwickshire are on independent quires, and a second set of Gloucestershire material starts at the beginning of quire 7. The Warwickshire material is presently misplaced, the original order probably having been 1–6, 14, 15, 7–13.

70. Ker, "Hemming's Cartulary," 69–70.

71. See *Hemingi Chartularium Ecclesiae wigorniensis* (ed. Hearne) 1:283–85; letter in R. A. Brown, *Origins of English Feudalism*, no. 42, pp. 133–35.

72. Lawson, "The Collection of Danegeld and Heregeld," *English Historical Review* 393 (1984): 721–38, esp. 727.

73. See Hyams, "'No Register of Title,'" *Anglo-Norman Studies* 9 (1986): 127–41.

74. Mason, *Saint Wulfstan of Worcester*, 209, 270, 294–95.

75. On the cartulary as history, see Brett, "John of Worcester," in *The Writing of History in the Middle Ages*, ed. Davis and Wallace-Hadrill, 102, 104.

76. "Hunc tantummodo codicem de menbranulis in unius libri cumulavimus corpus, ut, si forsan quis istius loci possessionum investigandarum fuerit avidus, ad hunc recurrat; ibi numerum et nomina invenire poterit quantocius sub pretitulatione annorum dominicae nativitatis vel tunc temporis cuiuslibet regis abte coniunctum, prout nostrae erat possibilitatis, sed non omnia, quoniam multa ab antecessoribus nostris neglecta sunt, partim librorum incensione, partim demolita vetustate." MGH SS XIII, 608.

77. Guérard, *Cartulaire de l'abbaye de Saint-Bertin*, 15 and 155.

78. Berlin MS 79. This is a composite manuscript that included seven charters on fols. 93r to 128r. Except for the charter of the founder, Bishop Berthefridus of Amiens, all the documents are papal (Bulls of Benedict III and Nicholas I) or royal (two of Clothar III, one of Chilperic II, and one of Theuderic III.) See Levillain, *Examen critique des chartes . . . de Corbie.*

79. *Cartulaire de l'abbaye de Saint-Père de Chartres* (ed. Guérard) 1:3.

80. "Expletis denique cartis scribendo quasi novi esse profuturas, illas esse relinquendas existimavi in quibus rememorando nulla utilitas ad presens putatur." Ibid., 1:119.

81. "sicut ab antiquorum dictis vel scriptis didicimus" (ibid., 1:4).

82. Ibid., 1:54.

83. *The Cartulary of Flavigny, 717–1113*, ed. Bouchard, 5–6.

84. Ibid., 6.

85. Iogna-Prat, "La geste des origines," *Revue bénédictine* 102 (1992) 135–91. See also Maria Hillebrandt, "Les cartulaires de l'abbaye de Cluny," *Mémoires de la Société pour l'Histoire du Droit* 50 (1993): 7–18; and Iogna-Prat, "La confection des cartulaires," in Guyotjeannin, *Les Cartulaires*, 27–44.

86. These consist of a "prefatio in libro de cartis in tempore domni Bernonis abbatis" (fol. 7r–v); the "Testamentum Willelmi ducis Aquitanorum de constructione cluniacensis" (7v–9r) and the "Testamentum domni Bernonis Abbatis" (9r–10r).

87. Composed of fols. 1, 2, 3, 4, 5, 6, 11, and 12. See Iogna-Prat, "La geste des origines," 153–56, for a codicological description of the cartulary.

88. See Iogna-Prat, "La geste des origines," 154–57.

89. *Inventaire des manuscrits*, ed. Delisle, 350–51.

90. Iogna-Prat, "La geste des origines," 153.

91. They were edited as an appendix to *Recueil des chartes de l'abbaye de Cluny* (ed. Bernard and Bruel) 5:843–46. That of Odo was also edited by Ernst Sackur, *Die Cluniacenser* 1:377–78.

92. "Quapropter ne et nos socordiæ eorum participes efficiamur, donationes cunctas pio justorum voto retroactis temporibus nostro monasterio collatas, et veneranda priorum sagacitate plurimis in scedulis nobis relinctas, uno in volumine decrevimus congregare, et . . . denotare." *Recueil des chartes de l'abbaye de Cluny* (ed. Bernard and Bruel) 5:844.

93. "Igitur exordium nostræ narrationis tempus et gesta domni continebit Bernonis et quomodo ipse dono Willelmi excellentissimi principis nostro loco donatus eum proprio alodio quod Alafracta dicitur, nobilitavit." Ibid., 5:844.

94. Rosenwein, *To Be the Neighbor of Saint Peter*, 173–76.

95. "quanta et qualia, prelibati patris industria, usibus monachorum in Cluniacensi loco degentium perseverant adquisita." *Recueil des chartes de l'abbaye de Cluny* (ed. Bernard and Bruel) 5:844–45 (fol. 37r).

96. A. Bruel, "Note sur la transcription des actes privés dans les cartulaires antérieurement au XIIe siècle," *Bibliothèque de l'Ecole des Chartes* 36 (1875): 445–56.

97. See Iogna-Prat, "La geste des origines," esp. 157–58, 163–64.

98. I am grateful for the advice and assistance of Hartmut Atsma and Thomas Waldman in the preparation of the following section on St. Denis.

99. Cited by Levillain. "Études sur l'abbaye de Saint-Denis," *Bibliothèque de l'Ecole des Chartes* 87 (1926) 20–97, 245–346.

100. Ganz, "Bureaucratic Shorthand," in *Ideal and Reality in Frankish and Anglo-Saxon Society*, ed. Wormald et al., 58–75; Ganz and Goffart, "Charters Earlier Than 800 from French Collections," *Speculum* 65 (1990): 906–32, esp. 913.

101. Waldman, "Saint-Denis," in *Religion et culture*, ed. Iogna-Prat and Picard, 191–97.

102. Waldman, "Saint-Denis," 192–93.

103. Nebbiai-Dalla Guarda, *La bibliothèque de l'abbaye de Saint-Denis*.

104. BN MS lat. 10846, *Vita et acta S. Dionysii*.

105. BN MS lat. 7230, *Praeceptum Dagoberti regis*. It is of the ninth century, but fol. 1 contains a copy from the tenth century of the *Praeceptum Dagoberti regis de fugitivis*, which also appears in the cartulary of the eleventh century.

106. BN MS nouv. acq. lat. 326, *Privilegia ecclesiae Sancti Dionysii*.

107. Spiegel, *The Chronicle Tradition of Saint-Denis*, 40.

108. *Inventaires et documents* (ed. Tardif), 152–53 n. 242.

109. "Quoniam a tempore Karoli tercii imperatoris usque ad presens, in tantum a multis eorum ejusdem beati martyris neglectus est locus, ut ordo sacrae religionis monastici scilicet ordinis usque ad secularem pompam devenisset, quo circa bona illius loci indique depopulata, distracta, atque dispersa, ab illo tempore multis modis videntur, idemque locus multis calamitatibus oppressus, qui libertatem ac dignitatem, prae omnibus hujus regionis coenobiis, adeptus fuerat." *Inventaires et documents* (ed. Tardif), 158–59 n. 250.

110. On the attempts of the monks to persuade Hugh Capet and Robert to force Archbishop Gerbert of Reims to celebrate mass in the monastery during the Council of 994, see Waldman, "Saint-Denis," 192–93 and n. 21.

111. K 20, n. 4; *Inventaires et documents* (ed. Tardif), 287; *Recueil des actes de Philippe Ier*, ed. Prou, 114–17, no. 40.

112. BN MS nouv. add. lat. 326, *Privilegia ecclesiae Sancti Dionysii*, fols. 1–18v. Such collections, prepared since the ninth century in order to obtain papal confirmation, were common. As part of his attempt to win recognition of Micy's property, around 1030 Abbot Albert had suggested to Pope John XIX that the pope provide his seal for two collections he termed "tomes" (PL 139:439). See Head, *Hagiography and the Cult of Saints*, 229. The earliest "cartulary" of Grenoble, the so-called Cartulary of Saint Hugues, is a slightly later example of such a collection intended to secure papal confirmation (see Geary,

Aristocracy in Provence, 12–21). Also common was the practice of including forged documents to this end. Compare, for example, the efforts of Abbo of Fleury on behalf of his monastery (discussed by Head, *Hagiography and the Cult of Saints*, 247).

113. *Revelatio S. Stephani* (PL 89:1023); Waldman, "Saint-Denis," 192.

114. Actually, one must be cautious in saying that only three others existed. As we shall see, some of the eleventh-century forgeries at St. Denis used two or three originals to make sufficiently large sheets of papyrus. The two lost documents may also have been composed of several originals.

115. DM 16.

116. Santifaller, *Beiträge zur Geschichte der Beschreibstoffe im Mittelalter*, 66, 109; Marini, *I papiri diplomatici, raccolti ed illustrati*, n. 145; Van Hoesen, *Roman Cursive Writing*, n. 112.

117. *Chartae Latinae Antiquiores* (hereafter, ChLA) 558.

118. *Regesta pontificum romanorum* (ed. Jaffé) 2718.

119. Tessier, "Originaux et pseudo-originaux carolingiens du chartrier de Saint-Denis," *Bibliothèque de l'École des Chartes* 106 (1945–46): 35–69, esp. 62–63.

120. Such an examination would be impossible without the extraordinarily well-prepared volume 13 (Zurich, 1981) of the *Chartae Latinae Antiquiores*, ed. Atsma and Vezin.

121. It is not clear that K 1 n. 9 (ChLA 554), in which Dagobert I confirms the division of properties of his *fidelis* Ursinus and his brother Beppoleno, was in the archives of St. Denis; K 2 n. 4 (ChLA 559), a confirmation, presumably by Clovis II, of the possessions of one Amanchildis, does not expressly mention St. Denis and may either support David Ganz's theory presented in "Bureaucratic Shorthand" or indicate that at a later date St. Denis inherited property from Amanchildis.

122. The eight royal privileges included:

(1) a confirmation by Clothar II of a testament in favor of St. Denis (k 1 n. 4, ChLA 550); (2) a confirmation by Clothar II in 625 of a donation to St. Denis made by a *vir inluster* Daoberchthus (K 1 n. 7[1], ChLA 552); (3) a confirmation by Dagobert I in 632 of St. Denis's rights to the villa of Ursines (K 1 n. 5, ChLA 551); (4) a confirmation of protection, presumably by Clovis II, to St. Denis, ca. 639–657 (K 1 n. 10, ChLA 555); (5) a confirmation of the property of St. Denis at *Totiraco* on the Oise by Clovis II ca. 639–642 (K 2 n. 1, ChLA 556); (6) a confirmation by Clovis II of the privilege of Bishop Landry from St. Denis, 654 (K 2 n. 3, ChLA 558); (7) a confirmation, presumably by Clovis II of the property of one Amanchildis, 639–657 (K 2 n. 4, ChLA 559); and (8) a confirmation by one of the sons of Clovis II of the four given by Dagobert I to St. Denis in the Beauvaisis, 657–688 (K 2 n. 5, ChLA 560).

123. These were: (9) a judgment of Clothar III in favor of St. Denis concerning properties in the Rennais and the Vimeu from 659–673 (K 1 n. 7[3], ChLA 553); (10) a judgment, probably by Clothar III, that a villa donated by Erchinoald and his son Leudesius was to be divided between St. Denis and the church of Rouen (K 2 n. 2, ChLA 557); (11) another judgment, also probably by

Clothar III, confirming the decision of Count Chadoloaldus ordering In-goberga to return property to St. Denis left the basilica by her dead husband Ermelenus (K 2 n. 6, ChLA 561); and (12) another judgment, presumably of Clothar III, ordering Bishop Beracharius of Le Mans to restore property to St. Denis likewise taken from the estate of Ermelenus (K 2 n. 7, ChLA 562).

124. These were: (13) the testament of one Erminethrude from the sixth or seventh century, which had legacies to various Parisian churches including one "fratribus ad minsa baselicae sancti Dionisi"(K 4 n. 1, ChLA 592); (14) the testament of the son of Idda from the second half of the seventh century, which likewise included a legacy to the "Basilecae sancti domni Dionisi Parisius" (K 3 n. 1^2, ChLA 469); (15) a fragment of a private donation made in 619 or 620, probably to St. Denis (K 1 n. 3bis, ChLA 549); (16) an exchange between Abbot Magnoald of Tucionevalle (nephew of Abbot Chardericus of St. Denis, who had founded the monastery and had appointed his nephew abbot) and Lambert, abbot of Saint-Germain-l'Auxerrois ca. 691 (K 2 n. 9, ChLA 563); and (17) a letter from Abbot Maginarius of St. Denis to Charlemagne, written in Italy in 788, describing his mission to Benevento (K 7 n. 9^1, ChLA 629).

125. (18) Nicholas I 2718, which as we have seen may well have been a ninth-century forgery (K 13 n. 10^4) and (19) L 220 n. 4. Formosus (of which a fragment remains).

126. Atsma, "Le fonds," *Paris et Ile-de-France Mémoires* 32 (1981): 263.

127. See Krusch, "Ueber die *Gesta Dagoberti*," *Forschungen zur Deutschen Geschichte* 26 (1886): 161–91.

128. Among others, doc. nos. 22*, 23*, 25*, 26*, 27*, 34*, 35*, 36*, 37*, 38*, 40*, 41*, 42*, 43*, 44*, 45*, 46*, 47* 49* (all Dagobert I), 63* (Clovis II), and 68* (Childeric II).

129. ChLA 558.

130. ChLA 556.

131. ChLA 570.

132. ChLA 578.

133. ChLA 567.

134. Atsma, "Le fonds," 263.

135. Levillain, "Études sur l'abbaye de Saint-Denis," 256.

136. Krusch, "Ueber die *Gesta Dagoberti*," 175, doc. no. 12.

137. PL 141:992.

CHAPTER FOUR
UNROLLING INSTITUTIONAL MEMORIES

1. Chronicles in the form of *rotuli* are extremely rare prior to the thirteenth century. The earliest parchment *rotuli* from the West date from the Carolingian period. In subsequent centuries *rotuli* were largely used for solemn acts, imperial diplomas, inventories of relics, mortuary rolls, and in southern Italy, Exultet texts. See Fossier, "Chroniques universelles," *Bulletin de la Société Nationale des Antiquaires de France* (1980–81): 163–83. One should add that fiscal and ma-norial records could also be in the form of *rotuli*. One such exists from Novalesa

from the early twelfth century: Turin, Archivio di Stato, Novalesa, Mazzo II, 39. For a brief overview of *rotuli* see Bischoff, *Latin Palaeography*, trans. Dáibhí ó Cróinín and Ganz, 32–33.

2. *Chronicon Novaliciense* (hereafter, *CN*), Archivio di Stato di Torino, Coll. museo. See the introduction to Gian Carlo Alessio's edition, *Cronaca di Novalesa*, xli–l.

3. Wickham, "Lawyers' Time," *Studies in Medieval History*, ed. Mayr-Harting and Moore, 53–71 (the quote is from p. 61).

4. Wickham, "Lawyers' Time," 61.

5. See Geary, *Aristocracy in Provence*.

6. *Rotulus historicus* (hereafter *RH*), Munich Hauptstaatsarchiv. Benediktbeuern Lit. n. 9. The text is badly in need of a new edition. The edition by Wilhelm Wattenbach in MGH SS IX, 210–38, is incomplete and unsatisfactory. The only complete edition is in *Monumenta Boica* 7 (Munich, 1766), 1–17. See most recently Jahn, "Urkunde und Chronik," *MIÖG* 95 (1987): 1–51.

7. See MGH SS IX, 221.

8. Holzfurtner, *Gründung und Gründungsüberlieferung*, 57, cited by Jahn, "Urkunde und Chronik," 9–10 n. 34.

9. MGH SS IX, 210; cited by Jahn, "Urkunde und Chronik," 11 n. 39.

10. On the early history of Benediktbeuern see Prinz, *Frühes Mönchtum im Frankenreich*, 366–69; and Jahn, "Urkunde und Chronik."

11. Jahn, "Urkunde und Chronik," 18–20.

12. MGH SS IX, 224. See Störmer, *Früher Adel*, 121.

13. "per neglegentiam cuidam fratri abstulit [diabolus] memoriam" (*CN* 5.47).

14. MGH SS IX, 221–24. See Meyer, "Die Klostergründung in Bayern und ihre Quellen vornehmlich im Hochmittelalter," *Zeitschrift der Savigny-Stiftung für Rechtsgeschichte*, Kanonische Abteilung 20 (1931): 123–201, esp. 151–52 on Benediktbeuern; Patze, "Adel und Stifterchronik," *Blätter für deutsche Landesgeschichte*, n.s., 100 (1964): 8–81, and 101 (1965): 67–128; and, more generally, Kastner, *Historiae fundationum monasteriorum*, on the creation of foundation chronicles.

15. MGH SS IX, 223–24. Tegernsee prepared similar lists in the eleventh century, and one can imagine that Abbot Gotahelm, who brought monks from Tegernsee with him to Benediktbeuern, may have adopted the practice from the former monastery. See Jahn, "Urkunde und Chronik," 26, and Störmer, *Früher Adel*, 121–22.

16. MGH SS IX, 221. For the identities of these individuals, see Störmer, *Früher Adel*, 452–54.

17. *RH*, 11.

18. The phrase, taken from tradition notices, appears frequently in the *rotulus*. The founders gave their property "pro commemoratione sui" (*RH*, 1); Lantfrid gave his property in the pagus of the Housi "pro commemoratione sui Parentumque suorum vel omnium Christianorum" (*RH*, 3); and Gisila, the sister of Charlemagne, gave the monastery property "de juro suo . . . pro commemoratione sui" (*RH*, 5–6). Later "multi nobiles viri dederunt predia sua Elilando Abbate ad loca supra dicta, pro commemoratione sui" (*RH*, 7).

19. On Rodulfus Glaber see the perceptive comments of Karl Leyser in *The Ascent of Latin Europe*, 11–18.

20. Ortigues and Iogna-Prat, "Raoul Glaber et l'historiographie clunisienne."

21. The story is related in *CN* 5.9.

22. The now lost first section of the chronicle assigned the evangalization of the region to Saint Peter and described how Priscilla, the niece of the emperor Nero, had established a hermitage at Novalesa. Later, a religious woman traveling from Gaul to Rome with relics of Saint Peter settled at Novalesa. Later, Abbo, a lord on his way from Gaul to Rome, discovered her hermitage and, convinced by a miracle that the relics were genuine, founded the monastery.

23. *CN* 1.2.

24. *CN* 1.9. The "Theodoric" here was actually not Theoderic III, responsible for the expulsion of Columbanus, but rather Charles Martel's Theoderic IV.

25. Geary, *Aristocracy in Provence*, 40–41.

26. *Waltharius*, ed. Strecker, MGH Poet. Lat., V, 1–79. See Langosch, *Waltharius: die Dichtung und die Forschung*, for a traditional attribution to Ekkehard I of St. Gall, and Surles, *Roots and Branches*, 12–13, for a summary of the arguments placing the composition in the ninth century. For a further discussion of the debate, see *Waltharius and Ruodlieb*, ed. Kratz, xii–xiv.

27. The *moniage* tradition is by no means limited to Old French literature. The increasingly common practice of entering a monastery in old age resulted in the frequent appearance of the *moniage* in European literature. See, for example, Boberg, *Motif-Index of Early Icelandic Literature* (no. V476, "Warrior retires into monastery in his old days"), for items from Icelandic literature.

28. P. Becker, *Das Werden der Wilhelm und der Aimeregeste*; Bédier, *Les légendes épiques* 2:151–70; Lecoy, "Le *Chronicon Novaliciense*," *Romania* 67 (1942–43): 1–52.

29. Rajna, "Contributi alla storia dell'epopea e del romanzo medievale," *Romania* 23 (1974): 36–61; de Vries, "Die Heldensage," *Hessische Blätter für Volkskunde* 46 (1955): 8–25.

30. Lecoy, "Le *Chronicon Novaliciense*," 52. See also the most recent contribution to this debate in the introduction to *Cronaca di Novalesa*, ed. Alessio, xxx–xxxix.

31. *CN* 2.6–14.

32. *CN* 3.15.

33. See Geary, *Aristocracy in Provence*, 125.

34. Ibid., passim.

35. *CN* 5.8.

36. I am grateful to François Menant, who is preparing a study of northern Italian genealogical materials, for pointing out comparative examples.

37. *CN* 5.19.

38. *CN* Appendix.9. On the Arduini see Sergi, "Una grande circoscrizione," *Studi medievali*, 3d ser., 12 (1971): 637–712.

39. *CN* 5.23–24.

40. *CN* 2.12.

41. *CN* 2.7.

42. *CN* 5.23.

43. "est autem locus ubi predictae manent serpentes modicus; quae manent in petrarum forminibus" (*CN* 1.9).

44. *CN* 2.5.

45. *CN* 1.11.

46. *CN* 3.9.

47. *CN* 3.14.

48. *Monumenta Novaliciensia Vetustiora* (ed. Cipolla) 1:28.75–80.

49. Ibid., 1:28.79.

50. Guenée, *Historie et culture historique*, 80–81.

51. *CN* 2.5.

52. *CN* 2.13. See chapter 2, on Petronilla.

53. *RH*, 9.

54. *CN* 2.5.

55. *CN* 1.7.

56. *RH*, 9.

57. *CN* 2.11, 18, and 3.14; "hoc usque hodie" (*RH*, 9).

58. *Monumenta Novaliciensia Vetustiora* (ed. Cipolla) 1:312.

59. Newberry Library, Chicago, MS f3 fols. 1r–123v. See Cipolla, "Notizia di alcuni codici," *Memorie della reale accademia della scienze di Torino* 2, 44 (1894): 193–241.

60. Kastner, *Historiae fundationum monasteriorum*, 160, discusses how individual charters or tradition notices served as *Kristallisationskerne* to which narrative elements were attached.

61. Cipolla, "Notizia di alcuni codici," 78.

62. BN MS lat. 5313, fol. 78r.

63. See Jahn, "Urkunde und Chronik," 8–9, for the normal procedure in Bavaria, 12–13 for that followed in Benediktbeuern.

64. Geary, *Aristocracy in Provence*, chap. 2.

65. *CN* 2.18.

66. Ibid.

67. Corpus Inscriptionum Latinarum 5.2, no. 7231.

68. *CN* 2.3.

69. *CN* 4.2, 23. See Eco, *Il nome della rosa* (Milan: Bompiani, 1980), 43: "So che i seimila codici che vantava Nocalesa cento e più anni fa sono poco a petto dei vostri, e forse molti di quelli sono ora qui."

70. *CN* 3.20.

71. *RH*, 7.

72. No medieval necrologies from Benediktbeuern survive. The notices published in MGH Nec. I are a compilation from a necrology begun in 1681 which incorporated notices from earlier necrologies as well as three notices from a *computus* prepared in 1147.

73. *RH*, 5.

74. *RH*, 6.

75. *RH*, 7–8.

76. *Necrologium Benedictoburanum*, February 9: "In profesto S. Scholasticae virginis ac patronae nostri monasterii ann. Waldrami fundatoris huius loci et ab-

batis secundi" MGH Nec. I, 4. July 10: "In profesto commemorationis s. Benedicti abbatis et patroni nostri ann. Landfridi fundatoris huius loci et primi abbatis" MGH Nec. I, 6.

77. 10 November, *RH*, 10.

78. 21 February, *RH*, 11.

79. 10 June, *RH*, 11.

80. 16 September, *RH*, 11.

81. 31 August, *RH*, 12.

82. 2 May, *RH*, 12.

83. *RH*, 9: "emisit spiritum XVII Kal. Decembris: sepultus est juxta domum Abbatum L. W. Ely."

84. *RH*, 14.

85. See chapter 3, on Bavarian tradition books.

86. *RH*, 4.

87. *RH*, 7.

88. *RH*, 9: "Qualiter vel quomodo istud monasterium rexerint, minime compertum habemus."

89. *CN* 2.25.

90. *CN* 2.20.

91. *CN* 5.49. See *Chronaca di Novalesa*, ed. Alessio, 311 n. 49.

92. Schmitt, "Les revenants dans la société féodale," *Le temps de la réflexion* 3 (1982): 287, and most recently, *Les Revenants*, esp. 77–98.

93. *CN* 2.14.

94. See Geary, *Aristocracy in Provence*, passim.

95. Jahn, "Urkunde und Chronik."

96. *Breviarium Gotscalchi*, MGH SS IX, 223–24.

97. The preface, as edited by Wilhelm Wattenbach as the *Chronicon Benedictoburanum* in MGH SS IX, 232–37, makes the relationship between the chronicle and the *traditionsbuch* unintelligible. One must still consult the edition in the *Monumenta Boica* 7.

CHAPTER FIVE
POLITICAL MEMORY AND THE RESTRUCTURING OF THE PAST

1. Arles, Bibliothèque municipale MS 881, no. 38.

2. Baron du Roure, ed., "Histoire de Montmajour," *Revue Historique de Provence* (Aix, 1890–91), 265. In general, du Roure's editions are to be used with extreme caution, and one should refer to the originals whenever possible. With characteristic sloppiness, du Roure cites this document as evidence of the living memory of its foundation although it mentions nothing whatsoever about it.

3. On the divorce, see McNamara and Wemple, "Marriage and Divorce in the Frankish Kingdom," in *Women in Medieval Society*, ed. Stuard, 108–113.

4. *Recueil des chartes de l'abbaye de Cluny* (ed. Bernard and Bruel) 1:20.

5. *Cartulaire de l'abbaye de Saint-André-le-Bas de Vienne*, ed. Chevalier, no. 11*.

6. On the details of the political history, see Poupardin, *Le royaume de Provence*, 164–242.

7. The mid-nineteenth-century study of Hugo by Gingins-La-Sarraz, *Mémoires pour servir à l'histoire des royaumes de Provence et de Bourgogne-Jourane*, vol. 2, *Les Hugonides*, contains some useful suggestions concerning the networks of religious foundations and patronage constructed by Hugo and his family. For the most recent analyses of the "Bosonids," the group of kindreds to which Hugh belonged, see Rosenwein, *To Be the Neighbor of Saint Peter*, 180–81; and Bouchard, "The Bosonids," *French Historical Studies* 15 (1988): 407–31.

8. Hlawitschka, "Die verwandtschaftlichen Verbindungen zwischen dem hochburgundischen und dem niederburgundischen Königshaus," in *Grundwissenschaften und Geschichte*, ed. Schlögl and Herde, 28–57, esp. 45–46.

9. BN MS lat. 2812, fol. 98r.

10. *I diplomi di Ugo e di Lothario di Berengario II e di Adalberto*, ed. Schiaparelli, Dip. Ugo 46 and 47.

11. Poly, *La Provence*, 32–34.

12. Althoff, *Adels- und Königsfamilien*, 31–132. A major difference is that Lüneburg was founded before, not after, the family's reversals (although in both cases the monasteries perpetuated family memory after defeat).

13. Marseilles, Arch. départ. Bouches du Rhône (hereafter, ABR) 1 H 5, no. 12.

14. *Chronica Monasterii Casinensis* 1.6, ed. Wattenbach (MGH SS VII, 623): "Hugo . . . cum iam ab eo utpote senex vilipendi coepisset, et molestias quasdam atque ingratitudines pati, relicto ei regno, ipse in Burgundiam cum omni thesauro suo recessit; ibique monasterium de propriis sumptibus extruens, quod Sanctus Petrus de Arle nuncupatur, illudque sufficientissime ditans, in eodem monachus est effectus."

15. Gingins-La-Sarraz, *Mémoires* 2:133.

16. ABR, 2 H 11 l bis; "Histoire de Montmajour," ed. du Roure, 25.

17. Rouquette, *Provence romane*, vol. 1, *La Provence rhodanienne*, 334–36.

18. Unfortunately, the capitals were recently defaced by an unknown vandal.

19. Poly, "Listes épiscopales de Provence Xe–XIe siècles" (Ph.D. diss., University of Paris, 1972), 45; Amargier, "L'an mil à Montmajour," *Provence historique* 23 (1973): 263–69.

20. *Cart. Arles*, Archives communales, *Authentique de S. Trophime*, fols. 13v–14v.

21. *Liber memorialis von Remiremont*, ed. Hlawitschka, K. Schmid, and Tellenbach, 56v. Note that the *Liber memorialis* contains *memoria* of the family of Waldrada.

22. ABR, 2 H 11 l bis; *Cart. Arles*, 14v.

23. ABR, 2 H 9, no. 2; *Cartulaire de l'église d'Apt*, ed. Didier, Dubled, and Barruol, no. 18; BN MS lat. 13915, fol. 327v (Necrology of Montmajour), Chantelou, *Mons maior seu Historia*.

24. Poly, *La Provence*, 69–72.

25. Among others, ABR, 2 H 15, nos. 42 and 45; 2 H 11, no. 5; 2 H 12, no.

11. See also *Cartulaire de Notre Dame des Doms d'Avignon*, ed. Duprat, no. 54, etc. These groups were identified with the assistance of the *Gruppensuchprogram* developed at the University of Münster by the research team of Joachim Wollasch. On the program see Westerhoff, *Gruppensuche*, and Rosenwein, *To Be the Neighbor of Saint Peter*, 20–24.

26. Liudprand of Cremona, *Antapodosis* 5.31. See Poly, *La Provence*, 32.

27. BN MS lat. 13915, fols. 24r–25v (Chantelou, *Mons maior seu Historia*).

28. ABR, 2 H 13, no. 15; *Cartulaire de l'abbaye de Saint-André-le-Bas de Vienne*, ed. Chevalier, no. 22* = I diplomi di Ugo, no. 43.

29. ABR, 2 H 9, no. 3. We do not know when Theucinda died. Her undated "testament" (Arles, Bib. mun. MS 881, no. 2) is a *brevis memoria* of property which, after her death and that of her nephew Riculf, was to go to the monks of Montmajour.

30. Nimes, Arch. départ. du Gard, H 106, fols. 21v–22r; Manteyer, *La Provence* 1:513–14.

31. Nimes, Arch. départ. du Gard, H 106, fols. 18v–19r; Manteyer, *La Provence* 1:520–22.

32. Nimes, Arch. départ. du Gard, H 106, fols. 15r.–v; Manteyer, *La Provence* 1:517.

33. *Recueil des chartes de l'abbaye de Cluny* (ed. Bernard and Bruel), no. 2866; Poly, *La Provence*, 176.

34. See Amargier, "L'an mil à Montmajour," 263–69; Poly, *La Provence*, 70–71.

35. Amargier, in "L'an mil à Montmajour," suggests that the reasons for the retirement of Archinricus to Carluc were that he found the life at Montmajour "trop exclusivement cénobitique" and that he preferred the eremitic tradition of Cassian.

36. BN MS lat. 13915, fols. 327–328v (Chantelou, *Mons maior seu Historia*).

37. BN MS lat. 12702, fol. 138v.

38. See Geary, *Aristocracy in Provence*, map 2, for Abbo's holdings and passim for his kin and allies.

39. Manteyer, *La Provence* 1:152 n. 1.

40. Poly, *La Provence*, 32–33.

41. Ibid., 32.

42. On this sense of the truth in a created past, see Constable, "Forgery and Plagiarism in the Middle Ages," *Archiv für Diplomatik* 29 (1983): 20–21, and in general Fuhrmann, "Von der Wahrheit der Fälscher," in *Fälschungen im Mittelalter* 1:83–98.

43. See most recently Werner, *Histoire de France* 1:438.

44. Waldman, "Saint-Denis," 191.

45. On the political meaning of Charles's diplomatics, see Wolfram, ed., *Intitulatio II*, 115–23.

46. Wolfram, ed., *Intitulatio II*, 110–13.

47. McKitterick, *The Frankish Kingdoms*, 309, citing *Recueil des actes de Charles III le Simple*, ed. Lauer, 108.

48. Flodoard, *Annales*, ed. Lauer, a. 922.

49. Richer, *Histoire de France* (ed. Latouche) I, 14 (1:34). On the surname *Simplex* see Eckel, *Charles le Simple*, 110–44.

50. Flodoard, *Annales*, ed. Lauer, a. 923. See Sot, "Les élévations royales de 888 à 987," in *Religion et culture*, ed. Iogna-Prat and Picard, 145–50.

51. On Dudo's image of Charles see the work of Eleanor Searle, especially "Fact and Pattern in Heroic History," *Viator* 15 (1984): 119–37; "Frankish Rivalries and Norse Warriors," *Anglo-Norman Studies* 8 (1985): 198–213; and generally on Dudo, *Predatory Kinship*, 61–97.

52. MGH SS IX, 365–66. On the *Historia* see Ehlers, "Die *Historia Francorum Senonensis*," *Journal of Medieval History* 4 (1978): 1–25.

53. "Karolo vero a cede belli victore revertente, occurrit illi Herbertus infidelium nequissimus, et sub fictae pacis simulatione in castro quod Parrona dicitur ut hospitandi gratia diverteret conpulit. Et sic eum dolo captum retinuit. Habebat enim idem Robertus sororem istius Herberti in oniugio; de qua ortus est Hugo Magnus." MGH SS IX, 366.

54. Aimoin of Fleury, *De regibus francorum*, MGH SS IX, 375.

55. Rodulfus Glaber, *Historiarum libri quinque* (ed. France) 1.i.5, 10–11. France suggests that the story of Herbert's agonizing death, which Rodulfus attributes to his treason, may have come from the house of Blois (xlvi–xlvii). This is not impossible, but the description of his deathbed ravings ("There were twelve of us who swore to betray Charles") sounds so much like the twelve betrayers of their oath to St. Emmeram that one suspects a typological overlay, provided perhaps by a monastic source such as Rodulfus himself, rather than the faithful report of a family story.

56. "Fuit enim hic Hugo filius Rotberti, Parisiorum comitis, qui uidelicet Rotbertus breui in tempore rex constitutus et ab exercitu Saxonum est interfectus; cuius genus idcirco adnotare distulimus, quia ualde in ante repperitur obscurum." Rodulfus Glaber, *Historiarum libri quinque* (ed. France) 1.ii.6, 14.

57. Schmidt-Chazan, "Les origines germaniques d'Hughes Capet," in *Religion et culture*, ed. Iogna-Prat and Picard, 231–44, esp. 233.

58. Rodulfus Glaber, *Historiarum libri quinque* (ed. France) 1.ii.12.

59. See most recently Bur, "Adalbéron, archevêque de Reims, reconsidéré," in *Le roi de France et son royaume*, ed. Parisse and Barral i Altet, 55–63, esp. 56–67.

60. On the often repeated history of the Capetian accession, see Andrew Lewis, *Royal Succession*, 17–88, and his bibliography.

61. "Secundo anno post eius mortem Robertus princeps rebellavit contra Karolum Simplicem." MGH SS IX, 366.

62. "Eodem anno rebellavit contra Karolum Hugo dux Francorum." Ibid., 367–68.

63. "tradit[or] vetul[us], qui erat episcopus falsus Laudunis et consiliarius Karoli." Ibid., 368.

64. Rodulfus Glaber, *Historiarum libri quinque* (ed. France) 1.ii.50.

65. I am most grateful to Richard Landes for sharing his new edition of Ademar with me prior to its publication.

66. "Defuncto rege Ludovico regnavit pro eo filius eius Carolus cognomento Insipiens vel minor. Tunc Franci, coniurantes contra Carolum iuniorem eiciunt eum de regno et Odonem ducem Aquitaniae elevant. . . . Iterum Carolus minor regnum suscepit. . . . Contra quem iterum Francorum proceres conspirati, eum regno pellentes, Robertum ducem sibi constituerunt regem. tunc inter se divisi sunt Franci, sed major pars Roberto favebat. Carolus denique accito ab Otone imperatore auxilio cum multo exercitu partim de Baioaria partim de Francia regressus Franciam conserto praelio Rotbertum interfecit. Regnumque recuperans Ugoni filio Rotberti ducatum permisit regendum. Karolo migrante Ludovicus pro eo regnavit." BN MS lat. 6190, fols. 53–57. I am grateful to Richard Landes for this transcription.

67. Again, I am grateful to Richard Landes for sharing with me the proofs of the edition that he is preparing for the *Corpus Christianorum* edition of Ademar's works.

68. See Landes, "L'accession des Capétiens," in *Religion et Culture*, ed. Iogna-Prat and Picard, 151–66, with the texts of the three recensions (164).

69. "Hac de causa episcopus Montis Leudenensis, Ascelinus, ebdomada majora in qua est Coena Domini et Parasceve et sabbato ante Pascha velut Judas Christum tradidit, tradidit Carolum" (ibid., 164). Version β: "Hac de causa episcopus Montis Leudenensis, Ascelinus, ebdomada majora ante Pascha in qua est Coena Domini velud Judas Christum, et ipse tradidit Carolum."

70. A. Schmid, *Das Bild*.

71. See chap. 1, in section titled "Bavaria."

72. "gloriosus dux noster Arnulfus, virtute ex alto indutus, fortitudine clarus et victoria enituit eximius, quia de progenie imperatorum et regum est ortus, et per ipsum populus christianus de sevienti gladio paganorum est redemptus et in libertatem vite translatus." MGH SS XVII, 570; reproduced with other sources relative to Arnulf in Reindel, *Die bayerischen Luitpoldinger*, 112. On this text, unique for all of Europe in the tenth century, see Wattenbach and Holtzmann, eds., *Deutschlands Geschichtsquellen im Mittelalter*, vol. 1 (ed. Schmale), 264–65; and A. Schmid's discussion in *Das Bild*, 7–9.

73. See Reindel, *Die bayerischen Luitpoldinger*, 103–106, for the sources; A. Schmid, *Das Bild*, 16–17.

74. A. Schmid, *Das Bild*, 17–25.

75. See Geary, "Die Provence zur Zeit Karl Martells," in *Karl Martell und seiner Zeit*, ed. Jarnut et al., on the revisions currently under way in the appreciation of the secularizations supposedly initiated by Charles Martel.

76. A. Schmid, *Das Bild*, 21.

77. Ibid., 20.

78. Schmid cites the return of estates in the South Tyrol to Freising (*Das Bild*, 20–21).

79. Reindel, *Die bayerischen Luitpoldinger*, no. 49, pp. 80–92.

80. See chap. 4.

81. A. Schmid, *Das Bild*, 25–46.

82. Thietmar of Merseburg, *Chronicon* (ed. Holtzmann) 1.73 (MGH SSRG, IX, 34); A. Schmid, *Das Bild*, 36.

83. Bibliothèque royale de Belgique, Cod. Brux. 1814–1816; A. Schmid, *Das Bild*, 24.

84. According to Andreas of Regensburg (ca. 1380–ca. 1448), Arnold was buried in St. Emmeram, but later his remains were removed and thrown into a lake. However, the original tomb could still be seen in Regensburg (Reindel, *Die bayerischen Luitpoldinger*, 177). A. Schmid, in "Die Herrschergräber," *Deutsches Archiv* 32 (1976): 333–69, argues that the tradition of his burial at St. Emmeram reported by Andreas is a later elaboration of Regensburg monks and suggests Tegernsee as a more likely location since the abbot of St. Emmeram was a royal supporter at the time of Arnulf's death. Just why Andreas would create an alternative tradition (since by the time that Andreas was writing, the black legend of Arnulf was well established) is unclear.

85. "Postquam monasterium beatissimi martiris Emmerammi, quod prius extra fuerat, coepit esse intra muros Ratisbonensium civitatis, quos Arnolfus dux, inter optimates opere diviso, cito construxerat sub rege Heinrico." PL 141:1006.

86. See A. Schmid, *Das Bild*, 24. On the entry in the necrological annals of Fulda, see K. Schmid, ed., *Die Klostergemeinschaft von Fulda im früheren Mittelalter* 1:328.

87. See chap. 1, in section titled "Bavaria."

88. Reindel, *Die bayerischen Luitpoldinger*, no. 65.

89. See ibid., 133.

90. A. Schmid, *Das Bild*, 24 n. 89. The same error appears in the Reichenau necrology: Schmid, citing *Archiv für österreichische Geschichte* 19 (1856): 261.

91. A. Schmid, *Das Bild*, 24 n. 89. The necrology of the Cathedral Chapter of Salzburg gives the donation of Erding and Petting made by Arnulf of Carinthia to St. Peters as the reason for the memorialization.

92. A. Schmid, *Das Bild*, 60.

CHAPTER SIX
REMEMBERING PANNONIAN DRAGONS

1. Arnoldus S. Emmerammensis, *De miraculis S. Emmerammi libri duo*, PL 141:989–1090, partial edition MGH SS IV, 543–574. References are to the PL text, which is badly in need of a new edition. For a short introduction and recent literature, see Morsbach, "Arnold von St. Emmeram," in *Ratisbona Sacra*, 196–97.

2. PL 141: col. 1039–41.

3. See Sigal, "Le travail des hagiographes," *Francia* 15 (1987): 149–82 and, on the professed importance of eyewitness accounts, esp. 151–52, 157–58.

4. One of the best examinations of the judicial materials in a hagiographical dossier is that of Platelle, "Crime et châtiment à Marchiennes," *Sacris erudiri* 24 (1980): 155–202.

5. "et cartam, quam sibi monachi Sancti Martini fecerant, per consensum totius capituli, nobis reddidit, quae, usque in praesentem diem, inter alia agio-

graphia, penes nos servatur." *Cartulaire de l'abbaye de Saint-Père de Chartres* (ed. Guérard) 1:167 (chap. 39).

6. Clanchy, *From Memory to Written Record*, 117.

7. He may have seen images of dragons in the bestiary known to be in his library: "De natura bestiarum et volcurum," G. Becker, *Catalogi bibliothecarum antiqui*, no. 42, item 453, p. 128.

8. "Vae vobis, quia Draco venit ad vos cum ira magna, sciens quod modicum tempus habeat."

9. Isidore of Seville, *Etymologiae*, L. XII, orig. cap. 4.

10. G. Becker, *Catalogi bibliothecarum antiqui* 1:128.

11. "squammis horribilibus compactum, et ceu parmis, vel scutis ferro munitus."

12. "corpus illius quasi scuta fusilia et conpactum squamis se prementibus" (Job 41:15; in Vulgate, Job 41:6).

13. "Vae vobis, quia Draco venit ad vos cum ira magna, sciens quod modicum tempus habeat."

14. "Vae terrae et mari quia descendit diabolus ad vos habens iram magnam sciens quod modicum tempus habet" (Apoc. 12:12; the translation is the Douai version).

15. On memoria *ad res* or verbatim memory in the Middle Ages, see Carruthers, *The Book of Memory*.

16. Bartlett, *Remembering*. See above introduction, 19.

17. Landes, "*Millenarismus absconditus*," *Le Moyen Age* 98 (1992): 355–77; Fried, "Endzeiterwartung um die Jahrtausendwende," *Deutsches Archiv* 45 (1989): 381–473.

18. Rodulfus Glaber, *Historiarum libri quinque* (ed. France) 78–79.

19. *Annales Floriacenses* (MGH SS II, 254–55). See Rodulfus Glaber, *Historiarum libri quinque* (ed. France) 78–79 n. 2.

20. See, most recently, the summary by Freise, "St. Emmeram zu Regensburg," in *Ratisbona Sacra*, 182–88.

21. PL 141:1064.

22. PL 141:1063.

23. "Sed contrario admodum amaricabar in gestis videlicet domesticis, clarissimi patroni nostri Emmerammi martyris, dudum a quodam, qui se Cirinum, id est heredem, nominat, Frisingensis ecclesiae episcopo, ut puto recte scriptis, ante nos autem majorum negelgentia depravatis." PL 141:992.

24. PL 141:992. See also note 18 in the introduction, above.

25. *Vita Landiberti episcopi Traiectensis auctore Stephano* (MGH SSRM VI, 385).

26. Vitalis of Fleury, *Vita S. Pauli Aureliani*, c. I, 112, cited by Head, *Hagiography and the Cult of Saints*, 68. On the rewriting of hagiographical texts generally see Genicot, "*Discordiae concordantium*," *Académie royale de Belgique: Bulletin* 51 (1965): 65–75.

27. See Arbeo of Freising, *Vita et passio Sancti Haimhrammi martyris*, ed. Bischoff, 93–95.

28. On the importance of the present for medieval historiography in general,

see Goetz,"Die Gegenwart der Vergangenheit," *Historische Zeitschrift* 255 (1992): 61–97, esp. 72–81.

29. Arbeo of Freising, *Vita et passio*, ed. Bischoff, 95. The recensions are edited by Bruno Krusch in MGH SSRM IV, 452–526.

30. Arbeo of Freising, *Vita et passio*, ed. Bischoff, 52.

31. MGH SSRM IV, 501. See Arbeo of Freising, *Vita et passio*, ed. Bischoff, 96.

32. "Hoc igitur modo fidelis in Baioarios fines, qui meridiem versus, Alpibus; ad orientem Ungris; ad aquilonem vero Hircano nemori limitem Germaniae protendunt, non hac conterritus meta, devenit. Ubi cum defluentis Histri fluminis imperium sequeretur. Ratisbonam accessit urbem quae olim totius Germaniae, et nomine et dignitate principum, et adhuc eiusdem gentis metropolis antiquae prosapiae caput." PL 141:975–76.

33. "ut infra paucos annos immature mortis falce praecisi, pene omnis vita difficulter extorta, pro innocuo martyris sanguine discerperentur." PL 141:984.

34. PL 141:1009.

35. Dollinger, *L'évolution des classes rurales en Bavière*, appendix II, 504–12.

36. "Quanto honore et qua reverentia, quo affectu principes beatum Emmerammum coluerint, inter cetera sibi ab his collata predia seu preciosa donaria testantur." PL 141:1002.

37. *Arnold:* "Attestatur quoque territorium Ratisponense et praedium regale, quod a fastigio montis meridiani inter vias publicas usque ad muros ipsius monasterii a Carolo Magno traditum est beato Emmerammo et monachis eius sub imperiali testamento" (PL 141:1003). *Compare* DKar. I, 176.(BM 321): "id est a parte meridiana ipsius monasterii terra culta et inculta iugera ducenta sexuaginta et sex et de prata in totum iuxta fontem cuius vocabulum est Uiuarias, ubi potest colligere fenum carradas quinquaginta octo; est autem spacium longitudinis de sepe giro ipsius monasterii posita usque ad ipsum fontem perticas decim pedas quatringentas duodecim et de ipso fonte sursum in monte perticas centum quadraginta et septem et supra ipso fonte habet in latitudine de via publica usque ad aliam publicam perticas centum quinquaginta et in medio spacio de ipsa via publica usque ad aliam viam noviter factam perticas centum quadraginta, iuxta sepem vero monasterii, ubi latissimum est, perticas ducentas septem." Later in the eleventh century, this diploma would be used by Otloh of St. Emmeram to forge BM 352, granting St. Emmeram immunity from episcopal control.

38. "Duces vero, qui ante hunc principem sub regibus Francorum Baioariae regebant ducatum, quae bona beato Emmerammo contulerint, pitacia eorum et testamenta penes nos satis indicant inventa." PL 141:1003.

39. BM 1012.

40. BM 1349. D.L. II, no. 174.

41. Arnold PL 141:1002–1003: "ad orientem provinciae huius Lunaelacus optimo pisce vividus, unde regius cibus, ad occidentem vero vinifer cespes Spalticus, e quo regius potus." DL II, 1. no. 24, 30.

42. "Ex his autem omnibus qui Christi martyrem reverenter colebant seu cum reverentia diligebant, eo quod pre ceteris eiusdem cultui deditus esset, ex-

cipiendum mihi rectius puto persuavis memoriae Arnolfum, Carolomanni filium, primo Baioariae ducem, deinde Franciae regem, novissime autem ob beati Petri defensionem, post victorias mirificas, Romae factum imperatorem." PL 141:1003.

43. BM 1777, 1844, and 1938.

44. "domino suo Arnolfo filio regali permittente" (no. 86, 876–80).

45. "in presentia igitur Arnulfi ducis" (no. 102, 883–87).

46. "anno Arnulfi regis secundo" (no. 148, 889–91).

47. BM 1938, D. Arn. 160.

48. D. Arn. 190. See A. Schmid, "Die Herrschergräber," 333–69.

49. "amorem et honorem scilicet patroni nostri et preciosi dei martiris Emmerammi." Ibid.

50. "elegit beatum Emmerammum vitae suae ac regno patronum." PL 141:1003.

51. D. Arn. 12. BM 1777, 160; BM 1938.

52. D. Arn. 75, BM 1844.

53. Munich Clm 14000. See the literature in Freise, *Ratisbona Sacra*, 197–99.

54. See A. Schmid, "Die Herrschergräber."

55. PL 141:1005.

56. "ut regio jure ac potestate, suorum utpote qui fuerit antecessorum, sibi vindicaret prescriptum magni precii librum." PL 141:1005.

57. "Qui venientes cum humilitate ac tremore sunt intromissi et non infructuose admissi." PL 141:1010.

58. "Nobiles quidam viri, cognatione nobis et tempore noti, quorum nomina silemus." PL 141:1009.

59. "Nam capita cum manibus religiose altari imponentes, professi sunt se martiri perpetuos censuales" (PL 141:1010). Presumably, noble *censuales*, such as Arnold is apparently describing, differ greatly from unfree *servi* given as *censuales* to the monastery. Dollinger, *L'évolution des classes rurales en Bavière*, 340–41, gives examples of such *censuales* who are and who remain free.

60. "Aliqui tradiderunt servos et ancillas, ut in conspectu tanti patroni invenirent gratias." PL 141:1010.

61. "Alii vero contulerunt possessiones prediorum, ne ultra starent in parte reorum." PL 141:1010.

62. "cum eiusdem manibus attractis more Baioarico testibus retradidit predia, uti antea fuerant tradita" (PL 141:1010). "More Baioarico" refers apparently not only to the presence of witnesses but to the custom of donations by women being done through the agency of a male advocate—as in a donation of ca. 1020, in which a certain Bertha makes a donation through "Hartwicus, advocatus cum manu Perehte, Guntperti fratris eius vidue, tradidit Pertold." *Die Traditionen des Hochstifts Regensburg* (Widemann, ed.), no. 304.

63. PL 141:1011.

64. Fols. 18v and 23v. *Die Traditionen des Hochstifts Regensburg* (ed. Widemann), no. 210 *a* and *b*, 190–91. On the double entries see Berthold Bretholz, "Studien zu den Traditionsbüchern von S. Emmeram in Regensburg," *MIÖG* 12 (1891): 24–45.

65. "ad seruitium monachorum deo inibi famulantium et ut inde pauperes ac peregrini uictu et uestitu consolarentur uel recrearentur." *Die Traditionen des Hochstifts Regensburg* (ed. Widemann), 190–91.

66. *Das Martyrolog-Necrolog*, ed. Freise, Geuenich, and Wollasch, fol. 5r [January 15]: "Perehtoldus comes."

67. See Freise's introduction to the manuscript, esp. 35–40, as well as his "Kalendarische und annalistische Grundformen der Memoria," in *Memoria*, ed. K. Schmid and Wollasch, 441–577, esp. 450–52.

68. *Das Martyrolog-Necrolog*, ed. Freise, Geuenich, and Wollasch, 72–75.

CHAPTER SEVEN
CONCLUSIONS

1. See Kraus, *Die Translatio S. Dionysii Areopagitae von St. Emmeram in Regensburg.*

SELECT BIBLIOGRAPHY

PRIMARY SOURCES

Manuscript Sources

Arles
Archives communales: *Authentique de S. Trophime.*
Bibliothèque municipale MS 881.

Chicago
Newberry Library: MS f3, Miscellany from Novalesa.

Ivrea
Biblioteca Capitolare: MS 31 (LXXXVI), Sacramentarium Episcopi Warmundi.

Marburg
Fulda Kopialbuch, Hessisches Staatsarchiv, Marburg, K 424.

Marseilles
Archives départementales des Bouches du Rhône
   Serie 3 G: Archevêché d'Arles.
   Serie 4 G: Chapitre cathédral de Saint-Trophime d'Arles.
   Serie 5 G: Evêché de Marseille.
   Serie 1 H: Abbaye de Saint-Victor de Marseille.
   Serie 2 H: Abbaye de Montmajour.

Munich
Bayerische Hauptstaatsarchiv
   Benediktbeuern Lit. n. 9. *Rotulus historicus.*
   Hochstift Freising Lit. 3a. Cozroh's *Codex traditionum.*
   St. Emmeram KL Lit. 5 1/2 (earliest fragments of Regensburg *Traditions-buch*).
   St. Emmeram KL Lit. 5 1/3 (Anamot's *Codex traditionum*).
   St. Emmeram KL Lit. 5 1/4 *b* (fragments of St. Emmeram *Traditionsbücher*).
   Hochstift Passau Lit. 1. Passau *Traditionsbuch.*

Nimes
Archives départementales du Gard
   H 106 Cartulaire ou livre "A" de Psalmody.
   H 116 Chartes de Psalmody.

Paris
Bibliothèque Nationale
   BN MS lat. 2812. Sacramentary of Arles.
   BN MS lat. 7230. *Praeceptum Dagoberti regis.*
   BN MS lat. 10846. *Vita et acta S. Dionysii.*
   BN MS lat. 13915. Claude Chantelou, *Mons maior seu Historia Monasterii sancti Petri Montis maioris.*
   BN MS lat. 17764. Cartulary of Corbie.

BN MS nouv. add. lat. 326. *Privilegia ecclesiae Sancti Dionysii.*
BN MS nouv. acq. lat. 1497–1498. Cartularies of Cluny.

Turin
Archivio di Stato
  Nuova collezione "museo." *Chronicon Novaliciense.*
  MS J. b. I. 15, *Bibla Magna.*

Published Sources

Actes concernant les vicomtes de Marseille et leurs descendants. Edited by Henry de Gérin-Richard and Émile Isnard. Monaco: Archives du Palais, 1926.
Ademar of Chabannes. *Chronique.* Edited by Jules Chavanon. Collection de textes pour servir à l'étude et à l'enseignement de l'histoire, 20. Paris: A. Picard, 1897.
Aimoin of Fleury. *De regibus francorum: Excerpta ex miraculis S. Benedicti.* MGH SS IX, 374–76.
Alcuin. *De animae ratione liber ad Eulaliam virginem.* PL 101:639–50.
Das älteste Traditionsbuch des Klosters Mondsee. Edited by Gebhard Rath and Erich Reiter. Forschungen zur Geschichte Oberösterreichs 16. Linz: Oberösterreichisches Landesarchiv, 1989.
Anglo Saxon Chronicle: Two of the Saxon Chronicles Parallel. Edited by Charles Plummer (revising Dorothy Whitelock). Vol. 1. Oxford: Clarendon Press, 1980.
Annales Bertiniani. MGH SSRG 5. Edited by Georg Waitz. Hannover: Hahn, 1883.
Annales Floriacenses. MGH SS II 254–55.
Annales Fuldenses sive Annales regni francorum orientalis. MGH SSRG 7. Edited by Friedrich Kurze. Hannover: Hahn, 1978.
Arbeo of Freising. *Vita et passio Sancti Haimhrammi martyris: Leben und Leiden des hl. Emmeram.* Edited and translated by Bernhard Bischoff. Munich: Ernst Heimeran, 1953. *Vita Ememarami: Vita vel passio Haimhrammi episcopi et martyris Ratisbonensis.* MGH SSRM IV, 452–526.
Arnoldus S. Emmerammensis. *De miraculis S. Emmerammi Libro Duo.* PL 141:989–1090 (partial edition MGH SS IV, 543–74).
Augustine. *Confessiones.* Edited by Luc Verheijen. Corpus Christianorum Series Latina 27. Turnhout: Brepols, 1981.
———. *De Trinitate.* Edited by W. J. Mountain. Corpus Christianorum Series Latina 50a. Turnhout: Brepols, 1968.
Breviarium Gotscalchi. MGH SS IX, 221–24.
Brevium Exempla ad describendas res ecclesiasticas et fiscales. MGH Capit. I, 250–56.
Cartulaire de l'abbaye de Cysoing et de ses dépendances. Edited by Ignace de Coussemaker. Lille: Imprimerie Saint-Augustin, 1883.
Cartulaire de l'abbaye de Lérins. Edited by Henri Moris and Edmond Blanc. Paris: H. Champion, 1883.
Cartulaire de l'abbaye de Saint-André-le-Bas de Vienne ordre de Saint Benoît suivi d'un appendice de chartres inédites sur le diocèse de Vienne (IXe–XIIe siècles). Edited by Cyr Ulysse Joseph Chevalier. Lyon: N. Schevring, 1869.

Cartulaire de l'abbaye de Saint Bernard de Romans. Edited by Cyr Ulysse Joseph Chevalier. (s.l.s.d.) [Romans: 1898].

Cartulaire de l'abbaye de Saint-Père de Chartres. Edited by Benjamin Edme Charles Guérard. 2 vols. Collection des cartulaires de France. Paris: Imprimerie de Crapelet, 1840.

Cartulaire de l'abbaye de Saint Victor de Marseille. Edited by Benjamin Edme Charles Guérard. 2 vols. Collection de Documents inédits sur l'histoire de France, 16. Paris: Ch. Lahure, 1857.

Cartulaire de l'église d'Apt (835–1130). Edited by Noël Didier, Henri Dubled, and Jean Barruol. Paris: Dalloz, 1967.

Cartulaire de Notre Dame des Doms d'Avignon. Edited by E. Duprat. Avignon: Musée Calver, 1932.

The Cartulary of Flavigny, 717–1113. Edited by Constance Brittain Bouchard. Medieval Academy Books, 99. Cambridge, Mass.: Medieval Academy of America, 1991.

Chartae Latinae Antiquiores: Facsimile Edition of the Latin Charters Prior to the Ninth Century. Edited by Albert Bruckner and Robert Marichal. Vols. 13–19, *France,* edited by Hartmut Atsma and Jean Vezin. Zurich: Urs Graf, 1981–1987.

Les chartes du pays d'Avignon (439–1040). Edited by Georges de Manteyer. Mâcon: Imprimerie Protat, 1914.

Chronica Monasterii Casinensis. Edited by Wilhelm Wattenbach. MGH SS VII, 574–844.

Chronicon Benedictoburanum. Edited by Wilhelm Wattenbach. MGH SS IX, 210–38.

Codex Diplomaticus Fuldensis. Edited by Ernst Friedrich Johann Dronke. Cassel: Theodor Fischer, 1850.

Cronaca di Novalesa. Edited by Gian Carlo Alessio. Turin: Einaudi editore, 1982.

Dhuoda. *Manuel pour mon fils.* Edited by Pierre Riché. Sources chrétiennes 225. Paris: Les Éditions du Cerf, 1975.

I diplomi di Ugo e di Lothario di Berengario II e di Adalberto. Edited by Luigi Schiaparelli. Fonti per la storia d'Italia, 38. Rome: Tipografia del Senato, 1924.

Flodoard. *Annales.* Ed. Philippe Lauer. Paris: A. Picard, 1905.

Fragmentum de Arnulfo duce Bavariae. MGH SS XVII, 570.

Genealogia Welforum. MGH SS XIII, 733–34.

Gesta abbatum S. Bertini Sithiensium. MGH SS XIII, 600–673; *Cartulaire de l'abbaye de Saint-Bertin.* Edited by Benjamin Edme Charles Guérard. Collection des Cartulaires de France, 3. Paris: Crapelet, 1840.

Gesta episcoporum Frisingensium. MGH SS XXIV, 314–31.

Guido of Arezzo. *Epistola Guidonis Michaeli monacho de ignoto cantu.* PL 141:423–32.

———. *Micrologus.* Edited by Jos. Smits van Waesberghe. Corpus scriptorum de musica 4. [Rome]: American Institute of Musicology, 1955.

Helgaud of Fleury. *Vie de Robert le Pieux: Epitoma vitae regis Rotberti.* Edited and translated by Robert-Henri Bautier and Gillette Labory. Paris: Éditions du Centre National de la Recherche Scientifique, 1965.

Hemingi Chartularium Ecclesiae wigorniensis. Edited by Thomas Hearne. 2 vols. Oxford: E theatro Sheldoniano, 1723.

Historia Francorum Senonensis. MGH SS IX, 364–69.

Inventaires et documents: Monuments historiques. Edited by Jules Tardif. Paris: J. Claye, 1866.

Letaldus of Micy. *Liber Miraculorum S. Maximini.* PL 137:795–824.

Liber memorialis von Remiremont. Edited by Eduard Hlawitschka, Karl Schmid, and Gerd Tellenbach. MGH Libri memoriales I. Zurich: Weidmann, 1970; Munich: Monumenta Germaniae Historica, 1981.

Liudprand of Cremona. *Die Werke Liudprands von Cremona.* Edited by Joseph Becker. MGH SSRG 41. Hannover: Hahn, 1915.

Das Martyrolog-Necrolog von St. Emmeram zu Regensburg. Edited by Eckhard Freise, Dieter Geuenich and Joachim Wollasch. MGH Libri memoriales et necrologia, n.s. 3. Hannover: Hahn, 1986.

Meginfred of Magdeburg. *De vita et virtutibus Beati Emmerammi.* PL 141:970–86.

Monumenta Benedicto-burana / Rotulus Historicus / Monumenta Boica 7. Munich: in Bibliopolio Academico (1766), 1–17.

Monumenta Novaliciensia Vetustiora. Edited by Carlo Cipolla. 2 vols. Fonti per la storia d'Italia. Rome: Forzani E. C. Tipografi del Senato, 1898 and 1901.

Necrologium Benedictoburanum. MGH Nec. I, 3–7.

"*Notitia Arnonis* und *Breves Notitiae.* Die Salzburger Güterverzeichnisse aus der Zeit um 800: Sprachlichhistorische Einleitung, Text und Übersetzung," Edited by Fritz Lošek. In *Mitteilungen der Gesellschaft für Salzburger Landeskunde* 130 (1990): 5–193.

Odilo of Cluny. *Die Lebensbeschreibung der Kaiserin Adelheid von Abt Odilo von Cluny (Odilonis Cluniacensis abbatis Epitaphium domine Adelheide auguste).* Edited by Herbert Paulhart. Graz-Cologne: Böhlaus Nach, 1962.

Odorannus of Sens. *Opera omnia.* Edited and translated by Robert-Henri Bautier and Monique Gilles. Sources d'histoire médiévale, 4. Paris: Éditions du Centre National de la Recherche Scientifique, 1972.

Peter the Venerable. *De miraculis: Libri duo.* PL 189:851–954.

Recueil des actes de Charles III le Simple roi de France (893–923). Edited by Philippe Lauer. Paris: Imprimerie nationale, 1949.

Recueil des actes de Philippe Ier, roi de France (1059–1108). Edited by Maurice Prou. Paris: Imprimerie nationale, 1908.

Recueil des actes des rois de Provence (855–928). Edited by René Poupardin. Paris: Imprimerie nationale, 1920.

Recueil des chartes de l'abbaye de Cluny. Edited by Auguste Bernard and Alexandre Bruel. 6 vols. Paris: Imprimerie nationale, 1876–1903.

Regesta pontificum romanorum. Edited by Philippe Jaffé. 2 vols. 2d ed. Leipzig: Veit, 1885–1888.

Rhétorique à Herennius. Edited and translated by Guy Achard. Paris: Les Belles Lettres, 1989.

Richer. *Histoire de France (888–995).* Edited and translated by Robert Latouche. 2 vols. Les Classiques de l'Histoire de France au Moyen Age, 12. Paris: Honoré Champion, 1930–1937.

Rodulfus Glaber. *Historiarum libri quinque*. Edited and translated by John France. Oxford Medieval Texts. Oxford: Clarendon Press, 1989.

Sacramentario del vescovo Warmondo di Ivrea: Fine secolo X, Ivrea, Biblioteca Capitolare, MS. 31 (LXXXVI). Ivrea: Priuli and Verlucca, 1990.

Thietmar of Merseburg. *Chronicon*. Edited by Robert Holtzmann. MGH SSRG IX. Berlin: Weidmann, 1935.

Die Traditionen des Hochstifts Freising. Edited by Theodor Bitterauf. 2 vols. Quellen und Erörterungen zur bayerischen und deutschen Geschichte n.f. 4, 5. Munich: Rieger, 1905.

Die Traditionen des Hochstifts Passau. Edited by Max Heuwieser. Quellen und Erörterungen zur bayerischen Geschichte n.f. 6. Munich: Rieger, 1930.

Die Traditionen des Hochstifts Regensburg und des Klosters S. Emmeram. Edited by Josef Widemann. Quellen und Erörterungen zur bayerischen Geschichte n.f. 8. Munich: C. H. Beck'sche Verlagsbuchhandlung, 1943.

Traditiones Wizenburgenses: Die Urkunden des Klosters Weißenburg 661–864. Edited by Karl Glöckner and Anton Doll. Arbeiten der Hessischen Historischen Kommission Darmstadt. Darmstadt: Hessische Historische Kommission, 1979.

Urkundenbuch des Klosters Fulda. Edited by Edmund E. Stengel. 2 vols. Marburg: N. G. Elwert, 1956.

Vita Landiberti episcopi Traiectensis auctore Stephano. MGH SSRM VI, 385–92.

Vita Mahthildis Reginae. MGH SS IV, 282–302.

Vita Mahthildis Reginae antiquior. MGH SS X, 573–82.

Vita Sanctae Odiliae virginis. MGH SSRM VI, 37–50.

Vitalis of Fleury. *Vita S. Pauli Aureliani*. AASS May II, 111–20.

Waltharius. Edited by Karl Strecker. MGH Poet. Lat., V, 1–79.

Waltharius and Ruodlieb. Edited and translated by Dennis M. Kratz. New York: Garland, 1984.

SECONDARY WORKS

Althoff, Gerd. *Adels- und Königsfamilien im Spiegel ihrer Memorialüberlieferung: Studien zum Totengedenken der Billunger und Ottonen*. Münstersche Mittelalter-Schriften 47. Munich: Wilhelm Fink Verlag, 1984.

Amargier, P.-A. "L'an mil à Montmajour: Archinric, scribe et abbé." *Provence historique* 23 (1973): 263–69.

"L'an mil: Rythmes et acteurs d'une croissance." *Médiévales* 21 (1991): 5–114.

Assmann, Jan. "Kollektives Gedächtnis und kulturelle Identität." In *Kultur und Gedächtnis*, ed. Jan Assmann and Tonio Hölscher, 9–19. Frankfurt am Main: Suhrkamp, 1988.

Atsma, Hartmut. "Le Fonds des chartes mérovingiennes de Saint-Denis: Rapport sur une recherche en cours." *Paris et Ile-de-France Mémoires* 32 (1981): 259–72.

Atsma, Hartmut, ed. *La Neustrie, les pays au nord de la Loire de 650 à 850*. 2 vols. Beihefte der Francia, 16. Sigmaringen: Jan Thorbecke Verlag, 1989.

Bachrach, Bernard S. "The Angevin Strategy of Castle Building in the Reign of Fulk Nerra, 987–1040," *American Historical Review* 88, no. 3 (1983): 533–60.

Bachrach, Bernard S. "The Idea of the Angevin Empire." *Albion* 10 (1978): 293–99.

———. "A Study in Feudal Politics: Relations Between Fulk Nerra and William the Great, 995–1030." *Viator* 7 (1976): 111–22.

———. "Toward a Reappraisal of William the Great, Duke of Aquitaine, 995–1030." *Journal of Medieval History* 5 (1979): 11–21.

Baddeley, Alan D. *Human Memory: Theory and Practice.* London: Erlbaum, 1990.

———. *The Psychology of Memory.* New York: Basic Books, 1976.

Baker, Keith Michael. "Memory and Practice: Politics and the Representation of the Past in Eighteenth-Century France." *Representations* 11 (1985): 134–64.

Barrière, Bernadette. "L'anthroponymie en Limousin aux XIe et XIIe siècles." In *Genèse médiévale de l'anthroponymie moderne*, 23–34. Tours: s.d. (1988).

Barthélemy, Dominique. "La mutation féodale a-t-elle eu lieu?" *Annales ESC* 47, no. 3 (1992): 767–77.

———. "Qu'est-ce que le servage, en France, au XIe siècle." *Revue Historique* 287, no. 2 (1992): 233–84.

———. *La société dans le comté de Vendôme de l'an mil au XIVe siècle.* Paris: Fayard, 1993.

Bartlett, Frederic Charles. *Remembering: A Study in Experimental and Social Psychology.* New York: Macmillan, 1932.

Bautier, Robert-Henri. "L'hérésie d'Orléans et le mouvement intellectuel au début du XIe siècle: Documents et hypothèses." In *Actes du 95e congrès national des sociétés savantes*, section de philologie et d'histoire jusqu'à 1610, I. *Enseignement et vie intellectuelle (IXe-XVIe siècle)*, 63–88. Paris: Bibliothèque National, 1975.

———. "La Place de l'abbaye de Fleury-sur-Loire dans l'historiographie française du IXe au XIIe siècle." In *Études ligériennes d'histoire et d'archéologie médiévales: Mémoires et exposés présentés à la Semaine d'études médiévales de Saint-Benoît-sur-Loire du 3 au 10 juillet 1969*, ed. René Louis, 25–33. Cahiers d'archéologie et d'histoire 4. Auxerre: Société des fouilles archéologiques et des monuments historiques de l'Yonne, 1975.

Beck, Patrice. "Évolution des formes anthroponymiques en Bourgogne (900–1280)." In *Genèse médiévale de l'anthroponymie moderne*, 61–85.

Becker, Gustavus. *Catalogi bibliothecarum antiqui*, vol. 1. Bonn: Max. Cohen et filium, 1885.

Becker, Philipp August. *Die Altfranzösische Wilhelmsage und ihre Beziehung zu Wilhelm dem Heiligen.* Halle: Max Niemeyer, 1896; rpt., Geneva: Slatkine Reprints, 1974.

———. *Das werden der Wilhelm und der Aimeregeste.* Leipzig: S. Hirzel, 1939.

Bédier, Joseph. *Les légendes épiques.* 4 vols. 3d ed. Paris: H. Champion, 1926–29.

Beech, George T. "Les noms de personne poitevins du 9e au 12e siècle." *Revue Internationale d'Onomastique* 26 (1974): 81–100.

Bischoff, Bernhard. *Latin Palaeography: Antiquity and the Middle Ages.* Translated by Dáibhí ó Cróinín and David Ganz. Cambridge: Cambridge University Press, 1990.

————. "Literarisches und künstlerisches Leben in St. Emmeram (Regensburg) während des frühen und hohen Mittelalters." In *Mittelalterliche Studien: Ausgewählte Aufsätze zur Schriftkunde und Literaturgeschichte* 2: 77–115. Stuttgart: Anton Hiersemann, 1967.

————. *Die Südostdeutschen Schreibschulen und Bibliotheken in der Karolingerzeit.* Vol. 1, *Die bayrischen Diözesen.* Weisbaden: Otto Harassowitz, 1960.

Bisson, Thomas N. "Unheroed Pasts: History and Commemoration in South Frankland Before the Albigensian Crusades." *Speculum* 65, no. 2 (1990): 281–308.

Bloch, Marc. *Feudal Society.* 2 vols. Translated by L. A. Manyon. Chicago: University of Chicago Press, 1961.

Boberg, Inger M. *Motif-Index of Early Icelandic Literature.* Bibliotheca arnamagnaeana 27. Copenhagen: Munksgaard, 1966.

Bois, Guy. *La mutation de l'an mil: Lournand, village mâconnais de l'antiquite au feodalisme.* Paris: Fayard, 1989. In English: *The Transformation of the Year One Thousand: The Village of Lournand from Antiquity to Feudalism,* trans. Jean Birrell. Manchester: Manchester University Press, 1992.

Bonnassie, Pierre. *From Slavery to Feudalism.* Past and Present Publications. Cambridge: Cambridge University Press, 1991.

Bouchard, Constance B. "The Bosonids, Or Rising to Power in the Late Carolingian Age." *French Historical Studies* 15, no. 3 (1988): 407–31.

————. "Family Structure and Family Consciousness Among the Aristocracy in the Ninth to Eleventh Centuries." *Francia* 14 (1986): 639–58.

————. "The Origins of the French Nobility: A Reassessment." *American Historical Review* 86, no. 3 (1981): 501–32.

————. *Sword, Miter and the Cloister: Nobility and the Church in Burgundy 980–1198.* Ithaca, N.Y.: Cornell University Press, 1987.

Bourin, Monique. "Bilan de l'enquête: De la Picardie au Portugal, l'apparition du système anthroponymique à deux éléments et ses nuances régionales." In *Genèse médiévale de l'anthroponymie moderne,* 233–46.

————. "Les formes anthroponymiques et leur évolution d'après les données du cartulaire du chapitre cathédral d'Agde (Xe siècle–1250)." In *Genèse médiévale de l'anthroponymie moderne,* 179–217.

Bournazel, Éric. "Mémoire et parenté (Le problème de la continuité dans la noblesse de l'an Mil)." In *La France de l'an Mil,* ed. Robert Delort, 114–24. Paris: Éditions du Seuil, 1990.

Bourrilly, V.-L. et al. *Les Bouches-du-Rhône: Encyclopédie Départementale.* Vol. 2, *Antiquité et Moyen Age.* Paris: Honoré Champion, 1924; Marseille: Archives Départementales, 1924.

Bransford, John. *Human Cognition: Learning, Understanding and Remembering.* Belmont, Calif.: Wadsworth, 1979.

Bransford, John and Robert Shaw, eds. *Perceiving, Acting, and Knowing: Toward an Ecological Psychology.* Hillsdale, N.J.: Lawrence Erlbaum Associates, 1977.

Breslau, Harry. *Handbuch der Urkundenlehre für Deutschland und Italien.* Vol. 1. Lepizig: Verlag von Veit, 1912.

Bretholz, Berthold. "Studien zu den Traditionsbüchern von S. Emmeram in Regensburg." *MIÖG* 12 (1891): 1–45.

Brett, Martin. "John of Worcester and His Contemporaries." In *The Writing of History in the Middle Ages: Essays Presented to R. W. Southern*, ed. Davis and Wallace-Hadrill, 101–26.

Brown, Peter. *The Cult of the Saints: Its Rise and Function in Latin Christianity.* Chicago: University of Chicago Press, 1981.

Brown, Reginald Allen. *Origins of English Feudalism.* London: Allen and Unwin, 1973.

Bruel, Alexandre. "Note sur la transcription des actes privés dans les cartulaires antérieurement au XIIe siècle." *Bibliothèque de l'École des Chartes* 36 (1875): 445–56.

Brunner, Karl. "Der fränkische Fürstentitel im neunten und zehnten Jahrhundert." In *Intitulatio II: Lateinische Herrscher- und Fürstentitel im neunten und zehnten Jahrhundert*, ed. Wolfram, 179–340.

Buchner, Rudolf. *Die Provence in merowingischer Zeit: Verfassung—Wirtschaft—Kultur.* Arbeiten zur deutschen Rechts- und Verfassungsgeschichte 9. Stuttgart: Verlag von W. Kohlhammer, 1933.

Bulst, Neithard. "Rodulfus Glabers *Vita domni Willelmi abbatis.* Neue Edition nach einer Handschrift des 11. Jahrhunderts (Paris, Bibl. nat., lat. 5390)." *Deutsches Archiv für Erforschung des Mittelalters* 30 (1974): 450–87. Reprinted and translated by John France in Rodulfus Glaber, *Historiarum libri quinque*, ed. France, 254–99.

———. *Untersuchungen zu den Klosterreformen Wilhelms von Dijon (962–1013).* Pariser historische Studien 11. Bonn: Ludwig Röhrscheid Verlag, 1973.

Bur, Michel. "Adalbéron, archevêque de Reims, reconsidéré." In *Le roi de France et son royaume*, ed. Parisse and Barral i Altet, 55–63.

Campbell, James, ed. *The Anglo-Saxons.* Harmondsworth: Penguin, 1991.

Carruthers, Mary. *The Book of Memory: A Study of Memory in Medieval Culture.* Cambridge: Cambridge University Press, 1990.

Cipolla, Carlo. "Notizia di alcuni codici dell'antica Biblioteca Novalicense." *Memorie della reale accademia della scienze di Torino*, ser. 2, 44 (1894): 193–241.

Clanchy, M. T. *From Memory to Written Record: England, 1066–1307.* 2d rev. ed. London: Blackwell, 1993.

Classen, Peter, ed. *Recht und Schrift im Mittelalter.* Vorträge und Forschungen 23. Sigmaringen: Jan Thorbecke Verlag, 1977.

Cody, Cheryll Ann. "There Was No 'Absalom' on the Ball Plantations: Slave-Naming Practices in the South Carolina Low Country (1720–1865)." *American Historical Review* 92, no. 3 (1987): 563–96.

Coleman, Janet. *Ancient and Medieval Memories: Studies in the Reconstruction of the Past.* Cambridge: Cambridge University Press, 1992.

Constable, Giles. "Forgery and Plagiarism in the Middle Ages." *Archiv für Diplomatik* 29 (1983): 1–41.

Corbet, Patrick. *Les saints ottoniens: Sainteté dynastique, sainteté royale et sainteté féminine autour de l'an Mil.* Beihefte der Francia, 15. Sigmaringen: Jan Thorbecke Verlag, 1986.

Dakhlia, Jocelyne. *L'oublie de la cité: La mémoire collective à l'épruve du lignage dans le jérid tunisien.* Paris: Éditions la Découverte, 1990.

Davies, Wendy. "The Composition of the Redon Cartulary." *Francia* 17 (1990): 69–90.

Davis, R. H. C. and J. M. Wallace-Hadrill, eds. *The Writing of History in the Middle Ages: Essays Presented to R. W. Southern.* Oxford: Clarendon Press, 1981.

Delisle, Léopold Victor, ed. *Inventaire des manuscrits de la Bibliothèque Nationale.* Fonds de Cluni. Paris: H. Champion, 1884.

De Vries, Jan. "Die Heldensage." *Hessische Blätter für Volkskunde* 46 (1955): 8–25.

Dittrich, Josef. "Personennamen im *Codex Odalberti.*" *Mitteilungen der Gesellschaft für Salzburger Landeskunde* 61 (1921): 55–60.

Dollinger, Philippe. *L'évolution des classes rurales en Bavière, depuis la fin de l'époque carolingienne jusqu'au milieu du XIIIe siècle.* Publications de la Faculté des lettres de l'Université de Strasbourg 112. Paris: Les Belles Lettres, 1949.

Dopsch, Alfons. *Die Wirtschaftsentwicklung der Karolingerzeit vornehmlich in Deutschland.* 2 vols. 3d ed. Weimar: Hermann Böhlaus Nachfolger, 1962; Darmstadt: Wissenschaftliche Buchgesellschaft, 1962.

Duby, Georges. *Le Chevalier, la femme et le prêtre: Le mariage dans la France féodale.* Paris: Hachette, 1981.

——. *La société aux XIe et XIIe siècles dans la région mâconnaise.* Paris: Armand Colin, 1953; rpt., Paris: S.E.V.P.E.N., 1971.

——. *Les trois ordres ou l'imaginaire du féodalisme.* Paris: Éditions Gallimard, 1978.

Du Cange, C. du F. *Glossarium mediae et infimae latinitatis.* Niort: L. Favre, 1885.

Dudai, Yadin. *The Neurobiology of Memory: Concepts, Findings, Trends.* Oxford: Oxford University Press, 1989.

Dunbabin, Jean. "Aristocratic Families and Their Perception of the Past in Twelfth-Century France." Forthcoming.

Ebbinghaus, Hermann. *Über das Gedächtnis.* Leipzig, 1885. In English: *Memory: A Contribution to Experimental Psychology,* trans. by Henry A. Ruger and Clara E. Bussenius. New York: Columbia University Teachers College, 1913.

Eckel, Auguste. *Charles le Simple.* Paris: É. Bouillon, 1899.

Eckhart, Lothar. "Die Kontinuität in der Lorcher Kirchenbauten mit besonderer Berücksichtigung der Kirche des 5. Jahrhunderts." In *Die Völker an der mitteleren und unteren Donau,* ed. Wolfram and Daim, 23–27.

Ehlers, Joachim. "Die *Historia Francorum Senonensis* und der Aufstieg des Hauses Capet." *Journal of Medieval History* 4 (1978): 1–25.

Fälschungen im Mittelalter. 5 vols. MGH Schriften, Bd. 33. Hannover: Hansche Buchhandlung, 1988.

Fentress, James and Chris Wickham. *Social Memory.* Oxford: Blackwell, 1992.

Fichtenau, Heinrich. *Living in the Tenth Century: Studies in Mentalities and Social Orders.* Translated by Patrick J. Geary. Chicago: University of Chicago Press, 1991.

——. *Das Urkundenwesen in Österreich vom 8. bis zum frühen 13. Jahrhundert.* MIÖG Ergänzungsband 23. Vienna: Herman Böhlaus Nachf., 1971.

Fine, Agnès. "L'heritage du nom de Baptême." *Annales ESC* 42, no. 4 (1987): 853–77.

———. "Transmission des prénoms et parenté en Pays-en-Sault, 1740–1940." In *Le Prénom, mode et histoire: Entretiens de Malher 1980*, ed. Jacques Dupâquier, Alain Bideau, and Marie-Elizabeth Ducreux, 109–25. Paris: Éditions de l'École des Hautes Études en Sciences Sociales, 1984.

Finnegan, Ruth H. *Literacy and Orality: Studies in the Technology of Communication*. Oxford: Blackwell, 1988.

Fossier, François. "Chroniques universelles en forme de rouleau à la fin du Moyen-Age." *Bulletin de la Société Nationale des Antiquaires de France* (1980–81): 163–83.

Freed, John B. "Medieval German Social History: Generalizations and Particularism." *Central European History* (1992): 1–26.

Freise, Eckhard. "Kalendarische und annalistische Grundformen der Memoria." In *Memoria*, ed. K. Schmid and Wollasch, 441–577.

———. "St. Emmeram zu Regensburg." In Freise, *Ratisbona Sacra: Das Bistum Regensburg im Mittelalter*, 182–88. Munich: Verlag Schnell und Steiner, 1989.

Fried, Johannes. "Endzeiterwartung um die Jahrtausendwende." *Deutsches Archiv für Erforschung des Mittelalters* 45, no. 2 (1989): 381–473.

———. "Neue Historische Literatur: Deutsche Geschichte im früheren und hohen Mittelalter, Bemerkungen zu einigen neuen Gesamtdarstellungen." *Historische Zeitschrift* 245 (1987): 625–59.

Friesinger, Herwig and Falko Daim, eds. *Die Bayern und ihre Nachbarn: Berichte des Symposions der Kommission für Frühmittelalterforschung*. Vol. 2. Veröffentlichungen der Kommission für Frühmittelalterforschung 9. Vienna: Verlag der Österreichischen Akademie der Wissenschaften, 1985. (For vol. 1, *see* Wolfram and Schwarcz, eds.)

———. *Typen der Ethnogenese unter besonderer Berücksichtigung der Bayern*. Vol. 2. Veröffentlichungen der Kommission für Frühmittelalterforschung 13. Vienna: Verlag der Österreichischen Akademie der Wissenschaften, 1990. (For vol. 1, *see* Wolfram and Pohl, eds.)

Frisch, Michael H. "The Memory of History." *Radical History Review* 25 (1981): 9–23.

Fuhrmann, Horst. "Von der Wahrheit der Fälscher." *Fälschungen im Mittelalter* 1:83–98, MGH Schriften, Bd. 33.

Ganz, David. "Bureaucratic Shorthand and Merovingian Learning." In *Ideal and Reality in Frankish and Anglo-Saxon Society: Studies presented to J. M. Wallace-Hadrill*, ed. Patrick Wormald et al., 58–75. Oxford: Blackwell, 1983.

Ganz, David and Walter Goffart. "Charters Earlier Than 800 from French Collections." *Speculum* 65 (1990): 906–32.

Geary, Patrick J. *Aristocracy in Provence: The Rhône Basin at the Dawn of the Carolingian Age*. Monographien zur Geschichte des Mittelalters 31. Stuttgart: Anton Hiersemann, 1985; Philadelphia: University of Pennsylvania Press, 1985.

———. "Échanges et relations entre les vivants et les morts dans la société du haut Moyen Age." *Droit et cultures* 12 (1986): 3–17; a revised translation,

"Exchange and Interaction Between the Living and the Dead in Early Medieval Society," appears in Geary, *Living with the Dead in the Middle Ages.*

———. "Ethnic Identity as a Situational Construct in the Early Middle Ages." *Mitteilungen der anthropologischen Gesellschaft in Wien* 113 (1983): 15–26. Reprinted in *Folk Life in the Middle Ages*, ed. Edward Peters, *Medieval Perspectives* 3 (1988) [1991], 1–17.

———. *Living with the Dead in the Middle Ages.* Ithaca, N.Y.: Cornell University Press, 1994.

———. "Moral Obligations and Peer Pressure: Conflict Resolution in the Medieval Aristocracy." In *Hommage à Georges Duby*, ed. Guy Lobrichon and Claudie Amado. In press.

———. "Die Provence zur Zeit Karl Martells." In *Karl Martell und seiner Zeit*, ed. Jarnut et al. Munich: in press.

Genèse médiévale de l'anthroponymie moderne. Études d'anthroponymie médiévale, Ie et IIe Rencontres, Azay-le-Ferron 1986 et 1987. Tours: University of Tours, s.d. (1988).

Genet, Jean-Philippe. "Cartulaires, registres, et histoire: L'example anglais." In *Le métier d'historien au moyen âge*, ed. Guenée, 95–138.

Genicot, Léopold. "*Discordiae concordantium*: Sur l'intérêt des textes hagiographiques." *Académie royale de Belgique. Bulletin de la classe des lettres et des sciences morales et politiques* 51 (1965): 65–75.

Gingins-La-Sarraz, Frédéric-Charles-Jean de. *Mémoires pour servir à l'histoire des royaumes de Provence et de Bourgogne-Jourane.* Vol. 2, *Les Hugonides.* Lausanne: G. Bridel, 1853.

Goetz, Hans-Werner. "Fälschung und Verfälschung der Vergangenheit: Zum Geschichtsbild der Streitschriften des Investiturstreits," *Fälschungen im Mittelalter* 1:165–88. MGH Schriften, Bd. 33.

———. "Die Gegenwart der Vergangenheit im früh- und hochmittelalterlichen Geschichtsbewußtsein." *Historische Zeitschrift* 255 (1992): 61–97.

———. "Serfdom and the Beginnings of a 'Seigneurial System' in the Carolingian Period: A Survey of the Evidence." *Early Medieval Europe* 2, no. 1 (1993): 29–51.

Goffart, Walter. *The Le Mans Forgeries: A Chapter from the History of Church Property in the Ninth Century.* Cambridge: Harvard University Press, 1966.

———. "The Privilege of Nicholas I for St. Calais: A New Theory." *Revue Bénédictine* 71 (1961): 287–337.

Gold, Penny Schine. *The Lady and the Virgin: Image, Attitude and Experience in Twelfth-Century France.* Women in Culture and Society. Chicago: University of Chicago Press, 1985.

Goody, Jack. *The Domestication of the Savage Mind.* Cambridge: Cambridge University Press, 1977.

———. *The Interface Between the Written and the Oral.* Cambridge: Cambridge University Press, 1987.

———. *Literacy in Traditional Societies.* Cambridge: Cambridge University Press, 1968.

———. *The Logic of Writing and the Organization of Society.* Cambridge: Cambridge University Press, 1986.

Goody, Jack and Ian Watt. "The Consequences of Literacy." *Comparative Studies in Society and History* 5, no. 3 (1963): 304–45.

Gruneberg, Michael M. and Peter E. Morris, eds. *Aspects of Memory*. London: Methuen, 1978.

Grüner, G. "Schwäbische Urkunden und Traditionsbücher: Ein Beitrag zur Privaturkundenlehre des früheren Mittelalters." *MIÖG* 33 (1912): 1–78.

Guenée, Bernard. *Histoire et culture historique dans l'Occident médiéval*. Paris: Aubier Montaigne, 1980.

Guenée, Bernard, ed. *Le métier d'historien au moyen âge: Études sur l'historiographie médiévale*. Publications de la Sorbonne: Études, 13. Paris: Publications de la Sorbonne, 1977.

Guerreau, Alain. "Lournand au Xe siècle: Histoire et fiction." *Le Moyen Age* 96 (1990): 519–37.

Guillot, Olivier. *Le Comte d'Anjou et son entourage au XIe siècle*. 2 vols. Paris: A. and J. Picard, 1972.

Guyotjeannin, Olivier et al., eds. *Les Cartulaires*. Paris: École des Chartes, 1993.

Hageneder, Othmar. "Die Kirchliche Organisation im Zentralalpenraum vom 6. bis 10. Jahrhundert." In *Frühmittelalterliche Ethnogenese im Alpenraum*, ed. Helmut Beumann and Werner Schröder, 201–35. Nationes 5. Sigmaringen: Jan Thorbecke Verlag, 1985.

Hajdu, Robert. "The Position of Noblewomen in the *pays des coutumes*, 1100–1300." *Journal of Family History* 5 (1980): 122–44.

Halbwachs, Maurice. *Les cadres sociaux de la mémoire*. Paris: Presses Universitaires de France, 1952.

———. *Mémoires collectives*. Paris: Presses Universitaires de France, 1950. In English: *The Collective Memory*, trans. F. L. Ditter, Jr., and V. Y. Ditter, with an introduction by Mary Douglas. New York: Harper and Row, 1980.

———. *La topographie légendaire des évangiles en terre sainte; étude de mémoire collective*. Paris: Presses Universitaires de France, 1941.

Hauthaler, P. Willibald. "Der Mondseer Codex traditionum." *MIÖG* 7 (1886): 223–39.

Havelock, Eric A. *The Literate Revolution in Greece and Its Cultural Consequences*. Princeton: Princeton University Press, 1982.

———. *Preface to Plato*. Cambridge: Harvard University Press, 1963.

Head, Thomas. *Hagiography and the Cult of Saints: The Diocese of Orleans, 800–1200*. Cambridge Studies in Medieval Life and Thought, 4th ser., 14. Cambridge: Cambridge University Press, 1990.

Herlihy, David. "Land, Family, and Women in Continental Europe, 701–1200." *Traditio* 18 (1962): 89–120; reprinted in *Women in Medieval Society*, ed. Susan Mosher Stuard, 13–45. Philadelphia: University of Pennsylvania Press, 1976.

Hillebrandt, Maria. "Les cartulaires de l'abbaye de Cluny." *Mémoires de la Société pour l'Histoire du Droit et des Institutions des anciens pays bourguignons, comtois et romands* 50 (1993): 7–18.

Hlawitschka, Eduard. *Franken, Alemannen, Bayern und Burgunder in Oberitalien (774–962): Zum Verständnis der fränkischen Königsherrschaft in Ita-*

lien. Forschungen zur oberrheinischen Landesgeschichte 8. Freiburg im Breisgau: Eberhard Albert Verlag, 1960.

————. "Die verwandtschaftlichen Verbindungen zwischen dem hochburgundischen und dem niederburgundischen Königshaus: Zugleich ein Beitrag zur Geschichte Burgunds in der 1. Hälfte des 10. Jahrhunderts." In *Grundwissenschaften und Geschichte: Festschrift für Peter Acht,* ed. Waldemar Schlögl and Peter Herde, 28–57. Münchener historische Studien, Abteilung Geschichtl. Hilfswissenschaften 15. Kallmünz: Verlag Michael Lassleben, 1976.

Holzfurtner, Ludwig. *Gründung und Gründungsüberlieferung: Quellenkritische Studien zur Gründungsgeschichte der Bayerischen Klöster der Agilolfingerzeit und ihrer hochmittelalterlichen Überlieferung.* Münchener historische Studien, Abteilung Bayerische Geschichte 11. Kallmünz: Verlag Michael Lassleben, 1984.

Hyams, Paul R. "'No Register of Title': The Domesday Inquest and Land Adjudication." *Anglo-Norman Studies* 9 (1986): 127–41.

Iogna-Prat, Dominique. "La confection des cartulaires," in Guyotjeannin, *Les Cartulaires,* 27–44.

————. "Continence et virginité dans la conception clunisienne de l'ordre du monde autour de l'an mil." *Académie des inscriptions et belles-lettres, comptes rendus* (1985): 127–46.

————. "La geste des origines dans l'historiographie clunisienne des XIe–XIIe siècles." *Revue bénédictine* 102 (1992): 135–91.

Iogna-Prat, Dominique and Jean-Charles Picard, eds. *Religion et culture autour de l'an mil: Royaume capétien et Lotharingie.* Actes du colloque Hughes Capet 987–1987. La France de l'an Mil, Auxerre, 26–27 June 1987; Metz, 11–12 September 1987. Paris: Picard, 1990.

Jahn, Joachim. "Urkunde und Chronik: Ein Beitrag zur historischen Glaubwürdigkeit der Benediktbeurer Überlieferung und zur Geschichte des agilolfingischen Bayern." *MIÖG* 95 (1987): 1–51.

————. "Virgil, Arbeo und Cozroh: Verfassungsgeschichtliche Beobachtungen an bairischen Quellen des 8. und 9. Jahrhunderts." *Mitteilungen des Gesellschaft für salzburger Landeskunde* 130 (1990): 201–91.

Johanek, Peter. "Zur rechtlichen Funktion von Traditionsnotiz, Traditionsbuch und früher Siegelurkunde." In *Recht und Schrift im Mittelalter,* ed. Classen, 131–62.

Johnson, Penelope D. *Equal in Monastic Profession: Religious Women in Medieval France.* Chicago: University of Chicago Press, 1991.

Jussen, Bernhard. *Patenschaft und Adoption im frühen Mittelalter: Künstliche Verwandtschaft als soziale Praxis.* Veröffentlichungen des Max-Planck-Instituts für Geschichte 98. Göttingen: Vandenhoeck and Ruprecht, 1991.

Kastner, Jörg. *Historiae fundationum monasteriorum: Frühformen monastischer Institutionsgeschichtsschreibung im Mittelalter.* Münchener Beiträge zur Mediävistik und Renaissance-Forschung 18. Munich: Arbeo-Gesellschaft, 1974.

Ker, Neil Ripley. "Hemming's Cartulary: A Description of the Two Worcester Cartularies in Cotton Tiberius A. XIII." In *Studies in Medieval History Presented to Frederick Maurice Powicke,* ed. R. W. Hunt, W. A. Pantin, and R. W. Southern, 49–75. Oxford: Clarendon Press, 1948.

Kraus, Andreas. *Die Translatio S. Dionysii Areopagitae von St. Emmeram in Regensburg.* Bayerische Akademie der Wissenschaften. Philosophisch-Historische Klasse. Sitzungsberichte Jahrgang 1972, Heft 4. Munich: Verlag der Bayerischen Akademie der Wissenschaften, 1972.

Krusch, Bruno. "Ueber die *Gesta Dagoberti.*" *Forschungen zur Deutschen Geschichte* 26 (1886): 161–91.

Ladner, Gerhart B. *The Idea of Reform: Its Impact on Christian Thought and Action in the Age of the Fathers.* New York: Harper and Row, 1967.

Lambert, Chiara and Renato Grilletto. "Le sepolture e il cimitero della chiesa abbaziale della Novalesa." *Archeologia Medievale* 16 (1989): 329–56.

Landes, Richard. "L'accession des Capétiens: Une reconsidération selon les sources aquitaines." In *Religion et culture,* ed. Iogna-Prat and Picard, 151–66.

————. "*Millenarismus absconditus*: L'historiographie augustinienne et le millénarisme du haut Moyen Age jusqu'à l'an Mil." *Le Moyen Age* 98 (1992): 355–77.

Langosch, Karl. *Waltharius: Die Dichtung und die Forschung.* Erträge der Forschung 21. Darmstadt: Wissenschaftliche Buchgesellschaft, 1973.

Lauranson-Rosaz, Christian. *L'Auvergne et ses marges (Velay, Gévaudan) du VIIIe au XIe siècle: La fin du monde antique?* Le Puy-en-Velay: Les cahiers de la Haute-Loire, 1987.

Lawson, M. K. "The Collection of Danegeld and Heregeld in the Reign of Aethelred II and Cnut." *English Historical Review* 393 (1984): 721–38.

Lecoy, Félix. "Le *Chronicon Novaliciense* et les 'Légendes épiques.'" *Romania* 67 (1942–43): 1–52.

Le Goff, Jacques. *Histoire et mémoire.* Paris: Gallimard, 1988.

Lemâitre, Jean-Loup. *Mourir à Saint-Martial: La commémoration des morts et les obituaires à Saint-Martial de Limoges du XIe au XIIIe siècle.* Paris: De Boccard, 1989.

Lesne, Émile. *Histoire de la propriété ecclésiastique en France.* Vol. 4, *Les livres "Scriptoria" et bibliothèques du commencement du VIIIe à la fin du XIe siècle.* Lille: Facultés catholiques, 1938.

Levillain, Léon. "Études sur l'abbaye de Saint-Denis à l'époque mérovingienne, III *Privilegium* et *immunitates* ou Saint-Denis dans l'église et dans l'état." *Bibliothèque de l'École des Chartes* 87 (1926) 20–97, 245–346.

————. *Examen critique des chartes mérovingiennes et carolingiennes de l'abbaye de Corbie.* Mémoires et documents publiés par la société de l'école des Chartes 5. Paris: A. Picard, 1902.

Lewis, Andrew. *Royal Succession in Capetian France: Studies on Familial Order and the State.* Harvard Historical Studies, 100. Cambridge: Harvard University Press, 1981.

————. "Successions ottoniennes et robertiennes: Un essai de comparaison." In *Le roi de France,* ed. Parisse and Barral i Altet, 47–53.

Lewis, Archibald R. "The Dukes in the *Regnum Francorum* A.D. 550–751." *Speculum* 51, no. 3 (1976): 381–410.

Leyser, Karl J. *The Ascent of Latin Europe: An Inaugural Lecture Delivered Before the University of Oxford on 7 November 1984.* Oxford: Clarendon Press, 1986.

————. *Rule and Conflict in an Early Medieval Society: Ottonian Saxony.* Bloomington: Indiana University Press, 1979.

Littger, Klaus Walter. *Studien zum Auftreten der Heiligennamen im Rheinland.* Münstersche Mittelalter-Schriften 20. Munich: W. Fink, 1975.

Lotter, Friedrich. *Severinus von Noricum: Legende und historische Wirklichkeit.* Monographien zur Geschichte des Mittelalters 12. Stuttgart: Anton Hiersemann, 1976.

Lynch, Joseph H. *Godparents and Kinship in Early Medieval Europe.* Princeton: Princeton University Press, 1986.

Magnani, Luigi. *Le miniature del sacramentario d'Ivrea e di altri codici warmondiani.* Codices ex ecclesiasticis Italiae bybliothecis delecti phototypice expressi iussu Pii XI pont. Max. consilio et studio procuratorum bybliothecae vaticanae 6. Vatican City: Biblioteca apostolica vaticana, 1934.

Manteyer, Georges de. *La Provence du première au douzième siècle.* 2 vols. Mémoires et documents publiés par la Société de l'École des Chartes, 8. Paris: Alphonse Picard, 1908, 1926.

Marini, Gaetano Luigi. *I papiri diplomatici, raccolti ed illustrati.* Rome: Stamperia della Sac. congr. de prop. fide, 1805.

Marino-Malone, Carolyn. "Les fouilles de Saint-Bénigne de Dijon (1976–1978) et le problème de l'église de l'an mil." *Bulletin monumental* 138 (1980): 253–91.

Mason, Emma. *Saint Wulfstan of Worcester, c. 1108–1095.* Oxford: Blackwell, 1990.

Mayr, Gottfried. "Neuerliche Anmerkungen zur Todeszeit des heiligen Emmeram und zur Kirchenpolitik Herzog Theodos." In *Typen der Ethnogenese,* vol. 1, ed. Wolfram and Pohl, 199–215.

McClelland, James L. "On the Time Relations of Mental Processes: An Examination of Systems of Processes in Cascade," *Psychological Review* 86 (1979): 287–330.

McKitterick, Rosamond. *The Carolingians and the Written Word.* Cambridge: Cambridge University Press, 1989.

————. *The Frankish Kingdoms Under the Carolingians, 751–987.* London: Longman, 1983.

McKitterick, Rosamond, ed. *The Uses of Literacy in Early Mediaeval Europe.* Cambridge: Cambridge University Press, 1990.

McNamara, Jo-Ann and Susanne F. Wemple. "Marriage and Divorce in the Frankish Kingdom." In *Women in Medieval Society,* ed. Susan Mosher Stuard, 95–124. Philadelphia: University of Pennsylvania Press, 1976.

Metz, Wolfgang. "Zur Geschichte und Kritik der frühmittelalterlichen Güterverzeichnisse Deutschlands." *Archiv für Diplomatik* 4 (1958): 183–206.

————. *Das Karolingische Reichsgut: Eine verfassungs- und verwaltungsgeschichtliche Untersuchung.* Berlin: Walter de Gruyter, 1960.

Meyer, Otto. "Die Klostergründung in Bayern und ihre Quellen vornehmlich im Hochmittelalter." *Zeitschrift der Savigny-Stiftung für Rechtsgeschichte,* Kanonische Abteilung 20 (1931): 123–201.

Molitor, Stephan. "Das Traditionsbuch: Zur Forschungsgeschichte einer Quellengattung und zu einem Beispiel aus Südwestdeutschland." *Archiv für Diplomatik* 36 (1990): 61–92.

Morsbach, Peter. "Arnold von St. Emmeram." In Freise, *Ratisbona Sacra: Das Bistum Regensburg im Mittelalter*, 196–97.

Nebbiai-Dalla Guarda, Donatella. *La bibliothèque de l'abbaye de Saint-Denis en France du IXe au XVIIIe siècle*. Documents, études et répertoires publiés par l'Institut de Recherche et d'Histoire des Textes. Paris: Éditions du Centre National de la Recherche Scientifique, 1985.

Nietzsche, Friedrich. *Vom Nutzen und Nachtheil der Historie für das Leben*. Vol. 2 of *Nietzsches Werke, Klassiker Ausgabe*. Leipzig: Alfred Kröner Verlag, 1922.

Nora, Pierre. "Mémoire collective." In *La Nouvelle Histoire*, ed. Jacques Le Goff, Roger Chartier, and Jacques Revel, 398–401. Paris: Retz, 1978.

Nora, Pierre, ed. *Les lieux de mémoire*. Vol. 1, *La République*; vol. 2, *La Nation*; vol. 3, *Les France*. Bibliothèque des Histoires. Paris: Gallimard, 1984—.

Oesterley, Hermann. *Wegweiser durch die Literatur der Urkundensammlungen*. 2 vols. Berlin: G. Reimer, 1885–86.

Oexle, Otto Gerhard. "Die Gegenwart der Lebenden und der Toten: Gedanken über *Memoria*." In *Gedächtnis, das Gemeinschaft Stiftet*, ed. K. Schmid, 74–107. Schriftenreihe der Katholischen Akademie der Erzdiözese Freiburg. Munich: Verlag Schnell and Steiner, 1985.

———. "Die Gegenwart der Toten." In *Death in the Middle Ages*, ed. Herman Braet and Werner Verbeke, 19–77. Louvain: Louvain University Press, 1983.

———. "Liturgische Memoria und historische Erinnerung. Zur Frage nach dem Gruppenbewußtsein und dem Wissen der eigenen Geschichte in den mittelalterlichen Gilden." In *Tradition als historische Kraft: Interdisziplinäre Forschungen zur Geschichte des früheren Mittelalters*, ed. Norbert Kamp and Joachim Wollasch, 323–40. Berlin: Walter de Gruyter, 1982.

———. "Memoria und Memorialüberlieferung im früheren Mittelalter." *Frühmittelalterliche Studien* 10 (1976): 70–95.

Ortigues, Edmond and Dominique Iogna-Prat. "Raoul Glaber et l'historiographie clunisienne." *Studi Medievali*, 3d ser., 26, no. 2 (1985): 537–72.

Parisse, Michel. "Die Frauenstifte und Frauenklöster in Sachsen vom 10. bis zur Mitte des 12. Jahrhunderts." In *Die Salier und das Reich*, vol. 2, *Die Reichskirche in der Salierzeit*, ed. Weinfurter, 465–501.

Parisse, Michel and Xavier Barral i Altet, eds. *Le roi de France et son royaume autour de l'an mil*. Actes du colloque Hughes Capet 987–1987. La France de l'an Mil (Paris: Senlis, 22–25 June 1987). Paris: Picard, 1992.

Patze, Hans. "Adel und Stifterchronik: Frühformen territorialer Geschichtsschreibung im hochmittelalterlichen Reich." *Blätter für deutsche Landesgeschichte*, n.s., 100 (1964): 8–81, and 101 (1965): 67–128.

Pelikan, Jaroslav. *The Mystery of Continuity: Time and History, Memory and Eternity in the Thought of Saint Augustine*. Charlottesville: University Press of Virginia, 1986.

Pfister, Christian. *Études sur le règne de Robert le Pieux, 996–1031*. Bibliothèque de l'École des Hautes Études 64. Paris: F. Vieweg, 1885; rpt., Geneva: Slatkine Reprints, 1974.

Platelle, H. "Crime et châtiment à Marchiennes: Étude sur la conception et le fonctionnement de la justice d'après les Miracles de sainte Rictrude (XIIe s.)." *Sacris erudiri* 24 (1980): 155–202.

———. "Le problème du scandale: les nouvelles modes masculines aux XIe et XIIe siècles." *Revue belge de philologie et d'histoire* 53 (1975): 1071–96.

Pocock, John G. A. "The Origins of the Study of the Past: A Comparative Approach." *Comparative Studies in Society and History* 4 (1962): 209–46.

Poeck, Dietrich. "Laienbegräbnisse in Cluny." *Frühmittelalterliche Studien* 15 (1981): 68–179.

Poly, Jean-Pierre. "L'oeuf du griffon: Les serments du roi de l'an mil." *Droit et cultures* 22 (1991): 99–121.

———. *La Provence et la société féodale (879–1166).* Contribution à l'étude des structures dites féodales dans le Midi. Paris: Bordas, 1976.

———. *La Société féodale en Provence du 10e au 12e siècle.* Thèse du doctorat en droit, Université de Paris II, 1972; Paris: Publications de l'A.U.D.I.R. Microeditions Hachette, 1973.

Poly, Jean-Pierre and Eric Bournazel. *La mutation féodale Xe–XIIe siècles.* 2d. ed. Paris: Presses Universitaires de France, 1991.

Poupardin, René. *Le royaume de Bourgogne (888–1038): Étude sur les origines du royaume d'Arles.* Paris: Librairie Honoré Champion, 1907.

———. *Le royaume de Provence sous les Carolingiens (855–933?).* Paris: Librairie Émile Bouillon, 1901.

Prinz, Friedrich. *Frühes Mönchtum im Frankenreich: Kultur und Gesellschaft in Gallien, den Rheinlanden und Bayern am Beispiel der monastischen Entwicklung (4. bis 8. Jahrhundert).* 2d ed. Darmstadt: Wissenschaftliche Buchgesellschaft, 1988.

Rajna, Pio. "Contributi alla storia dell'epopea e del romanzo medievale." *Romania* 23 (1974): 36–61.

Ratisbona Sacra: Das Bistum Regensburg im Mittelalter. Kunstsammlungen des Bistums Regensburg Diözesanmuseum Regensburg Kataloge und Schriften 6. Munich: Verlag Schnell und Steiner, 1989.

Redlich, Oswald. "Ueber bairische Traditionsbücher und Traditionen." *MIÖG* 5 (1884): 1–82.

Reindel, Kurt. *Die bayerischen Luitpoldinger, 893–989: Sammlung und Erläuterung der Quellen.* Quellen und Erörterungen zur bayerishen Geschichte, n.f. 11. Munich: Beck, 1953.

Reuter, Timothy. *Germany in the Early Middle Ages, 800–1056.* London: Longman, 1991.

Riché, Pierre. "Les bibliothèques de trois aristocrates laïcs carolingiens." *Le Moyen Age* 69 (1963): 87–104.

Rosenwein, Barbara H. *Rhinoceros Bound: Cluny in the Tenth Century.* The Middle Ages. Philadelphia: University of Pennsylvania Press, 1982.

———. *To Be the Neighbor of Saint Peter: The Social Meaning of Cluny's Property, 909–1049.* Ithaca, N.Y.: Cornell University Press, 1989.

Rouquette, Jean-Maurice. *Provence romane.* Vol. 1, *La Provence rhodanienne.* La Pierre-qui-Vire: Zodiaque, 1974.

Ruiz Domenec, José Enrique. *La memoria de los feudales.* Barcelona: Argot, s.d. [1984].

Sackur, Ernst. *Die Cluniacenser*. Vol. 1. Halle: Max Niemeyer, 1892.

Santifaller, Leo. *Beiträge zur Geschichte der Beschreibstoffe im Mittelalter: Mit besonderer Berücksichtigung der päpstlichen Kanzlei*. MIÖG Ergänzungsband 16, no. 1. Graz: H. Böhlaus, 1953.

Schmid, Alois. *Das Bild des Bayernherzogs Arnulf (907–937) in der deutschen Geschichtsschreibung von seinen Zeitgenossen bis zu Wilhelm von Giesebrecht*. Regensburger historische Forschungen 5. Kallmünz: Verlag Michael Lassleben, 1976.

———. "Die Herrschergräber in St. Emmeram zu Regensburg." *Deutsches Archiv für Erforschung des Mittelalters* 32 (1976): 333–69.

Schmid, Karl. *Gebetsgedenken und adliges Selbstverständnis im Mittelalter: Ausgewählte Beiträge*. Sigmaringen: Jan Thorbecke Verlag, 1983.

Schmid, Karl, ed. *Die Klostergemeinschaft von Fulda im früheren Mittelalter*. 3 vols. in 5. Münstersche Mittelalter-Schriften 8. Munich: Wilhelm Fink Verlag, 1978.

Schmid, Karl and Joachim Wollasch, eds. *Memoria: Der geschichtliche Zeugniswert des liturgischen Gedenkens im Mittelalter*. Münstersche Mittelalter-Schriften 48. Munich: Wilhelm Fink Verlag, 1984.

Schmidt-Chazan, Mireille. "Les origines germaniques d'Hughes Capet dans l'historiographie française du Xe au XVIe siècle." In *Religion et culture*, ed. Iogna-Prat and Picard, 231–44.

Schmitt, Jean-Claude. *La Raison des gestes dans l'Occident médiéval*. Paris: Gallimard, 1990.

———. *Les Revenants: Les vivants et les morts dans la société médiévale*. Paris: Gallimard, 1994.

———. "Les revenants dans la société féodale." *Le temps de la réflexion* 3 (1982): 285–306.

Schneider, Annerose. "Zum Bild von der Frau in der Chronistik des früheren Mittelalters." *Forschungen und Fortschritte* 35 (1961): 112–14.

Schonen, Scania de. *La Mémoire, connaissance active du passé*. Connaissance et langage 3. Paris: Mouton, 1974.

Searle, Eleanor. "Fact and Pattern in Heroic History: Dudo of Saint-Quentin." *Viator* 15 (1984): 119–37.

———. "Frankish Rivalries and Norse Warriors." *Anglo-Norman Studies* 8 (1985): 198–213.

———. *Predatory Kinship and the Creation of Norman Power, 840–1066*. Berkeley: University of California Press, 1988.

Sergi, Giuseppe. "Una grande circoscrizione del regno italico: La marca arduinica di Torino." *Studi medievali*, 3d ser., 12 (1971): 637–712.

———. *Potere e territorio lungo la strada di Francia: Da Chambéry à Torino fra X e XIII secolo*. Nuovo Medievo 20. Naples: Liguori editore, 1981.

Sigal, Pierre André. "Le travail des hagiographes au XIe et XIIe siècles: Sources d'information et méthodes de rédaction." *Francia* 15 (1987): 149–82.

Söhngen, Gottlieb. "Der Aufbau der augustinischen Gedächtnislehre: *Confessiones* x.c.6–27." In *Die Einheit in der Theologie: Gesammelte Abhandlungen, Aufsätze, Vorträge*, ed. Söhngen, 63–100. Munich: K. Zink, 1952.

Sot, Michel. "Les Élévations royales de 888 à 987 dans l'historiographie du Xe siècle." In *Religion et culture*, ed. Iogna-Prat and Picard, 145–50.

————. *Gesta Episcoporum, Gesta Abbatum*. Typologie des sources du moyen âge occidental 37. Turnhout: Brepols, 1981.

Southern, Richard W. *The Making of the Middle Ages*. London: Hutchinson's University Library, 1953.

Spiegel, Gabrielle M. *The Chronicle Tradition of Saint-Denis: A Survey*. Medieval Classics: Texts and Studies 10. Brookline, Mass.: Classical Folia Editions, 1978.

————. *Romancing the Past: the Rise of Vernacular Prose Historiography in Thirteenth-Century France*. New Historicism 23. Berkeley: University of California Press, 1993.

Stafford, Pauline. *Queens, Concubines and Dowagers: The King's Wife in the Early Middle Ages*. London: Bates Academic and Educational, 1983.

Stock, Brian. *The Implications of Literacy: Written Language and Models of Interpretation in the Eleventh and Twelfth Centuries*. Princeton: Princeton University Press, 1983.

Störmer, Wilhelm. *Früher Adel: Studien zur politischen Fürhrungsschicht im fränkisch-deutschen Reich vom 8. bis 11. Jahrhundert*. 2 vols. Monographien zur Geschichte des Mittelalters 6. Stuttgart: Anton Hiersemann, 1973.

Street, Brian. *Literacy in Theory and Practice*. Cambridge: Cambridge University Press, 1984.

Surles, Robert Leo. *Roots and Branches: Germanic Epic / Romanic Legend*. New York: P. Lang, 1987.

Taylor, A. E. *Plato: The Man and His Work*. London: Methuen, 1926.

Tessier, Georges. "Originaux et pseudo-originaux carolingiens du chartier de Saint-Denis." *Bibliothèque de l'École des Chartes* 106 (1945–46): 35–69.

Thelen, David. "Memory and American History." *Journal of American History* 75, no. 4 (1989): 1117–29.

Tonkin, Elizabeth. *Narrating Our Pasts: The Social Construction of Oral History*. Cambridge Studies in Oral and Literate Culture 22. Cambridge: Cambridge University Press, 1992.

Treitler, Leo. "Medieval Improvisation." *World of Music* 33, no. 3 (1991): 66–91.

Tulving, Endel. *Elements of Episodic Memory*. Oxford Psychology Series 2. Oxford: Clarendon Press, 1983.

————. "Episodic and Semantic Memory." In *Organization of Memory*, ed. Endel Tulving and Wayne Donaldson, 381–403. New York and London: Academic Press, 1972.

Van Hoesen, Henry Bartlett. *Roman Cursive Writing*. Princeton: Princeton University Press, 1915.

Verdon, Jean. "Recherches sur les monastères féminins dans la France du nord aux IX–XIe siècles." *Revue Mabillon* 59 (1976): 49–96.

————. "Recherches sur les monastères féminins dans la France du sud aux IXe–XIe siècles." *Annales du midi* 88 (1976): 117–38.

Verhulst, Adriaan. "The Decline of Slavery and the Economic Expansion of the Early Middle Ages." *Past and Present* 133 (1991): 195–203.

Vollrath, Hanna. "Konfliktwahrnehmung und Konfliktdarstellung in erzählenden Quellen des 11. Jahrhunderts." In *Die Salier und das Reich*, ed. Weinfurter, 3:279–96.

Von Wright, J. M. *Forgetting and Interference.* Helsinki: Helsingfors, 1959.

Waldman, Thomas G. "Saint-Denis et les premiers Capétiens." In *Religion et culture,* ed. Iogna-Prat and Picard, 191–97.

Walker, David. "The Organization of Material in Medieval Cartularies." In *The Study of Medieval Records: Essays in Honour of Kathleen Major,* ed. D. A. Bullough and R. L. Storey, 132–50. Oxford: Clarendon Press, 1971.

Wanderwitz, Heinrich. "Traditionsbücher bayerische Klöster und Stifte." *Archiv für Diplomatik* 24 (1978): 359–80.

Wataghin-Cantino, Gisella. "Prima campagna di scavo nella chiesa dei SS. Pietro e Andrea dell'Abbazia di Novalesa: Rapporto preliminare." *Archeologia Medievale* 6 (1979): 289–317.

———. "Le ricerche archeologiche in corso all'Abbazia della Novalesa." In vol. 1, *La Novalesa: Ricerche, Fonti documentarie, Restauri,* 329–357. Atti del Convegno–Dibattito 1981. Susa, 1988 (2 vols.).

———. "Seconda campagna di scavo nella chiesa dei SS. Pietro e Andrea dell'Abbazia della Novalesa. Rapporto preliminare: Le fasi preromaniche." In *Atti del V Congresso Nazionale di Archeologia Cristiana. Torino, Valle di Susa, Cuneo, Asti, Valle d'Aosta, Novara, 22–29 settembre 1979,* 89–101. Rome: Viella, 1982.

Wattenbach, Wilhelm and Robert Holtzmann, eds. *Deutschlands Geschichtsquellen im Mittelalter: Die Zeit der Sachsen und Salier.* 3 vols. (vol. 1, ed. Franz-Josef Schmale). Darmstadt: Wissenschaftliche Buchgesellschaft, 1967–71.

Weinfurter, Stefan, ed. *Die Salier und das Reich.* 3 vols. Sigmaringen: Jan Thorbecke Verlag, 1991.

Werner, Karl Ferdinand. "Bedeutende Adelsfamilien im Reich Karls des Großen." In *Karl der Große, Lebenswerk und Nachleben,* vol. 1, *Persönlichkeit und Geschichte,* ed. Helmut Beumann, 83–142. Düsseldorf: Verlag L. Schwann, 1965.

———. *Histoire de France.* Vol. 1, *Les Origines (avant l'an mil).* Paris: Fayard, 1984.

———. "Die literarischen Vorbilder des Aimon von Fleury und die Entstehung seiner *Gesta Francorum.*" In *Medium Aevum Vivum: Festschrift für Walther Bulst,* ed. H. R. Jauss and D. Schaller, 69–103. Heidelberg: Carl Winter, 1960.

———. "Les principautés périphériques dans le monde franc du VIIIe siècle." In *I problemi dell'Occidente nel secolo VIII* 2:483–532. Settimane di studio del Centro Italiano di studi sull'alto medioevo 20. Spoleto, 1973.

———. "Untersuchungen zur Frühzeit des französischen Fürstentums (9.–10. Jahrhundert)." *Die Welt als Geschichte* 18 (1958): 256–89; vol. 19 (1959): 146–93; and vol. 20 (1960): 87–119.

Werner-Hasselbach, Traut. *Die älteren Güterverzeichnisse der Reichsabtei Fulda.* Marburger Studien zur älteren deutschen Geschichte. Reihe 2, Stück 2, Heft 7–8. Marburg: N. G. Elwert, 1942.

Westerhoff, Friedrich-Wilhelm. *Gruppensuche. Ein Verfahren zur Identifizierung von Personengruppen in mittelalterlichen Namen-Quellen. Beschreibung des Verfahrens und der Programme.* Rechenzentrum Universität Münster. Schriftenreihe 61. Munster: December, 1988.

Wickham, Chris. "Lawyers' Time: History and Memory in Tenth- and Eleventh-Century Italy." In *Studies in Medieval History presented to R. H. C. Davis*, ed. Henry Mayr-Harting and R. I. Moore, 53–71. London: Hambledon, 1985.

Wilsdorf, Christian. "Le *monasterium Scottorum* de Honau et la famille des ducs d'Alsace au VIIIe siècle: Vestiges d'un cartulaire perdu." *Francia* 3 (1975): 1–87.

Wolfram, Herwig. *Die Geburt Mitteleuropas: Geschichte Österreichs vor seiner Entstehung, 378–907*. Vienna: Kremayr and Scheriau, 1987.

―――. "*Libellus Virgilii*: Ein quellenkritisches Problem der ältesten Salzburger Güterverzeichnisse." In *Mönchtum, Episcopat und Adel zur Gründungszeit des Klosters Reichenau*, ed. Arno Borst, 177–214. Vorträge und Forschungen 20. Sigmaringen: Jan Thorbecke Verlag, 1974.

―――. "Die *Notitia Arnonis* und ähnliche Formen der Rechtssicherung im nachagilolfingischen Bayern." In *Recht und Schrift im Mittelalter*, ed. Classen, 115–30.

Wolfram, Herwig, ed. *Intitulatio II: Lateinische Herrscher- und Fürstentitel im neunten und zehnten Jahrhundert*. MIÖG Ergänzungsband 24. Vienna: Hermann Böhlau, 1973.

Wolfram, Herwig and Andreas Schwarcz, eds. *Die Bayern und ihre Nachbarn: Berichte des Symposions der Kommission für Frühmittelalterforschung*. Vol. 1. Veröffentlichungen der Kommission für Frühmittelalterforschung 8. Vienna: Verlag der Österreichischen Akademie der Wissenschaften, 1985. (For vol. 2, *see* Friesinger, Herwig and Falko Daim, eds.)

Wolfram, Herwig and Falko Daim, eds. *Die Völker an der mitteleren und unteren Donau im fünften und sechsten Jahrhundert*. Veröffentlichungen der Kommission für Frühmittelalterforschung 4. Vienna: Verlag der Österreichischen Akademie der Wissenschaften, 1980.

Wolfram, Herwig and Walter Pohl. eds. *Typen der Ethnogenese unter besonderer Berücksichtigung der Bayern*. Vol. 1. Veröffentlichungen der Kommission für Frühmittelalterforschung 12. Vienna: Verlag der Österreichischen Akademie der Wissenschaften, 1990. (For vol. 2, *see* Friesinger and Daim, eds.)

Wollasch, Joachim. "Eine adlige Familie des frühen Mittelalters: Ihr Selbstverständnis und ihre Wirklichkeit." *Archiv für Kulturgeschichte* 39, no. 2 (1957): 150–88.

Yates, Frances A. *The Art of Memory*. Chicago: University of Chicago Press, 1966.

Zoepf, Ludwig. *Das Heiligen-Leben im 10. Jahrhundert*. Leipzig-Berlin: B. G. Teubner, 1908; rpt., Hildesheim: Verlag Dr. H. A. Gestenberg, 1973.

Zonabend, Françoise. *The Enduring Memory: Time and History in a French Village*. Translated by Anthony Forster. Manchester: Manchester University Press, 1984.

INDEX

Note: Illustrations are indicated with the following abbreviations: c = chart; m = map; pl = plate; t = table.

Date Due